RETHINKING THE POLITICS OF GLOBALIZATION

Rethinking the Politics of Globalization

Theory, concepts and strategy

IAIN WATSON
University of Durham, UK

ASHGATE

Published by
Ashgate Publishing Limited
Gower House
Croft Road
Aldershot
Hampshire GU11 3HR
England

Ashgate Publishing Company
Suite 420
101 Cherry Street
Burlington, VT 05401-4405 USA

Ashgate website: http://www.ashgate.com

British Library Cataloguing in Publication Data
Watson, Iain
    Rethinking the politics of globalization : theory, concepts
    and stategy
    1. Globalization 2. Protest movements
    I. Title
    337

Library of Congress Cataloging-in-Publication Data
Watson Iain.
    Rethinking the politics of globalization : theory, concepts and stategy / Iain Watson.
        p. cm.
    Includes bibliographical references and index.
    ISBN 0-7546-1968-0
        1. Social Movements. 2. Economic history--20th century. 3. Globalization. I. Title.

    HM881 . W38 2002
    303.48'4--dc21   2002024920

ISBN 0 7546 1968 0

Printed in Great Britain by Antony Rowe Ltd, Chippenham, Wiltshire

Contents

Preface

Whenever we listen to political debates today, the word globalization is never very far away. The term globalization implies that we are living in a new era of human history (Robertson, 1992; Scholte, 2000; Waters, 1994). For the optimists, this new era harbours a welter of economic, social, political and cultural opportunity. For others, globalization is an insidious process of global capitalism or even a malign class project/strategy that is naturalizing and legitimating a particularly harsh reality of neo-colonialism through the axiom 'there is no alternative' (TINA). Thus, economic, social, cultural and political global transformations are causing widespread intellectual and political anxiety (Amoore et al., 1997, 2000; Gills, 2000; Watson, 2001). Indeed, increasing electoral apathy, indifference, cynicism, boredom and irony have all, in the post-Thatcherite times, come to be, more or less, perfunctory insults thrown at an increasingly bewildered political establishment. Scepticism with the day to day relevance of the political process has been cultivated by ongoing soundbites and the making of election commitments (for better services of health, transport and education) which are of course, not always met. Such apathy is best exemplified by low election turn outs, nourished on a diet of maxims claiming that privatization and the market do work in this 'best of all possible worlds' (Falk, 1996; Klein, 2000, 2001). Protests such as those in France in 1995, Seattle in 1999 and Prague in 2000, have shown that 'challenge' in an age of globalization is occurring outside the democratic and political processes of the sovereign state and is becoming more and more virulent. Indeed, interdependence and globalization suggest the ongoing emasculation of state autonomy. Many protests consist of a variety of individuals, social movements and non-governmental organizations (NGOs) concerned with the social, economic, cultural and political vicissitudes of global capitalism, free trade, continuing Third World debt and global environmental risk to name just a few (Beck, 1992; Burbach, 2000; Jubilee, 2000).

Images of globalization now range from the iconic and incandescent symbolism of *Coca-Cola, Gap, McDonalds, Nike, Shell and Starbucks* to the growing perils of global environmental catastrophe (George, 2001; Roddick, 2001). In a post-Cold War age of a problematic globalization however, when 'politics' (in general) and the revolutionary doctrines of Marxism/socialism have been so besmirched and the political left is seen to be moving from its traditional leftist roots, then what kind of ideological and political alternatives to the globalization of capitalism and its institutions, can be, should be and are being constructed?

This book argues that the fact that the 'g' word is so ubiquitous, leads to the suspicion that the conventional horizons and the distinctions between national politics and international politics are becoming increasingly permeable, even outdated. Critics of *economic* globalization and free trade in particular, are being portrayed as at best, historically anachronistic or worse, intellectually self-indulgent, because, the argument goes, liberalization releases individuals from the shackles of the state to pursue their entreprenuerial ambition to create wealth which will 'trickle down' forging a world community of markets and democracy (Crook, 2000; Wheen, 1999). Yet, as one distinguished sociologist suggested recently, the:

> current scare word globalization, seemingly unavoidable in any public statement, points not to an end of politics *but to its escape* from the categories of the national state, and even from the schema defining what is political and non-political action (Bauman, 2000, p. 1, my emphasis).

Globalization is a descriptive *and* prescriptive term originally used by free-market economists who argued that the world economy was quite magnificently driven by ever larger institutions of business and finance that seemed to be outstripping the sovereign power of national government. The early architects of free market globalization wrote about a coming borderless world and the economic inefficiencies of state intervention. Writers such as Kenichi Ohmae (1985) extolled the virtues of a mass global market, the advantages to productivity and communication of new information technologies and business/strategic coordination. This galvanized multidisciplinary interest in global transformations (technological, political, social and cultural) and focused upon the *sociological* and *cultural* impacts of a new era of multinational capital and a concomitant development of an age of global modernity and the cultures of 'postmodernity'. We could also see the essence of globalization as generating a unique juxtaposition of time/space compression, social 'distanciation' and dsembeddedness, and a unique linking of the parochialisms of the local, to the political space of the global with the acceleration of change (Giddens, 1990). This is also predicated upon a subjective consciousness of the global space as a *concrete lived experience* rather than an *abstract* place 'out there' (Robertson, 1992). Debate surrounding 'globalization' clearly engenders issues and controversies surrounding the 'newness' of this social change (Barry-Jones, 1999;

Clarke, 1998; Falk, 1995; Waters, 1994). Global transformations wrought by the interactions of structures and agents have developed along with unique spatio/temporal structures which herald a distinctive extensity, intensity, velocity and impact of global flows running alongside distinctive patterns of institutionalization, and modes of economic, political, social and cultural contestation (Held and McGrew, 1998). Here, in this analysis, globalization is understood as the following.

1. A new form of geographical expansion.
2. A new form of information technology.
3. New normative demands for universal human rights.
4. Represented by new dominant actors such as TNCs.
5. Incorporating new issues through a polycentric world politics.
6. Forcing a breakdown of nation/society and territorial units.
7. Represented by new global organizations and new global issues.
8. The blurring of domestic and international politics.
9. A new global consciousness of the world as a single place.

The book shows that one particular form of globalization has attracted widespread condemnation from those on the streets and seminar rooms of Seattle, Prague and Davos. This is what is known as *free market economic* globalization, represented by big business and its affiliations, the International Monetary Fund (IMF), the World Trade Organization (WTO) and the World Bank. Businesswoman Anita Roddick stated recently:

> The result of Seattle will be a radicalization of the antiglobalization movement. Seattle has made the alternative possible on a global scale, the devestation caused by continued globalization is not inevitable, 'cooperation for the best, not competition for the cheapest' is a slogan that will carry us forward in this long fight (Roddick, 2000, p. 20).

It would be very easy to dismiss the recent protests at Seattle and elsewhere as merely 'end of millennium' anomie, soon to disappear, mosquitoe struggles of immense strategic/normative contradiction and of mere minor irritation to the institutional bastions of global capitalism. Indeed, can one take anticapitalist struggles seriously when they so plainly rely upon capitalist-technological innovations such as the World Wide Web (www), and where participants are so easily able to attend global demonstrations and to indulge in the newly crowned phenomenon of 'summit hopping'. Indeed, historically, it has always seemed to be the revolutionary vanguard, or the rich and the educated (who can afford to moralize), protesting *on behalf of* the world's poorer individuals and groups, a dangerously presumptious gesture borne of the Enlightenment.

The book argues that to dismiss such obvious conceptual and strategic inconsistencies would be to ignore that such paradoxes and contradictions form the conceptual and strategic *essence* of what it means to engage with a critical politics of globalization. The complexities of living and resisting in an age of globalization have challenged the older strategic 'dogmas' of the left and provoked considerable unrest with the concomitant hypocrises in this world of people and issue connections. The new politics of resistance to globalization is a reaction to the tragic legacy of revolutionary and ideological romanticism *but at the same time* calls for a *reworking* of Enlightenment sentiments of development, democracy, liberty, justice and rights, rather than invoking a so-called 'postmodern' or post-Enlightenment response. A politics of resistance to globalization will require a different conceptual and strategic perspective and I will be setting out what this means for critical IPE. The current ideological debate in IPE pits liberal advocates of the free market against their Marxist critiques who direct attention to the exploitative nature of neoliberal globalization/capitalism. and the institutions such as the World Bank, the IMF and the WTO whose agendas are unfavourably skewed towards the interests of the rich countries and the disingenuous power elite. There is also concern as to whether the free trade model known as the 'Washington Consensus' is the right kind of model to apply to those countries at a relatively early stage of development.

Consequently, it is the liberal advocates claim that solving the social exigencies and cycles of world poverty requires not a narrow minded policy of protectionism or of 'less globalization' but instead an enlightened and enriching policy of *more* free market globalization (Crook, 2000). In response to a variety of key concerns, it is becoming increasingly clear however, that the antiglobalization protests do not easily fit into the conceptual and strategic parameters of the old and new left. What *is* required, is an alternative conceptual and strategic perspective which rejects a privileged actor and/or privileged fixed logic of globalization, and cultivates an awareness of the inherent strategic paradoxes and ambiguities in the act of resistance. This, moreover, requires a rethinking of the themes of 'resistance' and 'power' in critical IPE. Such a perspective considers that one can resist and yet *simultaneously* benefit from the specific (and connected) economic, political, cultural and social processes concretely construed and perceived as 'globalization'. How is this so and how can (and should) one come to terms with this apparent contradiction? What does it all mean for cultivating emancipatory alternatives which derive a *commonality* of struggles rather than a universalized and monolithic alternative? The book argues that such questions and issues require *not only* a 'reclaiming of the political' in an age of globalization but a more fundamental question of 'what does it mean to be political' in an age of globalization?

The critical enquiry advocated in this book, recognizes that the economic, political, social and cultural locations are multifaceted, occur at concrete/specific locations and are experienced and resisted in different often paradoxical ways. This critical enterprise accepts the importance of current Marxist and neoGramscian approaches to 'struggle' but aims to cultivate an alternative critical framework. In particular, the perspective rejects a *reification* of global capitalism 'in the last instance' and accepts that the interrelationships between structures or ideas, institutions and social forces may work simultaneously with individual and collective actors in forming a complex relationship manifested at *concrete* locations. Moreover, under these circumstances the question 'What is to be done' invites a degree of arrogance that is all too visible in the behaviour of the dominant political forces, whether it be a right-wing authoritarian state or a revolutionary Marxist intellectual. The operation of global institutions and the markets seems, as the 'invisible hand', to have taken on a curious life of its own, a strange and self-fulfilling prophecy. Undoubtedly, this nightmarish almost 'Kafkaesque' *modernity* has been accelerated and brings up for debate the relationship between ethico-political consequences and responsibility, as protests in Seattle and Prague rejected the elite and abstract 'economic indicators' wrapped, paradoxically, in the curious nationalist blanket of the competition state (Cerny, 1995).

The book will consider, with examples, the impact of neoliberal globalization and the complex and creative objectives and strategies of antiglobalization protests such as the *Zapatistas* (EZLN), *People's Global Action* (AGP), *Reclaim the Streets* (RTS) and *Globalize Resistance.* Neoliberalism *is still* an ideological deity and yet there is a growing sense amongst the world's elite that the heady 1980s neoliberal experiment is causing much instability. Thus, connections have been made by several governments, indicated by recent global conference agendas (Johannesburg/Qatar) between increasing poverty, sustainable development and their implications for future state power, security and authority in the increasingly volatile global system (Annan, 1999; Blair, 1997). The book highlights the dangers of right-wing backlashes to globalization, new and extreme forms of fundamentalism/nationalism and 'alternative' global political economies such as new drug cartels and assymmetrical terrorist activities as new post-Cold War threats to state/global security. The book outlines an alternative way of thinking and practising a progressive politics of resistance to globalization which both 'reclaims the political' whilst at the same time, is rethinking the conceptual, theoretical and strategic issues concerning what actually is meant by 'being political'. This kind of engagement accepts the conceptual and strategic contradictions and ambiguities of living and resisting in the age of 21st century globalization, without a privileged actor, without a privileged logic and even necessarily, without a designated privileged goal.

Acknowledgements

My thanks to the following for nurturing my interest in the critical politics of International Relations and globalization: Jason Abbott, Louise Amoore, Richard K. Ashley, David Campbell, Richard Dodgson, Randall Germain, Barry K. Gills, Don Marshall, Adam Morton, Ronen Palan, R.B.J. Walker, and members of the Newcastle Research Working Group on Globalization. My thanks to my family for their encouragement and support.

Abbreviations

ACIEZ	Emiliano Zapata Peasant Alliance.
ADN	National Democratic Alliance.
AGP	People's Global Action.
ANCIEZ	Emiliano Zapata National Peasant Alliance.
APPANET	The Advanced Research Projects Agency.
ARIC	Association of Rural Collective Interests.
CCRI-GC	Clandestine Revolutionary Committee General Command.
CIA	Central Intelligence Agency.
CIOAC	Independent Organization of Agricultural Workers.
CIOAC-PWM	Mexican Peasant Communist Party.
CISEN	The Center of National Security Investigations.
CNC	National Campesino Union.
CND	Campaign for Nuclear Disarmament.
CND	National Democratic Convention.
CNN	Cable News Network.
CNOC	National Network of Coffee Growers Association.
CNPA	National Coordinating Commitee.
CNPI	National Coordination of Indian Workers.
CNTE	National Coordination of Educational Workers.
COCEI	Workers, Students and Campesino Coalition of the Isthmus.
COCOPA	Congressional Commission for Concord Peace and Conciliation.
CONAI	National Mediation Committee.
CONAMUP	National Coordination of Urban Popular Movements.
CONASUP	National Company of Popular Subsistence.
CONPAZ	Commmission for Non-governmental Organizations for Peace.
COPLNMAR	National Plan for Repressed Zones and Marginal Groups.

COREO	Chiapas Forestry Commission.
CT	Congress of Labour.
CTM	National Conferation of Workers.
DFID	Department of International Development.
ENCR	National Front Against Repression.
EPR	Popular Revolutionary Army.
EU	European Union.
EZLN	Zapatista Army of National Liberation.
FAC-MLN	Broad Front for the Construction of a National Liberation Movement.
FARC	Revolutionary Armed Forces of Colombia.
FDI	Foreign Direct Investment.
FNALIDUM	National Front of Women's Rights and Solidarity.
FIPI	National Front of Indian Peoples.
FLN	National Revolutionary Force.
FMLN	Sandinista Forces of National Liberation.
FZLN	Emiliano Zapata Front of National Liberation.
GATT	General Agreement on Tariffs and Trade.
GDP	Gross Domestic Product.
GNP	Gross National Product.
ILO	International Labour Organization.
IMF	International Monetary Fund.
IP	International Politics.
IPE	International Political Economy.
IR	International Relations.
ISI	Import Substitution Policy.
LFA	Livestock Promotion Law.
LIEO	Liberal International Economic Order.
MAI	Multilateral Agreement on Investment.
MGCRI	Indigenous Regional Movement of Workers and Farmers.
MNC	Multinational Corporation.
NAFTA	North American Free Trade Agreement.
NCDM	National Commission for Democracy in Mexico.
NGO	Non-Governmental Organization.
NIEO	New International Economic Order.
OECD	Organization for Economic Cooperation and Development.
OPEC	Organization of Petroleum Exporting Countries.

OPEZ	Emiliano Zapata Organization of Peasants.
PAAC	Department of Agricultural Affairs and Colonization.
PAN	National Action Party.
PARM	Authentic Party of the Mexican Revolution.
PDPR	Popular Democratic Revolutionary Party.
PEMEX	National Oil Company.
PFCRN	Cardenista Front of National Reconstruction.
PLM	Mexican Liberal Party.
PMS	Mexican Socialist Party.
PNR	National Revolutionary Party.
PP	Party of the Poor.
PRD	Party of the Democratic Revolution.
PRI	Partido Revolucion Institucional.
PRM	Party of the Mexican Revolution.
PROCUP	Worker's Clandestine Party of the People.
PROCUP-PDLP	Workers and the Revolutionary Party of the People.
PROGRESSA	Program for Education, Health and Nutrition.
PRONASOL	National Solidarity Program.
RICA	Intercontinental Network of Alternative Communication.
RMALC	Mexican Action Network on Free Trade.
RTS	Reclaim the Streets.
SALT	Strategic Arms Limitation Talks.
SAP	Structural Adjustment Policy.
STI	Syndicate of Indian Labourers.
STRM	Telephone Worker's Union.
TNC	Transnational Corporation.
UN	United Nations.
UNAM	National Autonomous University at Mexico City.
UNCTAD	United Nation's Conference on Trade and Development.
UNORCA	National Union of Regional Peasants.
UNT	New National Worker's Union.
UP	Union of the Poor.
US	United States.
WTO	World Trade Organization.

Chapter 1

Debating the Globalization Problematic: Ambiguities, Approaches and Controversies

Introduction

The chapter considers the current state of the debate on globalization as a source of historical, ideological, philosophical and cultural contention. The chapter points out that many approaches and debates are predicated upon multidisciplinary foundations. These debates and controversies raise important epistemological and ontological issues concerned with explaining and acting out the politics *and* critical politics of globalization.

A New World Order

During the Cold War, did glorious images of what it was like to live in the West flame revolutionary passions that perhaps even incredulously led to the events of 1989? (Klein, 2000). Throughout Eastern Europe and Russia the dominance of *McDonalds* establishments, the ubiquitous incandescence of *Pepsi* advertisements and the growing use of the Internet are powerful icons of Western Cold War victory manifested in the form of global capitalism. For critics of global capitalism and the US, this situation certainly makes the orthodox account of Cold War victory and the meaning and implications of 'victory' normatively problematic. Yet as Cold War geopolitical maps have begun to evaporate in front of our very eyes, (although Cold War mindsets may continue) new geopolitical coordinations and conceptual maps of the globe have now been required. The term and concept of 'globalization' has fitted the bill and has gone some way towards satisfying this descriptive, prescriptive and normative yearning for 'making sense of the world'.

From its obscure origins in French and American literature of the 1960s the term globalization now 'finds expression today in all the world's major languages and yet, inevitably perhaps, globalization is also in danger of becoming "the cliche of our times"' (Held, McGrew, Goldblatt and Perraton, 1999, p. 1). Globalization in its broadest sense means economic and technological opportunity for some, and to chronic fatalism, parochialism, seething fundamentalism and uncertainty for many others (Bauman, 2000). So what are we to make of this 'thing' globalization?

A Methodology for Globalization

The very word globalization implies a teleological and deterministic deity bereft of human agency or of political will. Economic and technological approaches to globalization have tended to regard globalization in a rationalist and scientific manner (Scholte, 2000). Economic, political and cultural forms of globalization are commonly associated with a reality 'out there' and we see this perspective daily in government policy proposals because, as they say, 'there is no alternative' to market discipline and the vagaries of the windswept global economy.

Many writers have in turn advanced a more critically astute assessment of global transformations. Here, the case is put that the characteristics that have come under the rubric of globalization are historically specific and have no single fixed logic. Hence, globalization is conceived as:

> a process (or set of processes) which embodies a transformation in the spatial organization of social relations and transactions, assessed in terms of their extensity, intensity, velocity and impact - generating transcontinental or interregional flows and networks of activity, interaction and the exercise of power (Held et al., 1999, p. 16).

Held et al. (1999) have argued for a *structurationist* approach to the causes/effects of global transformations. This perspective rightly privileges neither structures nor agents, but instead recognizes that a complex interaction between structures and agents occurs and that globalization must therefore be conceived at specific and complex nodes of economic, cultural, political and social interaction that emit both intended *and* unintended outcomes. This particular approach brings in the possibility of 'reclaiming the political' and forms a key strategic part of new Marxist and neoGramscian approaches to the issue of 'resistance' (Gill, 1993; Overbeek, 2000). This critical effort is dedicated to 'reclaiming the political' as a means of resisting and overturning the *economically* and *technologically* deterministic accounts of a socially and morally problematic globalization. Anthony Giddens argued:

> there is little point in looking for an overall theory of stability and change in social systems, since the conditions of social reproduction vary so widely between different types of society...we have to show how, in the context of the rationalisation of action, definitive practices are reproduced, how actors penetration of the institutions which they reproduce and through their practices, makes possible the very reproduction of these practices (1990, p. 215).

Giddens' structuration theory offers a plausible conceptual account of the dynamic of structure and agency. Here, the processes of globalization can be approached as a *politically* negotiated process of power and ideological relations between individuals, institutions, social movements, governments and capital at specific times and specific places. As a key architect and proponent of New Labour's 'Third Way' between Thatcherism and state-socialism, Anthony Giddens has argued that:

> I have proposed that the conception of structuration introduces temporality as integral to social theory; and that such a conception involves breaking with the synchrony/diachrony or static/dynamic divisions that have featured so prominently in both structuralism and functionalism...the general tendency, especially within functionalist thought has been to identify time with the diachronic or dynamic; synchronic analysis represents a 'timeless snapshot' of society. The result is that time is identified with social change (1990, p. 198).

Giddens (1984) suggested that structures should be understood as the rules, resources and power occurring in specific time and space which are simultaneously both enabling and constraining of social/political action and are the medium *and* the outcome of agency. The production of social interaction is seen from this perspective as a historically contingent accomplishment of the actions of knowledgable social actors. Consequently, present causes and outcomes of political actions are mediated through structures at *specific* points by reflexive agents who then rearrange the conditions for future actions. In this critical spirit Germain and Kenny (1998, p. 5) suggested that 'by insisting on the transformatory capacity of human beings' a 'radical embrace of human subjectivity, provides one way of avoiding a deterministic and ahistorical structuralism'. Germain and Kenny pointed out that structural limits of for instance resources and power:

are not fixed and immutable but exist within the dialectics of a given social structure. And whilst it is true that this social structure both constrains and constitutes social action, it is equally true that social action has a transformative impact upon its constraining structure (1998, p. 10).

The *orthodox* methodology of globalization encompasses the following:

1. Defines the global reality in terms of the physical world 'out There'.
2. Understands this reality in terms of objective and technicalenquiry.
3. Holds that there are both singular and privileged/universaltruths.
4. Enables people to solve their immediate problems within this reality.

The critical approach to globalization aims to inject a *political* dimension to the debate by challenging the rationalist and teleological readings of global transformations, and it is here where the critical responses to globalization are rightly evoked both conceptually and strategically (Amoore et al., 2000; Gills, 2000). Thus, this alternative move that initially lends itself to a 'structuration' approach accepts that:

> the course of social history results from mutually constituting agent choices and structural dispositions. Neither comes before the other: there is no chicken/actor without the egg/structure and vice versa. On the one hand, structural forces largely establish the range of options that are available to actors in a given historical context. Structures also generally encourage agents to take certain steps rather than others. At the same time, however, structures depend on an accumulation of actor decisions for their creation and subsequent perpetuation (Scholte, 2000, p. 91).

Using this critical sentiment, Cerny (1990, 1995) has suggested that globalization must be seen to be a complex set of economic and political structures and processes deriving from the changing character and value of goods and assets as held by different actors, individuals, institutions and/or states. Through this structurationist approach Cerny (1995) contended that structures are more or less those embedded sets, patterns, constraints and opportunities for action which are both enabling and dynamic patterns of interaction that take place on or across structured fields of action. These specific fields are made up of complex multilayered economic, political, cultural and social structures that incorporate distinct structural levels or different games with different payoffs for different agents. The multifaceted understanding of global transformations proves an invaluable insight into the complex processes at work at specific sites in the critical politics of globalization both intellectually *and* politically. My argument takes as its starting point a conceptual and strategic structurationist approach to the politics and critical politics of globalization.

From International Relations to the Hyperglobalists

According to Hoffman:

> international theory like the international system itself is undergoing profound transformation...this may sound like a trite observation but these recent efforts in international theory have in common a scepticism towards traditional social theory with its belief that there is a hierachy of forms of knowledge and toward the metanarratives of modernity with its overriding emphasis on technical or scientific forms of rationality (1991, p. 169).

Samuel Huntington (1998) controversially wrote of the possibility for a cataclysmic 'clash of civilizations' and a transgression of the essentially *European* understanding of geopolitical battles *between* Westernized sovereign states in the Westernized sovereign state system. Huntington (1998) identifies a religious tribal revival from 'second generation' Islamic fundamentalists, very educated and 'westernized' but also very determined to return to Islamic culture and customs as fostered by a rejection of the decadent West from where many once lived and worked. Huntington (1998) makes the profound point about the inability to 'dialogue' across civilizations. During the Cold War both Western and Soviet intellectuals and politicians could all debate and disagree on the nature of their modern political systems within the European international system of states and secular ideologies. Yet now, what real chance would a Western diplomat have *in really* understanding the meaning and cultural codes of a Russian orthodox perspective or a fundamentalist Islamic perspective concerning the nature of conflict and security? Indeed, Russia, like Turkey, resides on that very enigmatic and very tragic borderline that is the geopolitical and civilizational divide between the West and the East. To the West, the Eastern states, the cyrillic language, the folktales and the ambiance of 'Moscow by midnight' (and despite the *McDonalds* and *Pizza Huts*) is still that little bit different which all in all, makes for an uneasy cultural coexistence that may be profounder than Cold War hostility. Russia is of course, a janus or a 'torn' state; does it nervously turn to the European community (does a community that is concerned with having the Moslem state of Bosnia on its doorstep really want Russia?) or does it turn to and rediscover and consolidate its nationalistic, orthodox and Byzantine past? This contentious and seemingly irreconcilable dualism is manifested in the growing (and historical) competition between St Petersburg (looking to the European community) and Moscow, looking to the Russia of Western Asia. In the unnerving realignment of the new world order Huntington (1998) argues that a rethinking of the relationship between modernization and Westernization is under way. Throughout many Islamic states demands (particularly from the children of the rich) for a revival of Islam are growing as well as *within* the nation-states of the West, all concomitant with a sense of the 'decline of the West' is a growing source of disquiet in Europe and the US.

The recent terrorist attacks on the United States in September 2001 show perhaps, the alarming prescience of Huntington's argument which claimed that the resurgence of Islamic fundamentalism is as profound as the religious reformation in Western Christendom. The attacks on the World Trade Centre and the Pentagon clearly showed that the nature and practices of war and security have changed, maybe even forever as new civilizational fault lines that transgress the European state system continue to fracture. Whilst the international system as realists have pointed out, was conflictual, it was a system of anarchy, and yet it developed over time, a system of common norms and values, it became in actual fact, an 'anarchical society'. Something profound happened in 1989 and 2001, *not just* a new realignment of the European state system but rather, a new question mark hanging over the actual existence and very future of the European international system itself.

On the other hand, a posse of optimists enthusiastically talked of 'the end of history' and a spectre of the Hegelian spirit that portended an age without conflict, a rational age. As Brown put it:

> It seems difficult to deny that something momentous has indeed happened over the last few years, namely the fall of communism (Brown, 1995, p. 3).

Established security institutions in the West have now had to reassess what they understand to be the site and nature of security and their world view and it was conflict *within* states (Bosnia, Indonesia, Rwanda and Somalia) and itinerant terrorists which led to a new multidisciplinary understanding of the porous boundaries of the study and practice of International Politics (Kaldor, 1998). Global transformations were becoming a reality and not just another academic theory (Booth, 1997).

But it is not all bad news, one hopes. Exuberant optimism also greeted the new world order and carried the day in policy directives as the threat of a Cold War apocalypse evaporated and the Gulf War in 1991 suggested that sovereign states *were* willing to cooperate *and* intervene on humanitarian grounds through international law and international institutions to restrain and resist military dictatorships and to protect ethnic minorities from brutal persecution. New organizations challenged conventional approaches to state-sovereignty witnessed most starkly by the arrest of Slobodan Milosevic in June 2001 for alleged war crimes in Kosovo. Milosevic refused to accept the legitimacy of the War Crimes Tribunal in the Hague which challenged Yugoslavian state-sovereignty. This new era was begun in 1989, a change 'so striking that it marks the beginning of an era in world affairs' (Bush, 1990).

The language to describe this new world order is multifarious and it ranges from strategic suppositions that the world is no longer bipolar but unipolar, it is multipolar and polycentric, as new actors, new issues and new sources of power and authority now proliferated. As George (1994) noted 'the resultant sequence of events has been cause, generally, for widespread rejoicing at the new opportunities for personal and political liberty within the societies of, in particular, Eastern Europe. There has been smugness also' (George, 1994, p. 1). Elsewhere the ideational foundation of the neoliberal agenda was regarded as 'rooted in notions of progress and perpetual change' (Amoore et al., 1997, p. 179; Clinton, 2000; Fukuyama, 1991; Hilbert, 1997). Are the differences between the terms 'international', 'transnational', 'interdependence', and 'global' merely semantic differences, do the words correspond to different historical realities or do they all represent the same reality but with differing emphases? Language *is* a source of disquiet and antiglobalization groups such as *Reclaim the Streets* (RTS) have come up with alternative slogans such as 'Our world is not for sale' whilst global corporate advertizing continues to colonize their political space (Klein, 2000).

But the old questions remain. Is the age of globalization *qualitatively* different from other epochs, i.e. is it a break from the past? (Barry-Jones, 1995, 1999; Hirst and Thompson, 1996). Or are the processes commonly identified as globalization part of a *longer-duree* societal transformation or merely a *quantitative* acceleration of certain economic, political and social transformations? Such questions depend on which particular ontological, epistemological and ideological perspective one uses in conceptualizing history and social 'change' (Barry-Jones, 1995, 1999).

In their recent study on globalization Held et al. (1999) talk of the need to recognize the ensuing controversies and the political implications of these controversies insomuch as they focus on identifying the many different dynamics or causations of processes placed under the rubric of globalization. This is why understanding globalization through its processes and its trends has it seems, broken through some of the intellectual and political taboos concerning the power of disciplinary boundaries (Booth, 1997; Shaw, 2000; Wallerstein, 1989). In their earlier study, Held and McGrew (1998, p. 220) argued that:

> globalization refers to an historical process which transforms the spatial organization of social relations and transactions generating transcontinental or interregional networks of interaction and the exercise of power. It is possible to identify for analytical purposes different historical forms of globalization, from the epoch of world discovery in the early modern period to the present era of the neoliberal global project. These can be characterized by distinctive spatio-temporal and organizational attributes.

The debate on globalization was particularly pertinent for the discipline of International Relations (IR). During most of the 20th century international relations was dominated by the paradigm of realism. It has now been claimed, and with some justification, that we are moving into a post-realist age or even a post-international age because 'the world at the end of the short twentieth century is in a state of social breakdown rather than revolutionary crisis' (Shaw, 2000, p. 144).

From the Treaty of Westphalia in 1648 the modern state system developed through a European and Enlightened vision of where authority and politics does and should reside. The modern sovereign state developed through a centralization and monopoly of *legitimate* power and was considered the authentic site of progressive politics and community (Linklater, 1997; Walker, 1993). The founding and maintenance of state-*sovereignty* was a geopolitical act by making dominant one particular identity over others and within a bounded political space through the use of material *and* discursive practices (techno-territorial networks, communication/transport) and bringing diverse micro-spaces into one unitary/abstract national space (Giddens, 1985, 1990).

The modern state is based on the ideals of suffrage, democracy and 'the site of modern reason' (George, 1994, p. 202) and yet wielded 'the transplantation of unprecedented means of institutionalized violence and surveillance into political arenas' because 'the emergence of the modern state in Europe also produced some of the worst forms of terror in the twentieth century' (Giddens, 1985, p. 295). The creation of the state as an ordered national community relied upon both material *and* symbolic representational resources of political space and cultivated a distinctive structure and parameter for modern democratic politics (Watson, 2002, 2002a). As a universalizing concept of modern politics the institutions of state-sovereignty have developed through various political practices of exclusion and power to fix and bound the homogenous national community as legitimate political space.

The realist paradigm dominated International Relations after the brief sorte into post-World War One idealism. It was based upon the following assumptions of world politics:

1. The state was principal actor.
2. The state was a unified actor with a distinction being made between domestic and international politics, acting for its security, within an anarchical inte state system.
3. There was a hierachy of issues, i.e. high politics and low politics.
4. Power could be defined and measured in instrumental/military terms and as coercive 'power over'.

Thus, the end of the Cold War in 1989, was the end of a relatively stable bi-polar balance of power with its geopolitical symmetry. There was of course, intriguing uncertainty with what the post-Cold War world order might look like, and particularly with the apparent geopolitical instability as neorealists saw it, of a unipolar system. As George (1994) noted rather glibly perhaps, reality 'is not what it used to be in International Relations' (George, 1994, p. 1). Others focused upon the changing nature of the 'international' system and globalization (Clarke, 1998; Mayall, 1998). Many writers were cautiously optimistic with increasing economic, political and cultural convergence and institutions for global humane governance in the post-realist world (Falk, 1995, 1996). Held and McGrew (1998, p. 220) argued that contemporary globalization represents a challenge to the time and space of political realism through 'unique spatio-temporal and organizational attributes' with 'institutional modes of contestation, stratification and reproduction'.

The idea of a post-Westphalian order is a major part of the hyperglobalist thesis given that states will now seek to share their tasks of governance and security with a complex array of institutions, public and private, local, regional, transnational and global representing the emergence of 'overlapping communities of fate and risk' with the following patterns of change:

1. More emphasis put on cooperation and regional security.
2. A greater sensitivity between states.
3. The emergence of new threats to national security, such as terrorism.

Even before the events of September 2001 in New York, President George W. Bush talked of the new threat of fundamentalism/'cyberterrorism' and the changing geopolitical architecture by questioning the 1972 ABM Treaty with the Soviets which had been signed during the era of detente.

For those patiently waiting for their moment to gleefully disgard the ontologies of a prosaic realism, the morally debunked discourse of 'national security' with its 'ends justified the means' philosophy, globalization would signal a quite morally reverent challenge (Buzan, Held and McGrew, 1998; Elshtain, 1999; Held, 1995; Linklater, 1997; Smith, 1992). The emphasis here is placed on the possibility of extending political and moral community beyond the now *historical* boundaries of state territory, through this promotion of universal ideals of rights, justice and citizenship (Cox, 1999; Linklater, 1999; Shaw, 1994). These values and ideals are embedded within new global institutions of liberal humanism (Keohane, 1989, 1998). Global governance meant not simply formal and sovereign institutions through which the rules and norms governing the (neoliberal) world order are made. Governance implies a wider ranging approach to the site and nature of power and authority in the international/global system. As Keohane (1998, p. 1) noted, global institutions 'are persistent' and governance is maintained through 'connected sets of rules (formal and informal) that prescribe behavioural roles, constrain activity, and shape expectations'. From this perspective, to analyse world politics in the 1990s 'is to discuss international institutions' and the rules that govern 'elements of world politics and the organizations that help implement these rules' (Keohane, 1998, p. 82).

By the early 1970s it was being realized that international politics could no longer be separated from the emerging new international economic processes. At this time, new disciplines such as International Political Economy (IPE) developed new analytical importance of recognizing the networks between economic and political actors and issues. During the 1970s it became clear that the ontological parameters of state-centric classical realism were becoming increasingly limited as a means of explaining and predicting what seemed to be a new and complex reality of international politics (Keohane and Nye, 1977). Keohane and Nye (1977) acknowledged a 'complex interdependence' characterized by the blurring of boundaries between high and low politics, the development of non-state actors and a recognition of new actors and organizations (Keohane and Nye, 1977; Krasner, 1983). States could now be classed in degrees of their vulnerability and/or sensitivity, whilst neorealists reacted to recover a lost methodological parsimony (Waltz, 1979). Yet to the posse of onlooking critical writers of the 1980s neorealism had closed off the potential (albeit restricted) analytical richness of complex interdependence theory with just another *cul-de-sac* of strategic battlegrounds and *ahistorical* analysis. Neorealism was ontologically and epistemologically based upon the supposition that the world of international relations could be measured and predicted as a reality 'out there' (George, 1994). In other words, it claimed a scientific methodology and value free social scientific research, a credible perspective which was to continue to fuel critical approaches both in International Relations and Critical IPE (Cox, 1981, 1983). Others were concerned with imposing a new ideological and political bias or even a 'spooky kind of order, emanating from the multinational corporations and globetrotting financiers who animate McWorld' (Wright, 2000, p. 7).

It was interesting to note that these were American writers, all echoing the foreign policy objectives of President Carter on the 'dizzy complexity' of the world of international relations, a world where no state was independent and where issues overflowed state boundaries and state-sovereignty. This complexity and generation of instability in the international system (inflation, economic slowdown and the threat from the developing world shown by the oil price rises of OPEC in 1973) seemed to represent from a realist perspective the inevitable waning of US hegemony. Moreover, Strange and Stopford (1991) argued that power was in the hands of the economic institutions, firms and financial organizations and power was dripping away from the states. However, as Strange (1988) was to make very clear, power in the international system was not simply an instrumental device i.e. the 'power over' agents but power was also structural i.e. as maintained through ideas, the ownership of capital and the setting of ideological agendas both coercively and consensually. There was now a seemingly fundamental shift in the structure of the international system; with intergovernmental organizations, inter and intra state organizations, non-governmental organizations (NGOs) actors/institutions, a flow of peoples and exchange of ideas and the *complexities* of the international system. This was no longer the cocooned world of elite international diplomacy and moreover, Keohane and Nye (1977) argued that *all* states at specific times were increasingly *vulnerable* and increasingly *sensitive* to economic/political events around the world and that it was now more difficult to identify what was meant by a 'powerful' state. For instance, a state may have immense military power but may not be able to come to terms with the new threat of global environmental destruction and the threat of individual terrorists *within* state boundaries. The hierachies of realism came crashing and the definition and nature of security was changing along with an analytical and empirical blurring of domestic and foreign policy objectives. Such an international environment now required new forms of international cooperation achieved through new institutions and 'regimes' or - 'sets of implicit or explicit principles, norms, rules and decision making procedures around which actors expectations converge' (Krasner, 1983, p. 3).

The development of international cooperation seemed to belie the realist axiom that the international system was imbued with anarchy and distrust and yet cooperation was both a manifestation of self interest and a realization from states that states could no longer act on their own. It was accepted that there were now intended and unintended consequences of action and yet as later debates on 'global governance' were to show, the underlying problem with regime theory was of course, 'whose values are we talking about and engaging with'? The emergence of new actors suggested new forms of power and authority and the most powerful and symbolic manifestation of this power was the multinational corporation and the economic agents of big business. During the 1980s business magnates and moguls took advantage of a new free market ideology, structural adjustment and the 'rollback of the state'. For the left, the triumph of neoliberal capital accumulation has resulted in a 'triumphalist market system free to spread its graveyard dogmas over the entire planet' as all 'ideological conflict is supposed to have been laid to rest, as the rich have been transformed into revered 'wealth creators' whose exertions allow the poor to survive' (Seabrook, 1999, p. 23). As ever, the reality is different, as economic globalization in the form of big business and free marketeering 'permits money and goods to move around the world unimpeded, yet criminalizes the other indispensable element of production, labour, when it seeks to move to where it can command a decent livelihood' (Seabrook, 1999, p. 24). It is this tension that forms the politics of resistance to globalization.

If we consider the debates on *economic* globalization, then the fraught instabilities of the global economy recently witnessed in East Asia and the speedy transfer of money around the world have all cemented a view that we are living in new times. The sense of democratic alienation from the institutions and organizations of a global economy 'out there' is common. Mittelman (1995, p. 427) suggested that there has emerged a 'global coalescence of varied transnational processes and domestic structures' and that the 'state responds by becoming a transmission belt' between the seemingly dominant actors and institutions of economic globalization and the state which 'pulls in opposite direction using a variety of government interventions' (Mittelman, 1995, p. 439). Thus, through this complex interaction but with the balance of power seemingly with big business, globalization is 'a multilayered phenomenon' which incorporates the state and sustains some of its functions while at the same time altering its very essence and undermining its constitutional formation (Cerny, 1995, p. 123). Bayliss and Smith argued that globalization must be understood as:

> the process of increasing interconnectedness between societies such that events in one part of the world more and more have effects on peoples and societies far away...with increasing globalization comes increasing deterritorialization...greater insecurity...this in turn can render the need for old foundational myths of state territory and identity...economic and technological development led to an increase of interconnectedness between societies, results in a very different pattern of political world relations...states are no longer sealed units, if they ever were (1997, p. 3).

The Genealogy of Economic Globalization

Well fed, sipping perhaps a glass of vintage wine, globally mobile and wearing the latest fashion items; is this Western utopia based on the exploitation of the world's poor? Are we all, as Anita Roddick (2001) of the *Body Shop* recently asked, 'complicit' in perpetuating global poverty? For some, the recent antiglobalization protests represent Karl Popper's 'temptation of the tribe', a manifest nostalgia for a more secure and perhaps mythical past, a willingness to disengage from perhaps 'inevitable' historical processes. Yet this is to simplify matters. For advocates of free trade globalization such as Harold James (2001) of Princeton University, economically liberal globalization *has* raised living standards throughout the world because there are fewer starving people than during the 1960s. Moreover, the recent WTO meeting in Qatar showed that the current concern for many 'Third World' governments with is that, in fact, the rich countries, despite their rhetoric to the contrary, are still extremely protectionist, wielding political power to maintain their market advantage whilst, contrary to the protestors argument, the developing nations want *more* liberalization, though fairer, i.e. to engage *more* with economic globalization.

On the other hand, Ann Pettifer (2001) of the group *Jubilee 2000*, argued that the axiom of 'trickle down' i.e. the trickling of wealth from the rich to the poor is not working. Thus, the issue at stake here, seemed to be, that economic globalization produces employment opportunities for developing nations but the problems were that:

1. The jobs were low paid and with poor working conditions.
2. Individual economic self-sufficiency had gone.
3. The global market took over and individuals were then traded on the invisible hand of the market.

In other words, the argument went, that there was a job to go to; but, and crucially, there was no possibility of making a longer term *livelihood*. Pettifer (2001) went on to argue that it was now necessary to inject a political dimension and to actually 'pace' globalization. Indeed, whilst neoliberal institutions are flawed, they can be made to work better through a new dialogue and after the events of September 11 are 'willing to listen'. Globalization then, comes in many forms and dispute over its form and location requires conceptual and strategic complexity which recognizes a transformation of specific costs *and* benefits. As Scholte (2000) points out, globalization as extensive supranational economic, social and cultural flows can be measured and the figures are staggering. There are now over one billion commercial airline passengers per year, two billion radio sets and over a billion television receivers.

In this global malaise, the old cartography of a world divided into territorially and hermetically sealed units/states seems somewhat awkward and yet at a more subjective level, an awareness of *globality* is not necessarily new and as Scholte (2000) notes, Old Mother Skipton of Yorkshire had long ago prophesized that one day 'around the world thought will fly, in the twinkling of an eye' (Scholte, 2000, p. 64). In his recent study, Scholte argues that economic and technological global transformations can be dated from an incipient globalization from the 1850s-1950s and then manifested by two way telephone messages which first went across the Atlantic in 1926, and the formation of new companies such as the American Telephone and Telegraph Company (AT and T) whose brave new world was futuristically envisaged as a 'world bound together by telephone'.

So historical context *is* important and many do tend to get carried away with the ebulliant notion of 'new times'. But it is the objective and perceived *acceleration* of change that seems to me to be the crux of the debate and which plays a major part in forming a critical politics of globalization. There are four main themes identified: Firstly, the philosophical aspect to the debate, and a global secular existence on an earthly world, the planetary home of the human species living with accepted scientific truths. Secondly, the development of capitalist global markets, productive sourcing, accounting and global commodities. Thirdly, technological global innovations and finally, the development of new regulatory frameworks, standardization, and the liberalization and property rights for global capital.

With these changes, maybe qualitative, some call for a new paradigmatic shift in the social sciences in order to understand the processes of globalization. This will be in direct contrast to a disciplinary 'methodological territorialism' which took the state as natural society in terms of its economy and geography, history and sociology (Scholte, 2000, Shaw, 2000).

My own feeling here, is that any critical account of globalization must refrain from reifying and abstracting economic globalization as a privileged logic. Such an understanding unfortunately comes even from many critical accounts of globalization. As an ardent supporter of free markets and economic globalization Clive Crook writes that the global economy by 2001 will have grown by around four per cent. Good news for rich and poor, and yet the:

> US in particular and industrialized countries in general are being told to grow more slowly and detach themselves from the rest of the world. Tempting as it is to mock this view of the world, it is no laughing matter (2000, p. 14).

Consequently, there is growing concern from the orthodoxy, with the critical responses to globalization shown at Seattle and elsewhere. The seduction of the antiglobalization politics for Crook (2000), is a harmful and worrying influence, which unintentionally, aims to deny workers the best chance of escapting poverty because the economic opportunities in an age of globalization for attacking poverty are truly amazing. Instead of seizing them eagerly, much of the world will seemingly do so reluctantly and apologetically. This is particularly a concern for advocates of European regionalization and the feeling of many, that globalization is merely imperialism by US corporations, by another fanciful name. Here then, antiglobalization protests are seen by the liberals, to be challenging the wealth creators, big business, free trade and ineluctable democratization. For Crook, economic globalization and the freedom of capital is creating truly massive wealth. By the year 2000, world output had grown by a staggering four per cent, from a mere three per cent growth in 1999, and world trade was up from around five per cent in 1999 to a staggering ten per cent in 2000. As Pam Wodall (2000, p. 21) noted, by the end of 1995, actual US productivity was up by three per cent, yet by the year 2000 it was up by more than five per cent. Wodall (2000) noted that this was mostly due to the development of new information technologies which have, firstly, generated more corporate efficiency and the possibility of more wealth creation. Secondly, there is now much easier access to information and prices, and finally, there is a much easier diffusion of trade which greatly increases the possibility of cooperation between states.

For the liberal gurus then, to systematically disengage from this new historical prerogative of the market would be left-wing folly, and tantamount to economic suicide, even a return to the economic dark ages of the kind envisaged and created by the practitioners of 1930s protectionism and right-wing national fundamentalism. The liberals continue to argue that free trade increases the potential for efficient wealth 'trickle down' and growing democracy. But the protestors continue to state that globalization is not just about free trade and that the liberal argument willingly misses the growing mobility of productive and financial capital and the *immobility* of labour. This allows for a skewed bargaining relationship between capital and labour that is quite unfair. However, critics on the left have tended to regard these less than propitious circumstances to be the product of malevolent forces, as cultivated by a powerful conspiracy of big business and the institutional bastions of globalization, the IMF and the World Bank (Pilger, 1999). However, the theme of responsibility and accountability emerging from the left, the old guard so to speak, is too simplistic. This is shown in various debates on globalization, where individual representatives of economic globalization are often asked the rather crass questions of 'did you know' about human rights abuses in states which are recipients of foreign investment and if so (you certainly are now), 'what is your response'. This leads to the inevitable close down of debate and the taking of defensive postures. In fact, crucially, the 'debate' actually shows that a more complex understanding of the relationship between structures, agents, intentions/responsibilities and consequences is very much needed in leftist critiques. Clearly then, it is *economic* globalization that symbolizes the public's perception of globalization and the associated protests against big business (Gordon, 1988). According to Held and McGrew (1998) 20 per cent of world output is now globally traded, a phenomenon due to a greater magnitude, complexity and speed of financial flows. Global corporations now straddling the globe have an output of goods that is often bigger than the GNP of many countries. By 1996 there were estimated to be over 44,000 MNCs with 280,000 foreign affiliates accounting for $ seven trillion global sales or 25-33 per cent of world output and 70 per cent of world trade. Transformations in the economic sphere have their localized effects and no one seems to be immune.

Clearly, MNCs can be dated from the plantations of the Caribbean to Indonesia, to the factory owners of the sweatshops of Mexico and Taiwan. However, during the 1960s and 1970s economic downturns in the late 1970s put pressure on firms and distinctions were made between *multi-* and *trans*national/global firms. Global firms were more integrated and coordinated from the top down. In an age of economic liberalization, they were also increasingly centralized and streamlined. The global firms challenged the somewhat insular existence of local MNC affiliates and MNC management power was challenged by this new corporate emphasis on strategic rationalization and flexibility. Global firms had a global mindset and they were not parochially loyal to the disparate subsidies. This *Toyota Model* of corporate growth meant that strategically there were no *direct* TNC subsidiaries but instead what was cultivated was a localized network of subsidiaries which operated *as if* the global was a mass market, and the globe was a single entity.

Global firms liked this idea of a global culture, a mass market of billions of consumers with similar tastes. As Ohmae (1985) put it, in the regional Triad economies of the world (America, Europe and Asia) there were an estimated 600 million consumers with incredible purchasing potential, as well as wages and salaries could be maintained. However, the dictates of the ideas and institutions of neoliberal globalization on the state are putting real downward pressure on wages and salaries through continuing competition between states for foreign investment in the games of the global economy. A two tier labour force is beginning to emerge (Amin, 1994) with a low price mass market and a new and fragmented 'niche and branded' market. Mayall (1998, p. 248) suggested that 'globalization introduced change in the nature of international relations' and the term 'transnational' implies an epochal shift and a more seamless web of global interactions. According to Ohmae (1990, p. 213) this nice neoliberal sentiment accepts that 'we are not one big happy family in the world yet' but 'we may be closer than we think'. The new ability for large firms to utilize information technologies to streamline and coordinate strategies was aided by governmental emphasis on the free market as the fordist state system of developmentalism was eroded. The global revolution is seen as an:

> ongoing trend whereby the world has - in many respects and at a generally accelerating rate - become one relatively borderless social sphere...(G)lobal phenomena can extend across the world at the same time and can move between places in no time, they are in this sense supraterritorial (Shaw, 2000, p. 15).

Susan Strange emphatically wrote to the realists, 'Wake up Krasner, the world has changed!' (Strange, 1994). In the UK, antagonistic positions concerning further integration within Europe or the so-called 'Eurozone', particularly from the conservative right, continue to hold onto a belief in the ability of the government to control national economic destinies via interest rate policies, in an age when trillions of dollars from institutions and traders transverse the globe in just a matter of seconds. The unintentional quaintness of the new right argument is strangely reassuring in an age of global economic turbulence and democratic deficits.

What is also of particular interest here is the way that the old left were (and are) just as antagonistic to European integration (a conspiracy of big business) as the new right; strange bedfellows indeed. Essentially the state was now seen as a self-seeking unity scouring the global markets for investment opportunities and wealth *creation* by developing attractive investment climates for foreign capital. The creation of investment climates requires a dismantling of intervention strategies, an opening up of economies to foreign investment by cutting taxes and a rolling back of the interventionist state as a bargaining market player whilst the traditional pillars of state development and its lofty ideals such as maintaining labour rights, welfare and social production are being rendered obsolete or at best reduced to the lowest possible overhead costs. Prevalent business economists such as Ohmae (1990) termed this epoch as 'the borderless world'.

Linking Globalization and Neoliberalism

Economists almost inexorably link globalization to neoliberalism and the free market ethos. Yet, if we see globalization as a more complex interlinking of various economic, political, cultural and social processes then it emerges that one can both challenge neoliberal globalization and yet *simultaneously* benefit from globalization. Maybe, because 'as connections have formed across national lines, a different agenda has taken hold, one that embraces globalization but seeks to wrest it from the grasp of multinationals' (Klein, 2000, p. 445). According to Wodall (1999) financial institutions still tend to applaud the new market initiatives of Paul Volcker, President of the US Federal Reserve that erupted in the early 1980s. In contrast to the economic protectionism of the 1970s, capital, during the early 1980s, was liberated whilst it was argued that the workers have made great advances in many countries, especially those that have embraced global trends. The alternative to free trade is protection against competition and government subsidies which leads to bloated, inefficient companies supplying consumers with outdated, unattractive products. Ultimately factories will close and jobs will be lost. But according to Burbach free trade agreements such as NAFTA:

> will enable US corporate capital to take advantange of the cheap labour resources to the south and to better compete for markets on a global level. The drive to NAFTA and the Enterprise for the Americas is also a response to basic changes occurring within the Western hemisphere itself. Across the Americas, the boundaries of the nation state are being ruptured (1992, p. 241).

According to MacEwan (1994, p. 131) 'NAFTA, then, is quite explicitly an agreement that pushes out the boundaries of unfettered capitalist production, and in doing so, it limits democracy by limiting peoples power to exercise political control over their economic lives'. For many in IPE the shift to the Liberal International Economic Order (LIEO) was a class orchestrated project of material resources, institutions and ideas combining at a specific historical crossroads, dedicated to the development of *global* rather than *national* capitalism (Van Der Pijl, 1984). Influential groups such as the *Trilateral Commission* and the *Bilderberg Group* which include government officials and financiers who not only rejected state interference but have rejected the interests of capitalists operating at the national level. Cox wrote that:

> The hegemonic concept of world order is founded not only upon the regulation of inter-state conflict, but also upon a globally conceived civil society i.e. a mode of production of global extent which brings about links among social classes of the countries encompassed by it (Cox, 1983, p. 171).

Moreover, the internal economic, political, social and cultural institutions of states have had to be adjusted to the *seemingly* dominant forces of neoliberal globalization. However, there are contradictions. Beck quotes the following text:

> The bourgeoise has through its exploitation of the world market given a cosmopolitan character to production and consumption in every country...national one-sidedness and narrow mindedness become more and more impossible and from the numerous national and local literature, there arises a world literature (1999, p. 22).

In fact, this text is not taken from some glossy neoliberal manifesto but it *is* taken from Karl Marxs' Communist Manifesto (Beck, 1999, p. 22). Herein of course, lies a key paradox of neoliberal globalization where an expansion of global capital accumulation and the interests of the globalization of capitalism, clash dialectically with the interests and livelihoods of millions around the world, with many sparked into resistance because of the economic and social contradictions of capitalist accumulation. Wachtel (1990) argued that for the new transnationalists, economic regulation was no longer seen as a protection for the national common good but as a nuisance that hindered future economic growth and the interests of transnational/global capitalism. Given the new market ethos:

> The American corporation operates supranationally, by extending its labour market worldwide and conducting more of its productive activities outside the US (Wachtel, 1990, p. 5).

From 1980 to 1984, capital investment abroad by US corporations stood at $200 billion due to the end of the Bretton Woods agreement in 1970s and an emphasis on finance capitalism as eurodollars, petrodollars and 'stateless' money started swashing around the world of casino capitalism (Strange, 1985). There was a worldwide growth in the belief that markets were the solution to economic difficulties, where millions of dollars of portfolio money are now coursing through the global economy and call the shots. As a result, trade unions now dare not strike for fear of stalling inward investment and losing jobs to similar productive operations around the globe. As a Marxist historian, Meiksins-Woods (1996) is suitably unimpressed by the 'there is no alternative' and warns the left not to *buy into* bourgeois *ideology*. However, the economic *reality* is that governments dare not renationalize industry or reintroduce huge welfare measures for fear of losing present and future foreign investment. This is an interesting relationship, between ideology/reality, and the dangers of self-fulfilling prophecies. Pauly summed this scenario up:

> the advice for all countries was to adopt outward orientated trade and investment policies, monetary policies aimed at price stability, fiscal policies aimed at balance in the medium term...and liberal financial policies designed (1997, p. 121-122).

This kind of activity is causing unprecedented concern. Protests are being nourished.

Global Modernities: The Sociology of Globalization

The globalization of culture provokes critiques of 'cultural imperialism' and the 'McDonaldization' of a world becoming culturally homogenized and bland with the 'dumbing down' impact of global brands on local cultures/societies (Waters, 1994). Sociological approaches during the early 1980s talked of an emerging global society. The global society has heralded both opportunity of mobility and at the same time, new global risks such as nuclear apocalypse and global environmental destruction (Beck, 1992, 1999). Increasingly however, populations have become more reflexive and more aware of new global dangers and respond by challenging and protesting on a variety of issues.

Sociologists such as Anthony Giddens (1990) and Roland Robertson (1992) have linked globalization to a more overarching and perhaps even profound process of global *modernization* which has uncoupled our conventional understanding of the relationship between time and space which has been cemented around the concept of modern *national* society. Robertson argued that:

> globalization as a concept refers both to the compression of the world and the intensification of consciousness of the world as a whole (1992, p. 3).

For Robertson, globalization represents not only material/objective networks and flows of economics and politics but globalization also incurs a change in the subjective perception of the world as a *concrete* and authentic place to live, rather than an *abstract* place to live. The paradox is, as 20th century German philosopher Martin Heidegger pointed out, that an increasing sense of 'nearness' works parallel in modern society, with an uneasy feeling of 'rootlessness'. The genealogy of a global consciousness can be traced all the way back to those early and outstanding images of the Earthly orb as taken from NASA cameras, and which were published in a variety of leading periodicals in the early 1970s. At the same time sociologists have shown that the reality and perception of global cultural homogenization engenders a process of cultural fragmentation or this 'clash of civilizations'.

Yet the impact of the new technologies on our perception of space and time remains politically significant. On the one hand we find a *distanciation* or the condition under which time and space are reorganized so as to connect presence and absence. Alternatively the process of social and political *disembeddedness* occurs where social relations are lifted out of their local context and restructured (Giddens, 1990). Such developments have *strategic* implications for the politics of globalization. Yet a celebration of localism, even nationalism, is an understandably defensive reaction to a bewildering global politics. Globalization can thus be defined as this intensification of worldwide social relations which link distant localities in such a way that local happenings are shaped by events occurring many miles away and vice versa. This is a complex and dialectical process because local happenings may move in an obverse direction from the distanciated relations that shape them. Thus, if people in Tokyo can experience the same thing at the same time as others in Helsinki then they in effect live in the same place? Robertson (1992) prefers the term *glocalization* to connote the subjective and personal sphere and the constitution and invention of diverse localities through global flows and ideas.

The term globalization has been used to refer to processes such as the expansion and internationalization of financial markets, interactive networks (e.g., global corporate management, worldwide epistemic and interpretive communities), new structures (e.g., newly emerging power relationships deriving from changing global investment patterns), and new identities and cognitive discourses built upon postmodern global conditions (Falk, 1996, 1999). This means that we may perhaps have to look for political spaces other than those bounded by the parameters of the state system and we see a growing number of transnational networks orientated around common goals and boundaries. This relates as much to a way of thinking about the world as it does to a description of the dynamics of the political and economic relations within it.

The First Critiques of Globalization

Critics of globalization have tended to focus on the empirical accuracies of the 'ideal type' globalization thesis (Hirst and Thompson, 1996). I do not want to spend too much time on these empirical, historical and realist critiques as these have been well documented. My concern is with the way protests have understood and *perceived* globalization. Empirical studies have tended to focus upon the activity of multinational corporations and concluded that the level of production and financial flows inter/intra firms and states around the world still occurred within a framework of international politics. Indeed the point was made that the liberal international order of the late 19th century under the guise and protection of 'Pax Britannica' was in fact more 'global' than the era of the 1980s and 1990s.

Indeed, given the shift towards protectionism during the recession of the 1970s, protectionist barriers still remain a major policy initiative for states in the not so borderless world. Trade wars are a familiar story in this new 'tit-for-tat' diplomacy. Perhaps importantly, national differences remain as well. Indeed, as we have seen during the past ten years or so, the rise of new nationalisms around the world challenges the idea and ideal of there existing a homogenous and harmonious global society. Yet, Geoffrey Owen wrote in *The Spectator:*

> If there is one belief that unites the antiglobalisation protestors and their sympathisers it is that multinational companies have become more powerful than governments (2001, p. 22).

Realists of course, continue to claim that the state and state sovereignty with its sanction of military force remain the key theme of international relations. Realists claim that debates on globalization get carried away with the idea of 'novelty'. Indeed, with the US Presidency of George W. Bush, debates over the Strategic Defense Initiative and new diplomatic concerns with Russia and China indicate that the familiar realist cartography, whilst recognizing the new issues and new actors, *at the end of the day*, remains an adequate framework for understanding international affairs. Historical critiques of the hyperglobalist perspective point out that if we see globalization as an historical expansion of capital accumulation due to the inherent dynamics of capitalism, then the capitalist world system has in fact been globalizing for quite some time. Clearly for those schooled in the IR tradition, the idea that new actors and new issues were beginning to ask serious questions about whether distinctions between national and international politics were analytically and empirically valid, came as a shock. The idea of the 'borderless world' and the shift towards the new multidisciplinary approaches were seen as quite innovative and as quite profound. On the other hand, an understanding of 'globalization' from Marxists regarded the term as simply a 'buzzword' as some of the underlying dynamics of globalization of capital accumulation had not fundamentally changed. By this I am thinking specifically of the responses of classical Marxist, neoMarxist and neostructuralist perspectives (Clarke, 1997). As a Marxist historian, and former editor of the socialist journal *Monthly Review* (a journal which is highly sceptical as to the 'new times' theses and 'postmodernism'), Harry Magdoff wrote:

> to begin with capitalism was born in the process of creating a world market, and the long waves of growth in the core capitalist countries were associated with its centuries long spread by conquest and economic penetration (1992, p. 45).

Marxist theories of imperialism (Brewer, 1982) have shown that relations between states are not directed by realist 'self interest' but rather, that the foreign policies of states are a manifestation of the underlying crises tendencies and expansive dynamics of capitalism. Crises of overaccumulation and underconsumption forced MNCs to search for markets and cheap labour whilst the national state aimed to capture and protect these markets on behalf of its national bourgeoise. Not only did this allow profitability to be ensured but it allowed firms to stave off worker unrest at home through the promise of higher wages and propitious working conditions maintained through the distribution of this surplus extraction from the periphery. Consequently, as capitalism moved from competitive toward monopoly capitalism the state forged a distinctive relationship with the interests of capital as blocs of state/finance capital whilst debates within Marxist circles ensued as to the profundity of this relationship (Poulantzas, 1981). Marx and Engels once wrote that 'capital requires neither political nor social boundaries' (quoted in Rupert, 1998, p. 49). Hobsbawm (2000, p. 13) wrote that 'the global triumph of capitalism is the major theme of history in the decades after 1848' as it was a:

> triumph of a society which believed that economic growth rested on competitive private enterprise, on buying everything (including labour) at the cheapest price and selling everything at the dearest (Hobsbawm, 2000, p. 13).

The industrial revolution brought about a complex web of relationship and innovations. Hobsbawm asked:

> How did the world of the 1880s compare with that of the 1780s? In the first place it was now genuinely global. Almost all parts of the world were now known and more or less adequately or approximately mapped (2000, p. 15).

The early 20th century saw a new age of technological innovation and discovery. But even this age of Enlightenment and adventure had a history which directly or indirectly brought about an unprecedented expansion of capital relations. Explorers such as Columbus, Cortes and Magellan, yearning for adventure, began a trend of European discovery that paved the way for the introduction to remote parts of the world of European Enlightenment and capital. Paradoxically, both liberal and Marxist responses to the infiltration of capital relations shared a common set of assumptions borne of the Enlightenment, most notably the beliefs in progress and societal evolution (Hobsbawm, 2000a).

Undoubtedly, Marxism was a global theory with a global practice and yet Marx had never formulated a theory of internationalism/international relations *per se*. However in the periphery the export of capital was meant to develop the countries from traditional to modern society and inexorably to the point where the capitalist system could no longer sustain itself and world socialism would emerge. From this apocalyptic perspective NeoMarxist/world systems theory had critiqued classical liberal and Marxist theories of development on the supposition that both classical perspectives had taken the state as ontological unit whilst in fact the capitalist world economy, based upon the transfer of surplus through an unequal exchange of goods, has existed since the long 16th century (Haynes, 1996).

This was a dependency in the sense that the periphery was *dependent* on the economic development of the core countries and that this global *structural* inequality meant that the periphery could not act autonomously. Even during the post war era of political independence, neocolonial economic ties of exploitation manifested by the activity of MNCs and the local affiliates or 'comprador' class maintained this exploitative relationship. From this perspective, the main opponents of the capitalist world system were the working classes of core, peasants of periphery and the strong national bourgeoises responsive to local demands for public services, the diversification of economies and improvement of living standards. Clark (1997) suggested that globalization was both a new and intensive stage of global accumulation and as I read it, simultaneously a part of an 'historical evolution' (Clark, 1997, p. 31).

The crisis in radical development theory/neoMarxism based on the actions of the state and the apparent outdated theories of dependency (due to the East Asian Tigers and the growing income disparaties *within* Western states due to the onslaught of neoliberal restructuring) has led some to look for alternative paths to (and interpretations of) development. Responses have varied; from establishing 'better' scientific theories of explanation to the development of *subaltern* studies characterized by a rejection of grand programmatic alternatives by focusing upon the reflexivity of concrete agents and institutions (Mallon, 1994). Intellectual energy is thus directed to the concrete/specific development *studies* galvanized by new social movements activating in civil society and reacting to diverse issues such as protecting ethnic rights, the plight of the homeless, empowering democracy and social justice and protecting the environment. Such a politics operates at a community/grassroots level and outside conventional political institutions. Consequently, Burbach (1997, p. 1) argued that capitalism has gone through four major stages, evolving, though not progressing *per se*, from Colombus' age of discovery and the colonization of Latin America, to industrial capitalist development, to the dominance of finance capital and finally to globalization as manifested by a new and dictatorial global capital free to roam the world by tapping into cheap labour markets. It was also accepted that 'globalization is the international spread of capital exchange and production is a very painful process' (MacEwan, 1994, p. 130).

However, a focus solely on the expansion of capitalism, whilst important, must also be linked to other interpretations of what is meant by globalization as an economic social, political and cultural phenomenon. Through globalization, new cultural and political spaces are being created which *do not* correspond with state-sponsored cartography, but with marginalized and excluded sites, the privatization and commodification of public spaces (Klein, 2000).

During the Cold War there were the trusted friends 'in here' and there were the nefarious yet putative enemies 'out there'. Borders were defined as state centered. Now the enemies reside 'within' - not only through the activity of far right terrorists such as Timothy McVeigh and Islamic fundamentalists but through the segregation of major world cities between the marginalized and the underclass living side by side with luxury and the wealthy in the postmodern city, a city of high mobility and high security. This is the 'third world within', a two tiered society, even perhaps a return to the politics of the medieval walled city as there is a new and dichotomous 'global freedom of movement signalling social promotion, advancement and success and immobility exuding the repugnant odour of defeat, failed life and being left behind' (Bauman, 2000, p. 121). Those without property seek a job, selling their labour power on a recessionary market, dabbling with alternative political economies now that their economic self sufficiency has gone. The fires burn (Klein, 2000; Pilger, 1999).

Conclusion

The conceptual and strategical issue of 'overturning of globalization' is a particularly strong theme in critical IPE whilst these approaches have tended to regard globalization as a process of capital accumulation on the one hand and as a very *historically specific* manifestation of 'transnational' class ideas, institutions and interests. What is explicit in these approaches is the strong critique of the deterministic and teleological readings of economic globalization. Critical IPE has developed a broader based enquiry into the possibility of reclaiming the political and identified the major agents and institutions in this critical endeavour. Thus, focus was placed upon the development of the relationship between social movements and globalization. This focus will be discussed in the following two chapters.

Chapter 2

The Theory and Practice of Social Movements

Introduction

The purpose of this chapter is to outline the theoretical and conceptual interest in the activity of social movements. Attention is mostly drawn to a chronological account of the major social movement theories. Attention is then specifically drawn to an historical account of the emergence of the ideological movements of Marxism, liberalism and nationalism and through to the strategic debates incurred throughout the 19th and 20th centuries.

Social Movements and International Relations

The idea of changing the world is a very modern theme (Agnew, 1998). It is a theme which can only really make sense if the 'world' is understood as something 'to be worked upon' i.e. it is 'out there' and an entity that is somehow independent of political and social agents who, nevertheless, simultaneously live within it. This Enlightenment theme is at the core of the revolutionary social movement. For German philosopher Martin Heidegger, such a conception of the human relationship with (and to) the world through the human 'being' or *dasein* is an extremely alienating experience which ultimately leads to the domination of both humans over humans and of humans over nature. In a response to revolutionary aspirations, then emerges, as I will show here, a 'postmodern' response which is based upon, as Heidegger put it, a 'being in the world' and a rejection of modernity.

The idea and sentiment of change has been formulated in theory and practice at the level of the national state/society. Protests continue to lobby the national government and the idea of 'national elections' is standard and accepted in liberally democratic states. Moreover, revolutionary communist state Russia, shows so profoundly the way even the most radical politics would be enmeshed within the spatial and institutional parameters of the sovereign state system (Watson, 2001a). The study of social change began as a way of understanding the nature of social change within the *national* context. From the functionalist theories of Emile Durkheim and later, Talcott Parsons (1952), even to the Marxist conflict theories, the idea of society and social change has been historically tied to the bounds of the state and economically, politically and culturally coalesced within the state. We talk of national economy, national society and national institutions. In International Relations the 'inside' of the state was the realm of societal progress and the Enlightenment whilst the realm of the international was the time and the space of cyclical/perennial chaos and crisis. Indeed the sovereign-state system of 1648 marked a historically specific understanding of modern politics and of the relationship between time and space (Walker, 1993, 2000). Walker noted that:

> sovereignty is not properly understood as an expression of an extreme as constitutive of anarchy without or of order within - but precisely as a middle ground, as a point of intersection between extremes: between inside and outside, and between universality and particularity. It is in fact an expression of the characteristic manner in which the modern world has been able to answer questions about the relationship between one and many, between the multiplicity of things and people, on the one hand, and the unity of the world and humanity on the other, through a spatial differentiation between inside and outside (2000, p. 227).

Consequently, Sklair (1991, p. 30) wrote that 'the central feature of the idea of globalization is that many contemporary problems cannot be adequately studied at the level of nation-states, that is in terms of international relations, but need to be theorized in terms of global (Transnational) processes beyond the level of the nation-state'. For sociologists, this leap of faith was not only anathema to conventional moorings of what was meant by 'society' but it was also a highly *abstract* leap of faith. But what of protests, what of social movements? How does the idea of protest relate to these conceptual and political changes? For Sklair (1991), writing as a sociologist, the new anticapitalist movements are those that challenge the power of TNCs in the economic sphere, oppose the transnational capitalist class and its local affiliates and promote those cultures and ideologies antagonistic to capitalist global consumerism. Sklair (1998, p. 305) wrote:

although capitalism increasingly organises globally, the resistances to global capitalism can be effective only where they can disrupt its smooth running (accumulation of private profits) locally and can find ways of globalising these disruptions.

Historically the theory and practice of social movements, particularly those social movements resisting capitalism, its ideas and institutions have tended to be limited to the local and national spheres. Indeed, the problem for the Marxist internationals had always, as the First World War showed most starkly, been that nationalism was always going to seem a stronger ideology to die for than abstractions of 'workers of the world unite' (Falk, 1999). In the study of international politics conceptual and strategic limitations are also apparent. Walker (1993) argued that the geopolitical boundaries of 'inside' and 'outside' will restrict the strategic and imaginative shift to a different global politics of resistance because:

> once one crosses the official boundaries of the established conceptions of politics, the boundaries of the modern state, it is very difficult to speak about any kind of politics at all (Walker, 1994, p. 679).

Consequently, critical theories and practices must further challenge the 'codes of inner and outer, the account of spatial/temporal relations that informs the normative horizons of modern politics' (Walker, 1994, p. 672) as the 'ontological distinction of what goes on inside and outside the state' (Walker, 1994, p. 671). Marxism, neoGramscians and contemporary emancipatory projects work with the supposition that there could (and should) be a hierachy between the local, national and global. However, now, a future critical 'politics that encompasses the world' cannot 'be envisaged on the assumption that the world already exists along with the categories through which it must be known' (Walker, 1994, p. 700). Indeed I will argue that by working within the historically specific spatial and political *hierachy* of the local, national and global *other* forms and sites of a democratic politics of resistance are *potentially* excluded. And so, despite the inevitable problem of 'infinite regress', it emerges that 'to ask what does it mean to be political' is itself a political gesture (Walker, 2000).

Social Movements in Theory and Practice

How does a social movement differ from a political party? This is a difficult and often ambiguous question for political parties often began as social movements (Taylor, 1991, Wallerstein et al., 1991). If that is the case, how does the social movement become the political party? Is this transition quantifiable? Then, what about pressure groups, lobby groups, protest groups and non-governmental organizations (NGOs)? Where do these actors, institutions and organizations fit into the equation, if at all? Then, more politicized questions emerge. Do social movements really matter to the politics of the day? Are they effective social actors? Who joins social movements and why? For decades sociologists and political scientists have debated these issues, coming up with a variety of intellectual frameworks and theories through which to explain and understand the phenomenon of social change and the actors integral to this. Melucci (1984, p. 3) has argued that social movements are 'collectivities that comprize a number of individuals exhibiting at the same time and at the same place behaviour with relatively similar morphological characteristics'. For others, social movements 'bring about social change through challenging values and identities of social actors' (Scott, 1990, p. 18).

The term 'social' implies a broader concept of social change than that allowed by the term 'political' movement, a movement that is not restricted to the machinations of the modern bureaucratic political system but rather an overarching social transformation or may act in favour of one particular group or one particular issue. Charles Tilly (1978) wrote that social movements consist of people acting together in pursuit of interests they share. Social movements may be divided into categories such as revolutionary/transformative, reformist, redemptive and finally, alternative.

There has been a distinctive genealogy of efforts to explain *why* social movements emerge and *how* social movements attain their goals and objectives. Structural accounts tended to regard social movements as manifestations of a disfunctional society. The functionalist school of sociology based upon the legacy of the work of French writer Emile Durkheim who had regarded society as an organic entity or as a biological living entity where individuals and organizations were interconnected and all fitted neatly into the *gessellschaft* cog. Industrialization rendered old ways of mechanical feudal life obsolete and capitalist industrialization was the beginning of a complex modern society interwoven with new bureaucratic conglomerates. Durkheim regarded modern society as evolutionary and it was a society that could be measured and looked upon empirically because it was a society that determined individual action because it was 'out there'. Social conflict and unrest within this new interdependent entity were seen as manifestations of structural cleavage and required problem solving. Neil Smelser (1962, p. 3) in his 'Theory of Collective Action' aimed to find out why 'in all civilisations men take it upon themselves to engage in collective behaviour'. For writers of this ilk the answer was primarily a 'structural' account and the study of social movements has therefore been a central feature of the discipline of sociology and disciplines specifically concerned with the apparent traumas of social change. Many theories of social movements exist. Firstly, social movements are characterized as transformative or revolutionary. Secondly, social movements are characterized as seeking change but remaining within the existing political system. Thirdly, social movements are characterized as redemptive or which seek to 'rescue' people such as the new religious movements. Finally, there are alternative movements that seek to influence peoples' habits and behaviour, such as pressure and protest single issue groups. Structural accounts of social movement organization focused on the *location of grievance* or specifically *why* social movements mobilized and what their objectives were (Smelser, 1962). Smelser (1962) argued that movements also require definitive goals, beliefs, and are mobilized by many precipitating factors such as economic exploitation and a lack of political representation. What was required was a coordinated group and the success of the movement depends upon the reaction from the state or the authorities.

Moreover, such studies tended to regard the participants of social movements as showing the social dislocations in the social structure (Parsons, 1952). Secondly, there emerged a concern with the *strategies and tactics* of social movements or understanding why certain movements survived the passage of time and why others with similar grievances, did not. This 'resource mobilization theory' focused on the resources used by social movements. Here, social movements were not construed as deviant or 'irrational'. The earliest known 'theory' of social protest was Le Bon's theory of crowds (Rude, 1959). This highlighted reasons behind the development of intense mob frenzy in industrial areas and the psychological constituents of 'crowds' on the question of violence. For others, social movements were seen to attract rational and goal orientated individuals who were organized and who were motivated to efficiently use materials (economic) resources, support (political), organization and access to information technology and media outlets (Zald and McCarthy, 1977). And finally, in a rejection of a rather instrumentalist approach interest turned back to the question of grievance as shown in the development of the new social movements (Gladwin, 1994; Scott, 1990; Touraine, 1981). Indeed this chronological development impacted on conceptual distinctions made between the old and new social movements.

The societal dislocation generated by industrialization, as men and women were pushed from their feudal relations into the large factories of industrial towns such as London and Manchester generated social friction. Industrial capitalism turned humans into wage labour to be bought and sold on the labour market. This induced new social tensions and new forms of protest that differed from the fragmented and sporadic riots of the early modern period. Protests were also sentimental and reactionary as the Romantic Movement and the Luddite Movement later showed. Here, hankering for a premodern golden age of an idyllic rural setting as shown most vividly in the works of Blake and Wordsworth, a society in harmony with nature, seemed a little nostalgic, but in the turmoil of industrialization, it was understandable. Reactionary movements were thereby contrasted to those Enlightened movements which took advantage of the new and liberal values of capitalism and turned them against the selfsame capitalist system. Eder argued that:

> not every form of protest is a social movement...social movements are those directly and intentionally related to modernisation from the 17th century onward. In this sense there are only two, the first one appeared during the transition from traditional feudal domination to the early modern state...the second is the labour movement which challenged the restriction of emancipation to political emancipation. This notion of social movement clearly requires a reconstruction of their relation to modernity. Social movements are genuinely modern phenomena. Only in modern society have social movements played a constitutive role in social development (1993, p. 107).

These large collectivities directly related to the 18th and 19th centuries and bolstered by the new ideals of liberty, fraternity and suffrage brought forth by the 1789 French Revolution and Tom Paine's 'Declaration of the Rights of Man' (Hobsbawm, 2000). New and grand ideologies of nationalism and socialism were now beginning to emerge and following the French revolution, the 'tricolor of some kind became the emblem of virtually every emerging nation' (Hobsbawm, 2000, p. 73) and 'even provided the vocabulary and the issue of liberal and radical democratic politics for most of the world'. This was the new language of the

Enlightenment, a language of reform and suffrage but still, ultimately, a bourgeois revolution which pushed the *normality* of social change.

Nevertheless, the dawning of the Enlightenment and the revolutions of 1848 across Europe, along with the rise of the worker internationals indicated a new form of protest which worried the rulers and the elites. These old social movements mobilized against an exploitative capitalism and its class biased political institutions. The old social movements were particularly successful of course, in spreading the revolutionary ideals of liberty, equality, democracy and progress which have 'become part of the primary political structures of the modern world' (Walker, 1988, p. 26). The old social movements had transformative blueprints of 'what was to be done'. Strategically this would be achieved by capturing the state through violence or as a political party (Poulantzas, 1981; Scott, 1990; Taylor, 1991). Walker (1988) noted that socialists had an 'overriding concern with the state as the locus of political power' and however 'suspicious particular nationalists or socialists may have been of the state' both 'nationalism and socialism became organized in relation to state institutions' (Walker, 1988, p. 28). A modern social movement had a self image consciousness and a clear idea of who it was against and what it was for.

The cultivating of a socialist/worker internationalist or a new robust globalism, is key to the revival of Marxist theory and practice following the revolutions of 1989 and the new challenges of globalization. Indeed, the relevance of Marxism is clear given recent concern and developments of big business and the global financial community. Marx had always insisted that whilst the capitalists 'usurp and monopolize all advantages of this process of transformation' leaving a legacy of 'slavery degradation and exploitation' capitalism in turn also generates a unified revolution of workers, at a time when 'the monopoly of capital becomes a fetter on the mode of production' until even the capitalist 'expropriators are expropriated' (Marx, quoted in Mclellan, 1986, p. 56). *Internationalist* perspectives also underscore a distinctive understanding of the spatial and political relationship between national workers and the structural conditions of international/global capital. This brings in to the debate the intriguing conceptual and strategic relationship between the dialectically structural conditions of class conflict and 'class consciousness' (Sklair, 1998). Implicit in the theory and practice of Marxism therefore, was a distinctive spatial and temporal understanding of the site and nature of modern politics (even radical politics) mapped by the division of this world into territorially bounded states with supreme political sovereignty and a supreme distinction between the 'inside' and 'the outside' (Walker, 1991, 1993). The assumption for Marxism was capture of the national state apparatus and inevitable progress to world socialism as the dominos of the bourgeois state collapsed. Moreover there was implicit a spatial and strategic hierachy made from the insignificance of the local to the national and finally to the utopia of global transformation. Wallerstein noted (1992, p. 292) that it was 'the impact of the French Revolution the sense that the new is good and desirable' that formed the key ideological justification of mass revolutionary mobilization.

Marxists (and neoMarxists) have tended to focus on the development of the state in terms of the *development* of capitalism, its institutions and its material and ideological resources. This approach identified the state as an institution for the maintenance of capitalism. This was derivative of the Marxist axiom that the state was the executive of the ruling class (Marx and Engels, 1967). Indeed, historical materialism focused upon the interlinkages between production, ideas, institutions and social forces which injected an historical movement into the study of IR and challenged what were regarded as the politically moribund cyclical theories with a possibility of constructing alternative world orders (Cox, 1981, 1999). Such a focus on capitalism as the location of grievance and the principal mode of analysis linked to a theoretical heritage of the old social movements.

Traditionally understood as representing revolutionary nationalist and Marxist struggles, old social movements represented class struggle. Marxist struggles had an objective to destroy the exploitative development of capitalism, its bourgeois political institutions and to construct in their place a better economic, political, cultural and social development, namely socialism. Marxism emphasized the underlying material dialectic of class struggle as the inevitability of the grand narrative of world history. Marxism approached capitalism as a necessary stage towards communism within the dialectic and considered the capitalist mode of production and the exploitative relationship between the owners and non-owners of production as historically *specific*. Essentially, capitalist society was seen to be organized around the base/superstructure model and characterized by the two opposing classes of bourgeoise and proletariat, or more later, between developed core countries and developing peripheral countries (Meiksins-Woods, 1996, 1996a).

Thus, the 18th and 19th centuries were punctuated by short term protests, riots and political/social upheavals. Gradually, a grander and longer term objective was elucidated in the search for mass franchisement and equality. Ultimately, these were revolutionary desires for a better society as De Toqueville exclaimed, stating, what:

> to start with, had seemed to European monarchs and statesman a mere passing phase, a not unusual symptom of a nations growing pains, was now discovered to be something absolutely new, quite unlike any previous movement, and so widespread, extraordinary and incalculable as to baffle human understanding (1966, p. 35).

The French revolution of 1789 set the precedent. These revolutions were not meant to be a *coup d'etat* or the replacement of one set of coercive leaders by another. Instead, revolutions were, in theory, meant to lead to major changes by a mass social movement guided by the hope of freedom and the spirit of a better society. The values of liberty, equality, fraternity and democracy were manifested through struggles both in the developed and developing worlds. Revolutionary movements aimed to destroy the economic and political institutions of capitalism, aiming to generate a socialist, nationalist and democratic revolution and ultimately the transformation of society. According to Vilas:

> revolutions have to do with the transformation of the socio economic structure and the political system of a country; the transformation of the relations of power between the classes, of access to resources and of the administration of the means of production (1989, p. 31).

The Western vision struck a definitive normative chord with radicals attracted by the idea of the actual *normality* of social change. Yet paradoxically the capitalist world *and* the ideals of an unquenchably thirsty revolutionary socialism were reliant upon this 'liberalist' ideology (Wallerstein, 1992; Walker, 1988). Hobsbawm (2000, p. 9) noted that 'revolutions triumphed throughout the world' and that 'the years 1789 to 1848' were 'the greatest transformation in human history'.

Over the decades revolutionary fervour became distinguishable between solidly class based socialist movements galvanized by the proletariat and nationalist movements which tended to rely upon a distinctive alliance of classes. This latter scenario became very apparent in nationalist and often radical bourgeois movements in the Third World. The role of the peasantry as a revolutionary strikeforce was a hotbed for contestation as the fervent socialists did not regard the peasantry as a revolutionary *class for itself* (Hobsbawm, 1994; Marcos, 1994, 1994a).

The world bourgeoise had recognized that something different was happening.

Old Social Movements: Strategies and Tactics

Marxist writers developed a distinctive conceptual and interpretive device through which to explain and direct the strategies and tactics of resistances. For instance, Cox suggested that the:

> most open challenge to the impact of globalisation on social and political structures has come from a new type of revolutionary movement, the Zapatista rebellion of the Mayan Indians in the Southern Mexico state of Chiapas...a rallying force in civil society...*(T)he organic intellectual uses historical investigation and critical thinking and can open new territory for resistances on an informative and strategical level* (1999, p. 23, my emphasis).

The organic intellectuals were seen as the enlightened agents for strategically raising a radical political consciousness and serving 'to clarify the political thinking of social groups leading the members of these groups to understand their existing situation in society and how in combination with other social groups they can struggle towards a higher form of society' (Cox, 1999, p. 24). So how was a revolutionary movement to achieve this goal? This strategic puzzle concerned the strategic and tactical nature of the movements. It would spark debate on the justification of the use of *violence* and the bearing of arms. Indeed traditionally speaking, revolutions quite literally sought the destruction of capitalism and its political institutions. Revolutionary movements would attract and relied upon charismatic, sacrificial and heroic revolutionary leaders to 'raise the masses' into a revolutionary power.

During the 19th century and in the aftermath of the so-called year of revolutions (1848) debates ensued within Marxism concerning the link between the short and long term objectives of the revolutionary movement. Crucially, specific emphasis was placed on the role of the strategic role of the state which was construed as the location of class/political power. Marx and Engels (1967) had argued that the state was the executive of the ruling class and that political power is merely the organized power of one class oppressing another. Consequently, the state in essence, is the 'committee for managing the affairs of the bourgeoise'. Therefore the state would have to be destroyed. Debate raged as to whether the state merely aided a particular class *instrumentally* or whether the state aided *structurally* capitalist society as a whole. For instance, Poulantzas (1981) argued that structurally, the state incorporated both an ideological apparatus, (church, media and education) and a repressive apparatus, (army and the police) to maintain the efficient functioning of capitalism. For Marx and Engels (1967) and as stated in the last page of their Communist Manifesto it would be necessary to 'forcibly overthrow' the state and the existing social conditions, because the workers 'have a world to win'. Anarchists insisted that focus on the state would enmesh the revolutionary movement into the confines of capitalism's economic and political relations because the state was a functionary for maintaining class relations. On the other hand, the state was the revolutionary enabler and the first step towards global revolution (Taylor, 1991). What emerged was a strategic local-national-global matrix and once captured the destruction of the state meant the destruction of capitalist development and the ruling class.

There were those who thought that the state would need to be captured, even destroyed, through a violent Leninist style armed guerrilla insurgency. This was not violence for violence sake nor simply a cathartic release. Rather, violence was used efficiently and professionally. The alternative would be that the state would be captured through parliamentary means and the revolutionary movement would be organized and conducted as a political party.

Marxism then split between those strategically pushing for global revolution and those movements remaining at the level of national liberation. National liberation movements were based on the state and 'nationalism' became known as a progressive ideological force in representing a distinctive alliance of classes in the struggle against economic and political imperialism. It was also accepted (as Lenin pointed out during World War One) that nationalism was a 'bourgeois' ideology and could be gratuitously used to divide and rule the workers and take them away from their true and objective global solidarities. But nationalism *was* a powerful mobilizing force and the revolutions of the early twentieth century in Mexico and Russia were revolutions that according to Marxism could not, and should not have happened for the 'creative destruction' of capitalist relations had not been fully developed according to the dialectic of history. Walker noted that revolutionary movements in:

> contrast with most of the sporadic and fragmented movements that came before, these movements were remarkably successful. They have become part of the primary political structures of the modern world. This is not to say that their

great visions have been adequately realised. Far from it. But it is impossible to deny their impact on what we have now become (1988, p. 27).

World Systems and Antisystemic Movements

As I mentioned in chapter one, world systems analyses claim that the global market emerged during the 16th century. World systems writers questioned the 'national' strategic effort by anticapitalist revolutions for merely and unavoidably capturing the political structure of the capitalist world system, that is, the state. Anarchists such as the (in light of the 1989 events) prophetic Bakunin challenged the autarkic strategy during the 1860s. The Russian and Mexican revolutions suggested that capturing the state is an important revolutionary move and yet in the capitalist *world* economy:

> total economic withdrawal involves a major economic sacrifice, this is why the revolutionary movements once in power, have all without exception been beset by internal strains for the forces at work are contradictory...have fundamentally shaken the political structures of the capitalist world economy and the self confidence of the bourgeoise. But in their very success these movements have simultaneously strengthened the capitalist world economy and state system (Wallerstein, 1991, p. 23).

In the capitalist world economy the oppressed are too weak to manifest opposition constantly but when oppression becomes particularly acute people have risen up. These are the antisystemic movements that shake the bourgeoise. And they did. But they also became confined within the political superstructure of the world capitalist system, the inter-state system. Indeed, the global extent of the rebellions of 1968 indicated a profound disappointment with the old left. Attention was drawn to the authoritarianism of state-socialism and the imperialistic actions by the Soviet Union in Hungary in 1956 and Czechoslovakia in 1968 (Kundera, 1969). And in the West the post-war welfare state and the post-war compromize served to neutralize the aspirations of the really radical left as socialist party political governments maintained the economic and political stability of 'real world' capitalism. Socialist struggles helped spread the capitalist law of value and Khrushchev's 'we will bury you' became particularly ironic.

The counter-revolution revolutions of 1968 heralded in a new wave of protesting that baffled and annoyed the old left in terms of what they represented and what they wanted. It also heralded a new intellectualism. Intellectuals such as Jean-Paul Sartre supported 'the boycott of the 1968 Olympic Games in Mexico City, and on December 19, 1969, he gives a press conference to denounce once again the American massacre in Vietnam' (Cohen-Solal, 1991, p. 454). Sartre along with Michel Foucault also condemned the French War in Algeria. In response to the French authorities, Sartre protested, and 'If we were just a dozen intellectual simpletons playing at judging the world, they wouldn't bother us. So why do they fear us?' (Cohen-Solal, 1991, p. 456). On May 11 1968, the tenth anniversary of De Gaulle's rise to power, it was clear that these intellectuals were politicized 'by the Algerian and Vietnamese wars, and violently opposed to the practices of the Western communist parties' (Cohen-Solal, 1991, p. 457). New social movements represented a different world, and as such, cultivated different objectives and strategies. New social movements related to the development of a new kind of post industrial capitalism of growing complexity with the new technological production of symbolic consumer goods and symbolic struggles over ethical models by which a collectivity produces a culture. New social movements are located within civil society where the stakes of 'class consciousness' also involve the contestation of the main cultural patterns. Lyotard (1979, p. 3) argued that 'we no longer have recourse to the grand narratives we can resort neither to the dialectic of spirit nor even to the emancipation of humanity as a validation for postmodern discourse'. New social movements proffered the view that the proletariat was splintered and had lost its revolutionary vitality. The new social movements represented a 'crisis in confidence' with Western modernity (Grant, 1998, p. 29). Critical attention celebrated traditional cultures, philosophies and organizations which celebrated a 'politics of difference' and was *most commonly* understood to be a necessary move beyond modernity and revolutionary blueprints (Burbach, 1994). And other *single* issues such as feminism, culture, lifestyle, identity and gender politics emerged at the time. The new social movements questioned revolutionary strategies and objectives on the legacy of post-revolutionary state authoritarianism and cooption (Taylor, 1991). New social movements questioned the organizational deficiencies of old social movements because the bureaucratization of international communism clearly revealed the extent to which it had become an organ of Max Weber's bureaucratic capitalism. As such, new social movements favoured a strategically localized and pragmatic politics of resistance.

During the 1960s the old left remained somewhat convinced in the utility of the concepts and project of class struggle. But the model of diametrically opposed and ensuing cataclysmic struggle between the bourgeois and the proletariat seemed incredibly outdated. With the 'new deal' and the new information society, the old Marxist romanticism of the revolutionary proletariat was no longer a credible force in revolutionary solidarity, and a new and vibrant proletariat aristocracy, the 'nouveau riche' so to speak, was also emerging. This was where the threat to the middle class establishment was coming from; they put up the barricades. However, there were also new intra class cleavages and a cross cutting of 'contradictory' class positions and interests. Indeed it was said that other revolutionary subjects would now have to be found.

Undoubtedly, the Civil Rights Movement in the late 1960s, along with the halcyon youth movements of the time, from Mexico City, to San Francisco and to Paris, galvanized a staunch critique of the party political left and President Johnson's policy in Vietnam. Moreover, there was focus on the role of black Americans who were taking part in the Vietnam War. Malcolm X of the *Black Panthers* asked why the exploited of the West were fighting the exploited of the East. Chomsky (1969) argued that the rebellions of the late 1960s indicated a more than clear disdain for the fabric of the Cold War national security state where economic development had become inextricably linked to the arms race. Chomsky argued that 'there is a great many people who have been aroused by the Vietnam tragedy...there is a new mood of questioning and rebellion amongst the youth of this country, a very healthy and hopeful development' (Chomsky, 1969, p. 8). During the 1960s many groups and individuals began mobilizing on issues that were not based on class concerns. Emphasis was put on new issues and new grievances. Usually these were single issue movements focused on identity and lifestyle politics with a sense that capitalism was no longer, or perhaps never had been, the principal source of grievance (Gladwin, 1994). Many of those searching for revolutionary struggle went to the developing world. Consequently, a distinctive periodization was made.

The 'post-industrial society' rearranged previous class solidarities and work practices in the fragmented postmodern era. What emerged was a more outstanding questioning of the grand *ideology* of Western modernization, capitalist and/or communist. For instance, whilst white women were considered 'imperialists' by colonized peoples, a growing solidarity and empathy grew between white and black women who suffered the ignominy of patriachal dominance. This cross-over of issues and concerns somewhat diminished the rather mechanical versions of the world found in traditional Marxism. Indeed, Marx had not considered progress and technology as problematic *in themselves*, because the edifice of Marxism was still rooted in the narrative of rationality and the assumption of teleological progress/emancipation. Hence, contentious debates between Marxists and postmodernists ensued (Meiksins-Woods, 1996).

Whilst modernity was most commonly associated with a resounding break from tradition, superstition and liberation from the shackles of nature, it became clear that the project of modernity was not worthy of innate trust. Science and Enlightenment were creating a world of calculation, ruthless efficiency, environmental destruction and the neutralizing of human creativity and spirituality, whilst obscuring these perils through ideals 'in the name of progress'. The angst of Munchs' iconoclastic 'The Scream' and the later novels of Fyodor Dostoevsky showed the alienation of the human spirit in this modern world at the dawn of the twentieth century. Thus, new social movements began to be concerned with the overall fabric and direction of modern society (O'Neill, 1986). This so called 'colonization' of the lifeworld, meant much needed state welfarism, but which generated this somewhat stifling bureaucratization of society through the anonymous institutions of a database modernity, the Orwellian scenario. Ironically, the new right was also to respond vociferously to the 'nanny' state. Giddens (1990, p. 109) argued that to live in a 'universe of modernity is to live in an environment of chance and risk'. Modern society had created an ethic of 'distance' and the possibility of abrogating individual ethical responsibility to the new and anonymous bureaucratic chain of command, which ultimately led to the gas chambers of Auschwitz. According to George (1994), postmodernism 'whilst it is always directly (and sometimes violently) engaged with modernity' seeks 'to go beyond the repressive, closed aspects of modernist global existence' (George, 1994, p. 214). Walker noted that:

> whether understood as an extension of specifically Western cultural traditions, as a consequence of specifically capitalist forms of economic life, or even as a consequence of a particular form of patriachy, the culture of modernity is not so much universal in any absolute sense as it is an historical dominant expression of the claim to universality (Walker, 1988, p. 49).

Postmodernism intimated a celebration of cultural diversity and celebrated a romantic enchantment, in contrast to a homogenizing and mechanistic modernization. The prefix 'post' was imbued with, paradoxically, the temporal mindset of modernity/epochal progression. The Marxist ideology, in its state form, was dealt the final ignominious blow by the collapse of real existing socialism in 1989, and in 1990 when the Sandinistas lost the elections in Nicaragua. Burbach contended that:

> Marxism is in profound crisis. It is not due just to the collapse of actually existing socialism with the fall of the Berlin Wall and the Soviet Union. Marxism was in disarray in theory and praxis well before this, mainly because Marxism no longer has a revolutionary subject...today we need to go further particularly by exploring the major new arena of critical thinking referred to as postmodernism...the ideologies of the twentieth century will disappear completely. This has been a lousy century. It has been filled with dogmas that one after another have cost us time (1997a, p. 1).

New Social Movements/Postmodern Resistance: Strategies and Tactics

New social movements focused on the restrictive organizational aspect of the older struggles, the focus on the state as a strategical enabler and the spatial site of resistance. New social movements became concerned with the bureaucratic nature of the revolutionary movement and the older movements had become insurmountedly dislocated from their radical grassroots. Their internal politics and personal differences came to predominate strategical debates, as leaders and personalities clashed in an embittered Machiavellian 'cloak and dagger' and Michel's 'iron law of oligarchy' (Walker, 1988). In this sense new social movements favoured a grassroots and democratic form of organization which was not vertically organized and rejected the hierachical bureaucratization of the older struggles. On the strategic issue, emphasis on capturing the state was bound by difficulties as the state was characterized not only by class *power over* but also by discreet practices of power, discipline and governability. It followed that it made little sense to regard class struggle and the sovereign repressive state as the principal location of grievance. Thus there was more emphasis on cultural and identity politics. This had led to a decline in the attractiveness of the revolutionary 'grand narratives' (Alexander, 1995, p. 82). As such, it was suggested that the 'global theories are not in touch with concrete realities' (Schusterman, 1994, p. 392). On this basis the counter-revolutions of 1989 represented a resounding defeat for the project of totalizing order and repression. A postmodern resistance would instead attend to the sites of the local and the specific and without 'recourse to grand programmes' (Docherty, 1993, p. 4).

Reaction and Debate on the Political Possibilities of Postmodernism

It was Marxists who set the terms for the debate on the political possibilities of postmodernism. Marxists took exception to the idea of global/postmodern 'new times' and 'new issues' and the idea of an epochal break wrongly marginalized the continuing economic structure, the transformation of capitalism and the seemingly enduring and yet historically specific capital/labour tension (Meiksins-Woods, 1996). Concern was levelled at 'freezing' and reifying an *historically specific* mode of production and indulging in a politics of the affluent. Moreover, it was alleged that by accepting the fragmentation of class struggle new social movements had unintentionally played into the muddied hands of the ruling classes. By being enchanted by the seductions of the post-material issues of ethnicity and culture postmodernists had concentrated on issues somewhat archaic and reactionary when compared to the progressive dialectic of class struggle. Indeed, issues of culture and identity were regarded as the *superstructure* of a class ridden capitalism. The debate opened up controversy concerning the relationship between capitalism and modernization (Burbach et al., 1997; Nugent, 1995). Indeed, both capitalist and socialist development occurred within the rubric of the metanarrative of modernization and that it was necessary to engage with a critique of the particularly egregious tendencies of modernity and modernization located in capitalist and socialist societies alike. Indeed, the history of capitalism was closely linked to modernity whilst the failed socialist project was all about modernization. The Marxist response was pretty blunt, concluding that postmodernists were complicit in the ideological apparatus of the ruling class and helped obscure the exploitative transformation of capitalism (Nugent, 1995). Moreover, there was concern that postmodernists had too easily and quickly abandoned the revolutionary heritage due to the poor climate of real existing socialism whilst for others, a total rejection of the revolutionary ideals, democracy, socialism and emancipation would lead to a dangerous and barbaric 'descent into darkness'. Indeed it was said there:

> is something about this postmodern beast with which we are obsessed today that remains baffling: why has postmodernism been both acclaimed and decried by both ends of the political spectrum? What is it about postmodernism that has

caused it to be labelled both radically revolutionary and nostalgically neoconservative? (Hutcheon, 1988, p. 1).

So the political possibilities of postmodernism are causing heated debate. Indeed, many have asked 'where do the postmodernists come from?' (Eagleton, 1995; Meiksins-Woods and Bellamy-Foster, 1996). Do they come from the elite of the bourgeoise perhaps, sitting in ivory towers, enjoying the ethical seductions of nihilism and relativism and abdicating political responsibility and the need for action? For these writers so obviously of the old left, it was self evident that postmodernism was a political strategy manufactured to activate apathy and to destroy the left. It was suggested that the development of a postmodern politics during the 1970s was simply a kneejerk reaction to the defeat of the old left after 1968 and that postmodern nihilism was a mere recognition of the indomitable new right during the 1980s.

Strategically speaking, and given the world of exploitative and repressive global structures, a postmodern emphasis on rejecting the global programs of the past was virulently challenged on the basis that it simply led to an irrelevant and locally reformist struggle. Indeed, Sklair (1991) posited that such a celebration of localized struggle was not going to be radically useful in an age of globalization and that local struggle would invariably take attention away from the possibility of forging a more globally orientated resistance to globalization whilst simultaneously fragmenting the possibility of this coordination. Strikingly, what now emerged was a distinctive 'global/local' hierachy which implied that localized struggles must be deemed parochial and co-optable in the face of the forces of neoliberal globalization. Indeed, the argument was that the problems identified hitherto with the strategies for global emancipation and the strategic gambit of the state could now be bypassed. Indeed, paradoxically, globalization was for many on the left, opening up the opportunity for moving beyond the dilemmas of state co-option (Amoore et al., 1997). Neoliberalism and its maxim 'there is no alternative' coupled with the end of real existing socialism in 1989 seemed to have finished off Marxism, in theory and practice.

Whilst labour revolution to global capital on a global scale is pretty unlikely, resistances to neoliberal restructuring are occurring at an accelerated pace. However the old model of state-socialism and the reclaiming of economic and political sovereignty in the face of global structures also seems unlikely. Undoubtedly, the desire for a politics of robust globalism has introduced much criticism and injected much doubt into debates on resistance to globalization (Spegele, 1997). Indeed, alternative interpretations of the EZLN have tended to focus upon the way the EZLN has over the years and even in the early months of 1994 eschewed the grand revolutionary objectives and strategies of Central American 'guerrilla' outfits. Burbach (1994) proffered the view that the EZLN represented a distinctively *novel* politics of resistance *exactly because* it 'came in the wake of the collapse of the modern bi-polar world of the post-Second World War and the ideological exhaustion of most of the national liberation movements' (Burbach, 1994, p. 113). Burbach claimed that the:

> Indian rebellion that burst upon the world scene in January is a postmodern political movement. The rebellion is an attempt to move beyond the politics of modernity, whether it be the modernisation of the Salinas de Gortari government or of past national liberation movements (1994, p. 113).

Walker (1988) noted that:

> whether understood as an extension of specifically Western cultural traditions, as a consequence of specifically capitalist forms of economic life, or even as a consequence of a particular form of patriachy, the culture of modernity is not so much universal in any absolute sense as it is an historical dominant expression of the claim to universality (Walker, 1988, p. 49).

Indeed there is a debate in critical International Relations between emancipatory critical theory and intimations of postmodernism. George (1994) noted a debate 'between (broadly) emancipatory approaches and postmodernism in International Relations' (George, 1994, p. 186). Hoffman argued that:

> the potential for creating a new focus within the discipline of International Relations that is postrealist and post-Marxist...(which) provides the basis for the reintegration of International Relations into the broader traditions and concerns of social and political theory (1987, p. 247).

Critical theory had throughout the twentieth century and from the Frankfurt School onwards considered the traumas of rational/instrumental modernity which Marxism had missed. But at the same time critical theory retained a faith in a different emancipatory rationality. The Enlightenment in effect, required completion. Postmodernists queried the strategy wondering whether, given the legacy of the twentieth century, the project could be trusted anymore. The apparent intellectual 'appropriation' of revolutionary movements was challenged by American anthropologist the late Daniel Nugent (1995, 1995a). Nugent (1995, p. 127) was unimpressed by those academics who had fallen for 'the real seductive power' of the intellectual fad that is postmodernism and asked whether it was the actual role of these well meaning yet naive Northern academics to simply measure a brutal reality against trendy continental methodologies in pursuit of trendy deconstructionism and postmodern (pomo, as is the current vogue in many a common room) language games, (whatever they are)? Indeed, Nugent wrote:

> it should come as no little surprise that some postmodern/postcolonial critics, seem, or pretend not to know that the arenas of discourse in which their work circulates are several removes from the social reality they purport to represent. The privileges now enjoyed by intellectuals in the North have been so reduced that many seem to be compensating by providing to themselves an inflated sense of their own importance and the significance of purely intellectual or discursive practices (1995, p. 2).

The postmodern turn Nugent (1995) argued was inherently academic and inevitably, a million miles from the (real)ity of capital accumulation. He noted that postmodernism:

> is more a way of allowing some intellectuals to appropriate these events, to situate these complex historical developments on their own (intellectual) terrain, to assimilate them to a discourse that permits computer academics to feel good about themselves (1995a, p. 3).

For Nugent this enterprise lacked proper objective, scientific and critical enquiry being ostensibly in the mould of the romantics, an 'academia for academias sake'. Given the socialist aspect to Nugent's (1995) own critical enquiry he then noted:

> one way of summing up the difference between postmodernism and Marxism. It isn't that Marxism is uninterested in language, discourse, or meaning, and the best historical materialistic work deals precisely with the many different concrete referents that words like 'class' or 'work' can have in specific historical conditions. But here I simply want to underline that Marxism can understand the practices through which meanings are produced in relation to the actions of people on and in the world and not just in relation to other meanings. Practices are undertaken in particular places at particular times, by particular subjects in particular conditions and these have to be studied historically (1995, p. 1).

Postmodernists he suggested, proposed a *methodology* of anti-history and therefore, intellectual absurdity ensues, an inevitability 'to which the analysis can lead' (Nugent, 1995, p. 136). Indeed, if postmodernism is going to have anything to say to these other specific sites then it must not be 'in the form of yet another quest expressed in highly philosophical terms' (Wickham, 1990, p. 133). Continuing his socialist orientated criticism of postmodern intellectualism Nugent stated that:

> (T)he rest of us should be content to see our intellectual activity function as a critical instrument, as a challenge to ruling ideologies, maybe as a guide to political action when possible, but above all as a way of enhancing or broadcasting, but not replacing, the voices of those who oppose oppression (1995, p. 7).

These writers reported that there are now 'those of us in academia' who 'find its appeal to students and colleagues deeply depressing' and in a concluding attack on postmodern intellectualism Nugent, (1995a, p. 7) stated that 'the determinative power that postmodern intellectuals claim for their own discursive practices - the power to create reality itself - is, in the real world, possible only for the servants of a ruling class, with the power of the state underwriting their discourses'. Nugent asked of postmodernism specifically concerning the interpretation of the EZLN:

> So where does this leave us? The language of postmodernity has added nothing to our understanding of Chiapas. If anything it has obscured and detracted from what is valuable in Burbach's account. It is especially depressing to observe this effect in an otherwise illuminating and politically sympathetic study, and it is a measure of the price we have to pay for this surrender to fashion. Instead of bringing us closer to an understanding of a complex social movement, it simply serves to underline the profound distance between postmodern intellectuals and the activists or supporters of the EZLN (1995a, p. 7).

Postmodernists argued that societies and classes are fragmented, that workers, peasants, indigenous societies and other social groups have very specific identities depending on their location, culture, history and other factors, and that the proletariat is no longer the revolutionary force for change (Burbach, 1997). Burbach argued that:

> Marxism no longer has a revolutionary subject capable of transforming the world. Neither the working class, nor its major twentieth century ally, the peasantry show signs of taking up socialist banners as we approach the new millennium (1997, p. 1).

Conclusion

The conceptual development and the strategic make up of old and new social movements represent very different ideological ways of approaching protest. Undoubtedly the debate has intensified since the development of resistance to globalization and is now manifested, quite rigidly (and politically limiting), as a debate between Marxist accounts of resistance and postmodern accounts of resistance. Both perspectives have their very different ways of theorizing and strategically informing (via the role of intellectual) through the grievances and strategies and objectives of resistance. I will argue that contemporary protests against globalization render this debate conceptually and strategically limited and I will argue that new conceptual and theoretical avenues can now and should be discerned.

Chapter 3

A Politics of Resistance to Globalization: Marxist and NeoGramscian Responses

Introduction

The chapter considers the way that the theory and practice of social movements have been used in recent conceptual and strategic debates concerning the politics of resistance to globalization. Particular attention is directed towards outlining and discussing the new Marxist and neoGramscian approaches to resistance in an age of globalization. The chapter explores the impact of global social movements, the new internationalisms and the counter hegemonic project to that of transnational capital. The purpose of this chapter is to show how critical IPE has sought to explain and conceptualize the politics of resistance.

Globalization and its Discontents

As the protests at Seattle and Genoa showed, the politics of globalization are attracting considerable unrest and security concerns for many governments around the world. For the orthodox left, globalization 'is imperialism by another name' (Seabrook, 1999). The development of capitalism through the neoliberal doctrine is promoted by the market gurus and their government representatives as a new and enlightened cosmos. Marxists on the other hand, regard globalization as another expansion of a capital accumulation where 'all that is solid melts in the air' is coupled with a begrudging admiration of the bourgeois' innovation of industry and technology which would, in actual fact, inevitably sow the seeds of ruling class demise. Early copies of *Das Kapital* sold in their thousands, but ironically, *not* to the impoverished workers of the world, but instead, to the growing posse of new American entrepreneurs all interested in the quirks dynamics of the cut and thrust of competitive capitalism, desperate for ways to get ahead of their nearest and not so dearest competitors. One could ask maybe, what might have happened if Marx had not outlined the dynamics of accumulation and profitability (although it was originally supposed to be objective and teleological) in such apocalyptic terms.

With the 1994 Zapatista rebellion in Chiapas, the 1995 revolts in France, the 1999 'battles in Seattle' and May Day protests in London the ideas and institutions of neoliberal globalization are coming under more and more intellectual and political attack. In many cases it is the *politically* unaccountable institutions of finance capital and the major International Organizations such as the World Trade Organization (WTO) and the International Monetary Fund (IMF) that have attracted considerable disquiet with a growing rich versus poor.

From a Marxist and 'right wing' perspective (quite paradoxically), it is assumed that the new ruling classes of global capital (and faceless capitalism) are directing a new, coordinated and malign strategy of class power. Such an assumption as to the workings of the world, resonates with a centuries old myth of political/religious conspiracy and grand deception (Rupert, 2000). These are agent centered conspiracy theories who consistently maintain that 'structurally deterministic theories' are a smokescreen for the secret activities of conspirational groups such as the *Trilateral Commission* and the *Bilderberg* group, along with powerful and influential individuals such as Rupert Murdoch, Bill Gates and Klaus Schwab and financiers such as George Soros in a global conspiracy. Such a view has an unnerving resonance with pre-war distinctions made between industrial capitalism and Jewish finance capital.

Yet the emerging power of the *nouveau riche* individuals and their willingness and ability to 'work their system' during the 1980s was potently highlighted in Oliver Stone's 1987 film *Wall Street*, a parody of the 'yuppie' generation and the living off the buying and selling of others without, in a nostalgia for industrial capitalism, actually 'making' anything. The new capitalism of images, consumer fetishisms, symbols and brands consolidated throughout the 1990s. Indeed, the economic boom of the late 1980s was itself an illusion, bereft of longer term foundation, relying upon intense speculation and bull markets which cracked during the recession of the 1990s.

The idea of a malign group working within the 'limits of the possible' also forms a strategic part of the neoGramscian 'project' approach to the politics of globalization in critical IPE (Gill, 1995). The idea here, is that a new transnational class project is dedicated to institutionalizing 'neoliberalism' into the legal/political constitutions of states by locking them into both the present *and future* direction of economic/political policy.

Named after the Italian Marxist, Antonio Gramsci, these approaches have developed a complex understanding of the relationship between individuals and the world of structures in which they live, and, hope to transform. The complex analytical and political relationship between structure and agency is an important theme (Germain and Kenny, 1998). Overbeek (2000) writes that this kind of materialist philosophy is represented by.

1. An epistemological rejection of a positivist IPE i.e. which accepted a reality 'out there'.
2. An ontological break with ahistorical state centrism.
3. Rejecting structuralist or agent centered approaches.

This perspective draws upon a non-deterministic and teleological Marx who wrote:

> Men make their own history, but they do not make it just as they please; they do not make it under circumstances chosen by themselves, but under circumstances directly encountered, given, and transmitted from the past (Marx, quoted in Mclellan, 1986, p. 43).

From this perspective then, a reclaiming of social/collective agency in contradistinction to the teleological and deterministic readings of economic and technological globalization (as a logic) will require a coordinated global strategy. As suggested by Amoore et al. the:

> future success of resistance movements to neoliberal globalisation may be brought a step closer if resistance organisations themselves highlight the close relationship between the state and globalisation...to be successful resistance to neoliberalisation must be conducted in a coordinated manner on a local, national, regional and global level (1997, p. 194).

For classical Marxist writers (Meiksins-Woods, 1996) the exploitative wage relation of capitalism between the owners and non-owners of production remains thoroughly intact through the globalization of capital. Indeed this relationship is made more persuasive as the monopolization and mobility of capital outwits the democratic/political institutions of the state where once resided the traditional location of class struggle

(Poulantzas, 1981). In this sense, economic globalization 'neutralizes' the impact of these societal transformations with a comforting '*we* are all in this together' where the first person plural is crucial to the politics of the debate at a time when the owners of business and their workers seem to want to club together and collaborate to ward off the mighty evils that are the global markets and to stave off the inevitable threats of redundancies and bankruptcies, whilst the state takes a back seat, waving up its white flag in despair and saying 'we can't help, its globalization and its inevitable!'. Globalization is regarded as an autonomous force disembedded from *concrete* social and political relations, taken as a structural given 'under here' and 'out there' (McMichael, 2000).

If the imposing ideas and institutions of neoliberal globalization is causing social anxiety as protests at Seattle and Davos have suggested then the obvious solution is to alter its trajectory and to reverse and even overturn globalization. The danger here being that strategically speaking, globalization is still taken as a force 'out there'. Nevertheless, a politics of resistance to globalization will endeavour to 'reclaim' the political through individual and collective agency, in the form of social movements, through a desire to *repoliticize* globalization. Consequently, it is the relationship between theory and practice that has forged a distinctive critical niche in IPE and as a major proponent of this critical perspective Gill has argued that:

the dominant forces of contemporary globalisation are constituted by a neoliberal historical bloc...a set of ideas and practices with particular conditions of existence which are more or less institutionalised...the constraints of various discursive forms and for its emphasis on the way in which certain forms of power and knowledge serve to constitute particular aspects of civilisation (1995, p. 419).

Gill also argued that:

globalisation is part of a broad process of restructuring of the state...the neoliberal concept of globalisation suggests that the privatisation and transnationalisation of capital are either inevitable or desirable from a broad social viewpoint (1995, p. 422).

Whilst the cultivation of labour internationalisms is not new a strategic focus upon global capitalism and the construction of 'new internationalisms', counter hegemonic projects and global socialism is emerging (Amoore et al., 1997, 2000; Gills, 2000; Rupert, 2000;

Waterman, 1993, 1998). This has been an ideational and practical enquiry. The development of the metanarrative of 'robust globalism' has encountered 'postmodern' criticism (Burbach, 1994, 1996; Spegele, 1997).

Critical IPE: Brief History

Subcommandante Marcos (2000) of the Zapatistas has written much about what he considers to be the role of the intellectuals, through the theory/practice conundrum, or those who 'look at social facts and analyse the evidence, for and against, looking for anything ambiguous, that is neither one thing nor the other, revealing anything that is not obvious - sometimes even the opposite of what seems obvious'. Karl Marx had made it clear in his famous aphorism that it 'was not simply enough to interpret the world' but one must endeavour 'to change it'. The Paris Commune and the nationalistic revolutions of 1848 were undoubtedly symptomatic of this quite noble revolutionary gesture.

Intellectuals in IPE can (to an extent) be divided into what Cox (1981) terms the 'problem solvers' or the technical policy advisors who are doing their bit in the real world 'out there'. On the other hand, there are the more critically inspired intellectuals who offer a more emancipatory epistemology, a politics of alternatives. As Marcos (2000) put it, 'intellectuals must choose between their function as intellectuals and the role that activists offer them'. In other words, does one humbly 'play the system' or does one 'change the system'. If the latter were not tricky enough, there is the added bonus of accusations of policymaking irrelevance, and worse still, intellectual hypocrisy.

Before I commence on assessing what it is to be politically engaged in the theoretical and practical protest against globalization in critical IPE I would like to outline how a critical space for thinking and practice has emerged historically. IPE is a relatively new discipline whilst its intellectual heritage of political-economy stretches back to the classics of Adam Smith, David Ricardo and Karl Marx. Writers with very different political persuasions to be sure and yet they were all, and perhaps paradoxically, 'children of the Enlightenment' (Wallerstein, 1992). The development of IPE emerged when national economies were hitting crisis and when the phenomenon of stagflation contradicted the major economic theories of Keynesian demand management and fine tuning the relationship between consumption and investment. A large literature grew over the next decade so as to aim to come to terms with and to explain the apparent contradiction and the reason why national capitalism after twenty years of stability entered crisis. Theories or 'schools' ranged from classic Marxist approaches through to 'regulation theory' (Aglietta, 1979).

One common theme emerged; that an understanding of economies purely based at a national scale was inadequate to explain the contradictions of state intervention in an increasingly globalizing economy; to engage with a purely 'economic' or 'political' study (Business economics or international relations) was unlikely to help explain the new emerging dynamics in a world that was witnessing a very complex interrelationship between the state and the global economy (Strange, 1988; Strange and Stopford, 1991). What was required both conceptually and strategically was a complex analytical synthesis between politics and economics and a new multidisciplinary approach to understanding the interaction of politics *and* economics on an international/global scale (Shaw, 2000). This was a radical gesture because up until this point the study, site and nature of politics and 'society' had been assumed to work around and wedded to the state. IPE was initially a very positivist/empiricist orientated enterprise with the intention of relating theories to a reality 'out there'. As a consequence of course theories were assumed to be value free and the enquiry was objective (Cox, 1981; Murphy and Tooze, 1991).

The development of neoliberal globalization has precipitated two main strands of theory and practice within the 'discipline'. Indeed the term 'discipline' must be treated with analytical and political caution as the new IPE aimed to break down traditional boundaries. This was in contradistinction to the discipline of International Relations which had traditionally been closed off from the many debates within the philosophy of the social sciences and IPE also had to be careful not to *reinforce* boundaries between the disciplines of politics and economics. Theoretical positions were identified between on the one hand 'problem solving' theories (Booth, 1997; Cox, 1981). Since the turn of the century the development of the social sciences and the compartmentalization of intellectual expertise disciplines has been implicitly manifested in the current organization of University departments and inspired by the separation of the natural sciences (Shaw, 2000). From the emergence of positivism, the distinctive epistemological characteristics taken from natural science have been used to locate the workings of, and to elegantly develop, a unified explanatory device through which to understand the social world. This social world was independent and an object for enquiry 'out there'. On the other hand, a more critically aware IPE emerged during the 1980s. This took its intellectual cue from similar developments in critical International Relations Theory. There then developed scepticism both as to the objectivity of the scientific endeavour and of the possibility of applying scientific practices to the world of human beings (Ashley and Walker, 1990; George, 1994). Critical approaches not only identified the interpretive problem of being able to access an objective reality 'out there' but they also insisted that social reality is itself created in more complex and concrete ways. This opened a space for a politics of alternatives and change. In order to tease open a critical space for theory and practice, critical writers had to instigate a problematization and an unpacking of the most persuasive epistemological and ontological fundamentals of empirical/positivist IPE/IRT.

This was a problematization of the epistemology that the subject was split from an objective reality 'out there'. Emphasis was not only placed upon the difficulty of accessing this reality, but, and more crucially, driven by a scepticism on whether this 'reality' actually existed. Once the idea of the reality 'out there' was challenged then a space for change was opened up by introducing philosophical and sociological issues into a study of IR which could no longer be based on the closure of parsimony (George and Campbell, 1990; Cox, 1981; Waltz, 1979). This critical interest holds particular methodological, political and often prescriptive approaches, ranging from various forms of Marxism (Cox, 1981, 1983; Maclean, 1988), variations of critical theory (Hoffman, 1991; Linklater, 1986, 1990), feminist approaches and postmodernism (George, 1994).

Critical Emancipatory Theory and Globalization. Role of Intellectuals in Theory and Practice

It was the influential intellectual economic think-tanks of Reaganism and Thatcherism imparting the legacy of the 'philosophies' of Smith, Hayek and Friedman which unleashed, developed and legitimated the new market philosophy. Some saw it as a veritable Pandora's Box, but the liberal argument was quite seductive at this time. Inefficiency, bloated economies and a seeming unwillingness by workers to adapt to the new opportunities of the global markets were to be replaced by a comparative advantage in trade, the efficient allocation of resources and competition, providing the best goods and services, reduced government expenditure and therefore lower taxes, an end in effect to the 'nanny state'. But the ideological doctrine of neoliberalism, certainly in the UK and the US, now went hand in hand with a new conservatism that emphasized national pride and law and order *along with* the free market, rather strange and inconsistent, to say the least.

There seems of course, no reasonable respite for academics who denounced the 'ivory towers' and accusations of 'academia for academias sake' (Booth, 1997). But what does this inability to predict, indicate for the role and status of knowledge in a climate of globalization? Does it require better conceptual instruments and methodology or should this traditional project be abandoned? Is the quest for knowledge to be trusted based on the accumulation of facts? Recently it has been the economists who have come under criticism for not being able to predict the global economic markets and there is a concern that existing theoretical developments lag behind this complex reality. In the struggle against globalization, Cox (1999) suggested that given the normative ambiguities of neoliberal globalization there must also be a role for a critical and transformatory knowledge.

Thus, one of the intriguing aspects of critical interest in the politics of resistance is the role of knowledge and what type of intellectual is to be engaging in such work and finally of course, what are the normative/emancipatory goals involved. This was the rekindled intellectual Marxist understanding of theory as strategic guidance for action and in generating an alternative world order the *organic* intellectuals are critical agents for raising consciousness and clarifying the political thinking of social groups leading the members of these groups to understand their existing situation in society and how they can struggle towards a higher form of society. Critical intellectuals engage in a struggle with the ideas and philosophies of the intellectuals in power. Indeed, in reacting to neoliberalism the Zapatistas are placed within this critical framework and are said to be:

> indicative of something moving in different societies across the globe towards a new vitality of a bottom up movement in civil society as a counterweight to the hegemonic power structure and ideology. This movement is however relatively weak and uncoordinated. It may contain some of the elements but has certainly not attained the status of a counterhegemonic alliances of forces on a world scale (Cox, 1999, p. 7).

Transformative emancipatory movements such as the EZLN are interpreted as:

> The most open challenge to the impact of globalisation on social and political structures has come from a new type of revolutionary movement, the Zapatista

rebellion of the Mayan Indians in the Southern Mexico state of Chiapas...a rallying force in civil society...to create the beginnings of a counterhegemonic bloc (Cox, 1999, p. 7).

Cox noted that:

the critical agents for raising consciousness...are the organic intellectuals; they serve to clarify the political thinking of social groups leading the members of these groups to understand their existing situation in society and how in combination with other social groups they can struggle towards a higher form of society (1999, p. 7).

Such a strategic intellectual engagement is part of an emancipatory drive against neoliberal power, exploitation and repression where:

the war of position is a strategy for the long term construction of self conscious social groups into a concrete emancipatory bloc within society. It is only when the war of position has built up a combination of organised social forces strong enough to challenge the dominant power in society that political authority in the state can be effectively challenged and replaced. The war of position is contrasted to the war of manouevre which might seize state power before this groundwork of social organisation has been built up...would constitute a hollow victory...popular participation is an indispensable basis for durable political authority (Cox, 1999, p. 7).

Resistance to Globalization: Reapplying Marxism

The original works of Marxism have been interpreted in a number of ways. One continuous theme however, has been that the development of capitalism is an inherently exploitative and historically unstable *economic* process with an amazing capacity to waste human and environmental resources but which continues (on the basis of an abstract theory of the market) to exist, despite a multitude of crises throughout the last 150 years or so. From classic Marxism, to the post-war application of Marxism in International Relations (neoMarxism and historical materialism), such a perspective has been used to show how the historically specific capitalist mode of production has reproduced and maintained itself through the practices of coercion and consent, shown most notably through the parasitic institutions of the state apparatus. Undoubtedly, economic globalization, if we see it in these terms of a new bourgeois inspired project of global capitalism with its associated cultures, institutions and ideas, inspired by a new ruling class faction, renders the politics of Marxism again quite relevant, and the seemingly ignominious demise of Marxism following the East European revolutions of 1989 in states of *real existing socialism* becomes the historical release of *global* theory and practice. Indeed the spillage of global capital over national borders and the new technological developments we see emerging on almost a daily basis are exactly the kind of developments that Marx had predicted, as the bourgeoise are chased around the world in search of profits:

> The bourgeoise cannot exist without constantly revolutionising the instruments of production, and thereby the relations of production, and with them the whole relations of society (Marx and Engels, 1967, p. 22).

However, since the early 1980s a distinctive 'neoliberal' agenda *has* emerged and its institutional basis is located in the WTO and IMF. Such institutions have rallied against protectionism, advanced the benefits of the free market, the free movement of capital and the rollback of the state. To this end, critics of the IMF are left a little uneasy with the retort from these institutions that it is perhaps 'better to be exploited than not to be exploited' and whilst it is recognized by the institutions promoting neoliberalism, that structural adjustment may deliver social unrest, the IMF simple reply is, then 'what would be the alternative'; a world of inefficiency, low productivity and ultimately low economic growth to be sure, and this would not aid the world's poor. Clearly, within the *existing* state of global affairs they would be right. Critics in turn, both vehemently and on occasion, whimsically argue that accelerating global poverty exists *exactly because of* the policies of neoliberal globalization and cannot therefore be solved by simply adding *more* neoliberal globalization, then hiding under the cover of economic theory and the 'natural' tendencies of some inexorable market force that will somehow make things better. It makes one wonder of course, who really is living in 'the real world' and the sides are hermetically sealed, clearly talking past each other. Thus 'the analytical focus of the study of the globalization phenomena must therefore shift from the technical to the political' and resistance must be construed as 'a form of political action which should represent general or societal interest and with the potential to transform the political situation and produce a real alternative' (Gills, 2000, p. 3-4). The general problems identified are as follows. Firstly, an extensive capital accumulation and a homogenization of state policies towards the free market and a convergence and essentialist-teleology. Secondly, a threat to civil society of disembedded global financial markets which are seemingly more powerful than political and societal institutions. Thirdly, a growing lack of democratic power/accountability and transparency due to an ideological agenda of 'there is no alternative' to the market and an ensuing bellicose 'race to the bottom' as workers around the world are pitted against each other, to compete for global investment. Fourthly, a reduction in union power and a strange consensus between worker and industry to defend interests against a new/volatile global economy. Finally, there are new issues/dangers of culture/identity/risk and a olitical exclusion of dissident social forces. Moreover, globalization is presented instrumentally which requires a form of knowledge that is both technical and problem solving. This means that debate in national political institutions and democracy becomes technical and neoliberal globalization is *depoliticized*. Neoliberal globalization is construed as a paradoxical process both opens out economies and yet generates new forms of law and order, discipline and surveillance to promote a viable investment climate.

Undoubtedly, it is the rampant excesses of a 'wild and savage global capitalism' that is precipitating much concern and alarm (Falk, 1999). With the rise of neoliberal economics during the 1980s, structural adjustment programs and an epochal shift to a 'post-fordist' economy represented by the competition (rather than welfare) state, a new disenfranchised group marginalized and excluded from democratic political institutions and the new global information economy. Through the homogeneity of strategic economic advice given by the IMF technocrats, state policy is directed towards attracting foreign investment by producing those economies suited not to maintaining national production and consumption *à la* fordism but suited to the whims of mobile global capitalism. At the same time, market liberalization paradoxically develops along with the securing of borders through tight immigration policy and increasing coercive authoritarianism. Colin Hines (2000) stated that the *ideology* of globalization was 'cooked up' for the benefit of big business through the 'no alternative' school. In other words he is saying that globalization is a smokescreen to legitimate global business and its somewhat nefarious excesses, and so, 'don't fall for it, it's a conspiracy, an illusion!'. However, 'people all over the world are twigging' to this grievous falsity. The cross border NGO, *Maquila Solidarity Network* has current campaigns against the activities of global companies such as *Mattel* in Mexico and against *Phillips Van Heusen* in Guatemala support workers in these areas. The *Maquila Solidarity Network* has current campaigns against the activities of global companies such as *Mattel* in Mexico and against *Phillips Van Heusen* in Guatemala, and aims to support workers in these areas. In a *Maquila Update* (1996) it was reported that 'two recent wildcat strikes in autopart plants in Mexicos northern maquiladora region highlight growing worker dissatisfaction with their declining standard of living under the North American Free Trade Agreement'. The introductory flyer stipulated that with the spread of free trade workers and communities in Canada and throughout the Americas are subject to corporate blackmail. To compete for jobs and investment, we are told that we must accept lower wages, cutbacks in social services, poorer health and safety and environmental standards. As Marxist historian Eric Hobsbawm (2000b) has explained recently the idea that globalization is uncontrollable is mistaken and ideologically motivated because it could be controlled. Although some things are more difficult to control than others, control is possible simply because governments have done so whilst a new interest has centered upon the possibility of cultivating new forms of state/labour alliances, trade unionism and worker alliances. Institutions such as the International Labour Organization (ILO) are representing this carefully nurtured development (Hughes and Wilkinson, 2000).

In other words, a major niche of critical IPE uses Marxism to explicate *why* there have been structural changes and *who* is involved in this complex process. Capitalism has relied upon its various and inscrutable mechanisms and instruments of coercive and consensual legitimation to sustain its crisis ridden and historically specific mode of production. As Marx and Engels said in their classic maxim:

> in the social production of their existence, men enter into definite, necessary relations, which are independent of their will, namely relations of production corresponding to a determinate stage of development of their material forces of production. The totality of these relations of production constitutes the economic structure of society the real foundation on which there arises a legal and political superstructure and to which there corresponds definite forms of social consciousness (quoted in Mclellan, 1986, p. 40).

The controversies identifying the site and nature of ideology took place at the spatial and institutional level of the state. The debate on the politics of globalization has taken alternative political ideologies to a different spatial, conceptual and strategic level. Marxists have rejected the ideas and institutions of global corporate capitalism to cultivate a counter ideological project. This has induced interest in developing a critical politics of resistance to the actors, ideas and institutions to a *specific* neoliberal globalization. The French Revolution crystallized the 'naturalization' of ideologies and 'isms' of Enlightened political thinking. Whilst the British had their Industrial Revolution the French events of 1789 created a distinctive climate that gave the world the ideology of 'liberalism' and a passionate belief in the *normality* of social change and progress. It was in effect a world historic date and an ideology that lasted until 1989. The ideologies of liberalism, socialism, conservatism and nationalism were emblems of modernity as mindset *and* as socio-political era. Yet this belief in the 'metanarrative' of Marxism came crashing as the Berlin Wall, so tragically symbolic, was hacked down in late 1989. However, simultaneously, with ebuilliant optimism, a new grand ideology was emerging: this was 'globalism' and it went hand in hand with a revitalized ideology of neoliberalism.

Any understanding of the institutions, site and nature of ideology from both a liberal *and* Marxist perspective has been framed around the state and it follows, that if global forces are making objective and subjective political boundaries more permeable then this is altering our understanding of politics and ideology. Marxists have made a tentative leap of faith to reexamine the logic of capitalism, its contradictions and practices from a state to a global spatial/institutional level. The intriguing aspect of the globalization/state debate is that neoliberals and Marxists agree on the necessary retreat of the state even if they disagree with the political and ideological implications.

Indeed the globalization of capital is indicative of the prescient nature of Marxism if the revolutions of 1989 are alternatively interpreted as the historical release of Marxism and dialectic materialism as a global theory and practice. Marx and Engels classically stated:

> The ideas of the ruling class are in every epoch the ruling ideas i.e. the class which is the ruling material force of society, is at the same time its ruling intellectual force. The class which has the means of material production at its disposal, has control at the same time over the means of mental production, so that thereby, generally speaking, the ideas of those who lack the means of mental production are subject to it (1970).

The political counter-project is begun with a 'demystification' of ideology maintaining global capitalism through global civil society consensually. The new transnational classes are allegedly perpetuating the 'myth' of the powerless state which *naturalizes* the roll back of the state, cuts in welfare, policies dedicated to attracting foreign capital and reflecting the effectiveness of mobile global capital. There are two problematics. Firstly, to assess what does ideology actually do, who creates it and how? Secondly, where do the sites, institutions and practices of ideology and the formation of 'counter-ideologies' reside through the mechanisms of ideological diffusion? On the one hand ideology is seen as *naturalizing* what in effect is historically specific, arbitrary and imbued with interminable contradictions. Here, ideology has the capacity to distort and hide the truth and is manifested as the specific ideas of a ruling class and in capitalism the bourgeoise have the institutional means of material production at its disposal and control over the means of mental production. Yet only in modern times has a systematic cultivation of a *dominant ideology* been able to solidify, hypnotize and be disseminated effectively through the new mass media communication. The world of Marxism is a world of mirrors, ghosts and spectres, a world of false consciousness and false needs, where material 'reality' and the logic of history is increasingly difficult to locate, if it is there at all. This is more persuasive given the emergence of a global consumer culture. Ideologies can also have positive functions.

Internationalist perspectives also underscore a distinctive understanding of the spatial and political relationship between national workers and the structural conditions of international/global capital. This brings in the intriguing conceptual and strategic relationship between the dialectically structural conditions of class conflict, false consciousness and fermenting 'class consciousness' (Sklair, 1998). Clearly, the leaders of organized labour took a while to come to terms with the cunning nature of capital. Organized labour saw itself as the 'vanguard' and given sustenance by the ideas and dreams of the organic intellectuals.

Old social movements were caught between the possibility of global revolution and the strategic implications of capturing the state whilst objective economic conditions for global class struggle may have been structurally fermenting. Accusations of revolutionary betrayal have been hurled at the party-political left as it succumbed to Michels 'iron law' and the halcyon post-war consensus accepted by the left and the right. Concerns with global capital and its promises have now focused upon the reformist language and pronouncements of Global Compacts for 'globalization with a human face' manifested through packages of new 'new' deals and third ways. (Annan, 1999; Giddens, 1999). Since the recent global financial crisis (Smadja, 1999) there has been a feeling amongst those states and non-state actors who constructed the project of neoliberal globalization (such as transnational class alliances) that they are undermining their own interests through economic short termism. This is precisely the kind of contradiction that Marx envisaged and that whilst capitalism entered periodic crises during the 1970s this neoliberal doctrine maintained and legitimized capitalism during the 1980s and 1990s. What emerged was a disciplined neoliberal state based upon the rollback of welfare, the general lowering of wages, a flexible work force and the destruction of organized labour.

Such conditions seem ripe for protest and challenges to the social vicissitudes of global capital were stepped up. One manifestation was through new labour/union solidarities (Waterman, 1998). This has implied a desire for a counter project based upon a temporary unification of major social relations under a ruling coalition to the ideas and institutions of the ruling transnational capitalist class bloc. Many writers have become convinced that conditions for labour internationalism (finally) on a global scale are being sown and on this level, the clear ambiguity of globalization is that the globalization of capital is simultaneously cultivating an opposition to activate and coordinate globally.

Moreover, neoliberal discipline reduces the capacity of the state to quell or 'coopt' protest and using its coercive means of once enforcing law and order for a viable investment climate is economically suicidal in a world of global media attention. Moreover, there seems an uneasiness with the inability of political institutions at a national level to come to terms with this increasing sense of political powerlessness in the world of global structures. Implicit here, is a distinctive spatial and temporal understanding of the site and nature of modern politics (even radical politics) mapped by the division of this world into territorially bounded states with supreme political sovereignty and a distinction between the 'inside' and 'the outside'. The strategic assumption of world socialism was the strategic and enabling 'first stage' capture of the national state apparatus and then progress to world socialism would occur as the dominos of the bourgeois inter-state system collapsed. Crucially, Marxists had a very specific idea of where the location and boundaries of *power* and *politics* resided. However, the state was also regarded as the revolutionary enabler for global revolution (Taylor, 1991). Strategic debate raged as to whether the state aided a particular class instrumentally or whether the state structurally aided the interests of the capitalist society as a whole (Poulantzas, 1981).

If we see globalization as an extension of capitalism on a global scale with the concomitant discipline of national economies then we can ask questions as to whether the state is able to coopt resistance through promises of welfare by cultivating an aristocracy of labour, whether the structural and objective conditions are emerging for a global Marxist revolution as capital overspills boundaries as Marx envisaged and whether the state and the ideology of nationalism (the global revolutionary quislings) are challenged to the extent that global revolutionary movements are no longer neutralized by false consciousness?

NeoGramscian Approaches and Debates

There has of course, been some justifiable concern with applying the writings of an Italian Marxist from the 1920s to debates on neoliberal reconstruction (Germain and Kenny, 1998). Can Gramsci's writings on the development of national civil society and the practices of national ruling class bloc hegemony be applied to the dynamics of globalization some sixty years on? Nevertheless, according to Gill (1993), the following themes are now all intrinsically part of a neoGramscian program for change, concerning the critical politics of globalization.

1. To reconsider the epistemological and ontological aspects of the world.
2. To reconsider 'order' in the context of the past, present and future.
3. To reconsider methodological, theoretical and conceptual issues.
4. To reconsider the structure/agency debate.
5. To reconsider concrete studies of the emerging world order and the contradictions which limit and expand understanding of the politically and ideologically possible.
6. To address a number of ethical and practical approaches to the global problems, for shaping the collective future and the making of history.

Indeed, Gramsci is said to have provided a distinctive critical consciousness of the world, and praxis, as juncture from past, present and future. Gramsci (1971, pp. 34-35) noted that a critical consciousness 'provides a basis for the subsequent development of an historical dialectical conception of the world, which understands movement and change, which appreciates the sum of effort and sacrifice which the present has cost the past and which the future is costing the present'. It is also taken for granted that there is no *necessary* or teleological correspondence between class position and class ideology in this fluid approach. Indeed, Stuart Hall has argued:

> Ideologies may not be affixed as organic entities to their appropriate classes; but this does not mean that the production and transformation of ideology in society could proceed free or outside the structuring lines of power and class (quoted in Rupert, 1998, p. 430).

Ideology provides the mechanisms, discursive practices and shared meanings for individuals to form political projects and come to an emancipatory consciousness of their place in the world, to act on and change the world. This directly translates to the strategic resisting of the ideas and institutions of global capitalism whilst such a perspective relies heavily upon a vision of a coordinated counter-capitalist project and a translation of Marxist theory and practice to the global sphere. The sites of hegemonic power and authority are now changing due to the pressures of globalization. In contrast to a deterministic/structural Marxism where the ideological state apparatus were seen to hail and recruit concrete individuals into the structures of capitalism by transforming them into conforming human subjects, Gramsci sought to inject an antideterministic richness into the Marxist tradition and to understand how a specific mode of production was able to maintain and legitimate itself in the face of crisis tendencies. Gramsci argued that the dominant classes of capitalism maintained their leadership or hegemony through a conducive and coordinated (yet specifically situated) myriad of interlinkages of ideas, institutions and social forces. Class leadership was not only maintained through the coercive powers of the bestial state but was simultaneously (and more importantly perhaps) maintained by the practices of consent as located in and transmitted through the institutions of civil society through common sense (Germain and Kenny, 1998).

Moreover, Gramsci had sought to develop a distinctive role for the organic intellectual to show where the mystifications resided and were perpetuated. This *organic* intellectual aspired to scientifically unmask ideology and to understand the nature of ideology not only in terms of a class project but also as the residues of the shared norms, values and intersubjective meanings placed on the social world by concrete agents in their concrete economic, political, social and cultural environments. The 'organic intellectual' the 'enlightener' of the masses (and now a major figure in the counter-hegemonic project against the forces of economic globalization) Gramsci was aware that ideology was comprized of the everyday (usually contradictory) conceptions of the world created by conscious social agents whose consciousness was itself determined by a coagulation of economic, social, cultural and political factors and which consisted of echoes of past generations, past norms, diluted concepts, irrational prejudices and inherited and even mystical wisdoms. Gramsci was interested in the way the dominant institutions of capitalism related to and reinforced such narrow and false conceptions of the world, and he challenged the dichotomous relationship between subject and object, structure and agency by focusing upon both the real *and* perceived 'limits of the possible'.

His concepts were based upon the contests *within* the emerging nation state and not surprisingly such ideas have attracted considerable attention to disciplines such as international political economy and the possibility of cultivating alternative *world* orders to the world of neoliberalism. Gramsci's perspective on hegemony have been transposed to an understanding of how states maintain their power and influence by focusing upon the shifts to neoliberal economic accumulation on a global scale, new global class relations; how they are cultivated and legitimized through the interlocking and the strategic fit between the project of the ideas and institutions of transnational class blocs, international organizations and the emergence of new counter forces. Focus was placed upon the global shift to a neoliberal/new right agenda during the 1980s manifested by the policies of Reagan in the US, Thatcher the UK and the structural adjustment policies of the International Monetary Fund (IMF). It has also been inspired by Gramsci's understanding of the political potential of civil society and interest in the actors of global civil society such as global social movements, NGOs and the emergence of 'resistance to globalization'. Thus:

civil society is the sphere of class struggles and of popular democratic struggles. Thus, civil society is the sphere in which a dominant social group organises consent and hegemony. It is also the sphere where the subordinate social groups may organise their opposition and construct an alternative counter hegemony (Amoore et al., 1997, p. 185).

The possibility of creating a new vanguard/historic bloc is said to be becoming more and more likely. Undoubtedly, the nature of the debate has been quite virulent. The globalization debate and the debate on the politics of resistance to globalization have intensified the underlying features of social movement theory and practice that have emerged throughout three centuries of struggle dating back to the French Revolution of 1789. Strategic issues *have* centered around the state and the state as 'container' of politics. Such a perspective assumes a strategically hierachical relationship between the local, national and global sites and spaces of struggle which influence political protest within and outside conventional political institutions. Undoubtedly the original temptation was for many, and especially economists, to regard globalization as the key enabler of the free market, an historically unique transformation of state and society that had no limits and was inevitable in any case. Given the problems identified with globalization and the increasing sense that 1. people are being left behind in an emerging two tiered society between the core states and periphery states, *and* within the core and peripheries of the Western world cities, and 2. the neoliberal adage that 'it is better to be exploited than not to be exploited' is becoming a dangerous truism, such orthodox perspectives are now certainly challengeable.

Conclusion

The reclaiming of 'the political' and of political agency at the local, national and global level as implicit in Marxist and the neoGramscian approaches is limiting the development of a more broader conceptual and strategic critique of globalization and the meaning of 'the political' within the context of this debate and within critical IPE. My argument in the subsequent chapters is that whilst the critical perspectives outlined here are vital for reengaging with an emancipatory politics in an age of globalization, they continue to reside within (and perhaps even perpetuate) a quite limited conceptual and strategic understanding of what it means to be 'political', to be 'emancipatory' and to 'resist'. I argue that a reevaluation of the strategic direction of leftist responses to globalization is now required in order to identify the profundity of the new direction taken by new antiglobalization protests as currently seen in the media. And whilst it is clearly necessary to reclaim the political, at the same time surely it is necessary to rethink and reexplore what it is that is being reclaimed? It is my suggestion that developments in critical IR can add a further critical richness into the debates in critical IPE which will force a rethinking as to the meaning of *the political*, and of the intellectual routines (both traditional *and* radical) that keep us as we are.

Chapter 4

Rethinking the Politics of Resistance

Introduction

The chapter considers how *critical* social movements such as those mobilizing at venues such as Seattle and Prague and elsewhere re-explore the site and nature of politics. The chapter outlines an alternative conceptualization of the relationship between social movements and globalization, asking, what is meant by 'being political' and by the act of 'resisting'.

Critically thinking about Resistance

Undoubtedly, it was a sense of living in a dangerous and unpredictable post-Cold War world that forged critical thinking in International Relations Theory (IRT) and IPE. The fragmentation and collapse of states, emerging new forms of warfare and new parameters of threat and security have all combined to challenge the intellectual hegemony of realism. Moreover, critical approaches have eulogized the cause of the silenced, the marginal and the voices who were excluded from the grand politics of statecraft and elite globalization. There was a feeling that critical intellectuals might be able to play a part in cultivating a politics of alternatives (Ashley and Walker, 1990). As such, critical attention focused upon the site, the objectives and the strategies of social movements (Gladwin, 1994; Melucci, 1984; Scott, 1990; Touraine, 1981). To this end critical writers forged a problematization of the central ontological and epistemological constituents of realist and neorealist IRT (Ashley and Walker, 1990; George and Campbell, 1990).

In contrast to the intellectual Marxist engagement concerned with placing a resistance within ideological and strategic parameters, Walker (1988, p. 62) argued that there were in fact 'serious limits to the extent to which it is possible to categorize and analyse movements' and there was, and is, 'always a danger of imposing premature classification onto political processes that have not yet run their course' (Walker, 1988, 62). The difficulty of theorizing about social movements in general gives an indication why they have become so interesting to people seeking to find some way through the conventional horizons of contemporary political debate. Walker suggested that:

> although difficult to define, critical social movements are distinguishable in part by their capacity to recognise and act creatively upon connections among structures, processes and peoples that do not enter significantly into the calculations of conventional political actors...not only in struggles around specific problems but also in struggles that recognise the emancipatory potential inherent in certain kinds of connections and solidarities (1988, p. 3).

Whilst capitalism *is* recognized as a major historical development the critical enquiry also recognizes that the economic, political, social and cultural features of the grievance are multifaceted and occur at concrete/specific locations. The grievances are also experienced in different ways, at different times and at different spaces. Consequently, the abstracting out of a particular determining logic is a perspective that is rejected and instead, more emphasis is laid on the way critical social movements recognize *connections* between certain processes at these specific sites. This makes reductionist conceptual and abstract ideological apparatus difficult to sustain. Critical social movements favour a more pluralistic and open and yet inclusive dialogue of *commonality* rather than *a* suppressive and revolutionary *universality* through a politics of connections which delivers and principally accepts strategic ambiguity during the act of resistance.

Theme 1: Constructing an Inclusive and Fair Development

One of the most hotly contested and central themes of concern therefore, is with the rethinking of the meaning, nature and site of development. Critical social movements do not wish in effect to 'destroy' contemporary development, whether defined as capitalism, socialism or modernity, but instead are:

> placing considerable stress on the need to recognise the connections between economic processes and other aspects of our social life, contemporary labor movements and movements for alternative forms of economic development

repeat one of the most powerful messages being given by critical social movements everywhere (Walker, 1988, p. 63).

Of course, the theory and practice of modernization is alive and kicking and economists, (now neoliberal technocrats) continue to, and have:

> invented their own rather bizarre ideas about what constitutes rational behaviour. these ideas often jar disconcertingly with the way people act in practice. What is more serious is that these ideas have enabled people to stop thinking about how to create forms of economic life that are appropriate for human development (Walker, 1988, p. 68).

The conventional politics of development is economic modernization based around *top down* state planning. Even the developmentalism of the 1950s through to the neoliberal accounts of development strangely carried similar assumptions on the nature of modern progress. The pressure on states to dance to the beat of the new world economy has also of course, led to an often exploitative, violent and exclusionary climate. Consequently, there is increasing importance given to exploring alternative 'development movements' on the basis that 'attempts to encourage development from the top down have often been disastrous' (Walker, 1988, p. 84). Consequently:

> the insights of critical social movements may be used to show that other interpretations of development, other possibilities for human well being, remain open. These insights begin with a recognition that the spatial structuring of the world economy is being transformed. This insight necessarily leads not only to explorations of new ways of acting on economic problems but also to a rethinking of the basic categories in which the possibilities of human development are now envisaged (Walker, 1988, p. 129).

Consequently a recognition of multicultural plurality at a local, national and global level means an exploration of the way 'alternative conceptions of development must involve the creation of new understandings of work, production and ownership that are more meaningful socially than just processes of individual or aggregate capital accumulation' (Walker, 1988, p. 132). Of course a concern with the vagaries of modern life may turn into a romanticized idealization of premodern life but the critical social movements challenge a deeply rooted contrast between tradition and modernity so essential to dominant economic and political categories. Critical social movements look for alternative and specific developments which generate a potential dialogue on a development based on the theme of *inclusivity* yet aware that the demand for inclusivity *is not* the replacement of an arrogant ethnocentrism with a romanticized or relativistic appeal because this would merely reproduce the false choice between modernity and tradition. In this sense critical social movements engage with the most persuasive and deeply entrenched assumptions that constitute prevailing common sense. But as I will show in chapter seven, the EZLN forges a distinctive approach to this inclusive development (De Huerta, 1999; NCDM, 14 September 1998, 9 December 1998, 13 March 1999; Rodriguez, 1999). Walker argued:

> the concept of development has become problematic in an even more complex and far reaching way than that of security. It has long been subject to bitter theoretical and ideological dispute. As a synonym for progress it has been criticised for all the arrogance of a universalistic reading of History. As a synonym for economic growth, it has been embroiled in a century of debate about the character and consequences of capitalism, industrialism, imperialism and socialism. In some places it is still treated as short hand for the inevitable way forward. Elsewhere quotation marks around it symbolise increasing embarassment and anger (1988, p. 128).

The importance of radicalizing our understanding of just what is meant by the term 'development' in an age of global transformations, is in effect, a tentative exploration rather than an imperial assertion of what it means to 'be human' in a community, or in being a national/global citizen. Indeed, development for who, and how, or who pays the price and the burden? In rethinking the site, nature and direction of development which concomitantly pours such scepticism onto the grand narratives, both liberal and Marxist, as well as the 'postmodern' rejection of modernity, as a form of critique, alternative conceptions of belonging and responsibility/obligations begin to emerge. In this challenge to neoliberal development, according to Falk:

> Rethinking citizenship is crucial. The citizen, unlike the subject of a monarchy or authoritarian political order, is a participant in the polity...(I)f elections seem to avoid issues, to leave the electorate bored and indifferent and if political parties converge on a consensus, then other modes of participation need to be identified, and if necessary, invented, to avoid the atrophy of civic virtue (1996, p. 24).

The newly politicized citizen in an age of globalization will be a concretely understood and politically active, even astute, citizen and not a legal abstraction. This concrete form of modern citizenship should accommodate cultural diversity and the growth of citizen loyalty to an inclusive modern state, given the various localized and national cultural and political amalgamations generated by the forces of globalization (Camilleri and Falk, 1992; Held and McGrew, 1998). Walker made the point that:

> the primary message coming from the critical social movements in this respect, is again quite stark in its simplicity. It is the claim that in a world of connections and global structures, and yet a world also of increasing social and economic exclusion, ideas of development must be based on the principle of *inclusivity* and solidarity. An empowering development must be a development for all (1988, p. 132, my emphasis).

Thus, for critical social movements, the idea of development is not something to be grasped by the myth of history and modernization and it was recognized that traditional ways of life become *at least as* important for understanding the potentialities of different kinds of human community. This brings together peoples at their specific locations in their attempt to render a sense of *control* over their own lives and destinies. This is not therefore, a simple return to a premodern romanticism galvanized by a potentially absurd sentimentalism. Instead, the key theme is a modern development that is based on economic, political, social and cultural *inclusivity* in order to create an enriching, fair and non-excluding modernization.

Theme 2: Radicalizing Democracy

Critical social movements aim for a democratic revolution.and rework the meaning, nature and practice of democracy at a local, national and global level. Indeed, there has clearly developed a sense of individual powerlessness brought about by a lack of accountability of political institutions coupled with the instrumentalism of the globalization axiom that 'there was no alternative'. The current institutions of formal political democracy is often connected to life experiences dominated by bureaucratic stultification, authoritarian state, elite sponsored apathy and cynicism and conditions to which most people are excluded from the decision making process. Critical social movements like critical social theorists, have become engaged in a broader agenda involving the reconceptualization of emancipatory concepts and practices, such as democracy and progress. Critical social movements both aim to recover electoral institutions *and* nurture a consultary and direct form of radical democracy. This is a democratic revolution based upon a unique reworking of the ideals of the political institutions and a rethinking of the actual idea of a political institution because liberal democratic institutions are all 'indictments of boredom and irrelevance on the one hand, and cynicism on the other. A sense of powerlessness is apparent in many societies' (Walker, 1988, p. 133). Here, direct participation is to be promoted through the construction of different political institutions from the grassroots as the bureaucratization of politics, the 'iron law of oligarchy' is challenged. Crucially, there was also a willingness to work with the institutions that are available, imperfect as they may be. Hence the importance of the use of the existing constitutional legal mechanisms to introduce greater accountability into public life. But this was only the start. This is a:

> recognition that democratisation is not the equivalent of voting in periodic elections. It requires an ongoing insinuation of peoples participation into all aspects of public life. It requires constant vigilance about the preservation of substantive rights, about how the basic investment decisions of a society are made, about how production is organised and goods distributed, about how cultures, values, identities are constructed (Walker, 1988, p. 140).

Democracy is often reduced to a commercial pageant and has been largely reduced to bureaucracy and state planning. Thus, critical social movements 'seek not only to enhance democratic processes in the formal political arena but, perhaps even more so, to democratize within social processes' (Walker, 1988, p. 140). In their vision, Laclau and Mouffe (1985) have argued that 'the first condition of a radically democratic society is to accept the contingent and radically open character of all its values, and in that sense, to abandon the aspiration to a single foundation' (Laclau and Mouffe, 1985, 101). Consequently, the idea of a new and radically democratic revolution:

> does not pass through a direct attack upon the state apparatus but involves the consolidation and democratic reform of the liberal state. The ensemble of its constitutive principles, the division of executive, legislative and judicial powers, universal suffrage, multiparty systems, civil rights etc, must be defended and consolidated (Laclau and Mouffe, 1985, p. 105).

For Mouffe, (1992, p. 4) 'the task of rethinking democratic politics is more urgent than ever given the tragic experience of totalitarianism'. Forces for radical democracy such as the Emiliano Zapata Front of National Liberation (FZLN) set up by the EZLN and at the call of civil society in 1996, recognize the dangers of bureaucratic party politics. Walker noted that one of the main characteristics of the critical social movements is that they maintain:

> a suspicion of the urge to build institutions before underlying principles and ideas have been sufficiently worked through...there is a very powerful sense that existing political institutions embody the wrong principles and ideas...it is necessary to think what exactly is meant by a political institution...the very idea of a political institution embodies the underlying image of yet another structure that is somehow out there, another false dichotomy between structure and practice (1988, p. 137).

The project of radical democracy has been linked to new issues concerning the 'spatiality' or institutional site of politics and the generation of new sites of democratic struggle on both a local and global level (Massey, 1994, 1995; Mouffe, 1995). The use of global technologies inspires a belief that they are generating opportunities for enhancing democracy by generating new forms of radical citizenship at the local, national and the global level. Indeed, concern with image and daily opinion polls indicates a sense of *vulnerability* emanating from the elites which can be used as a new terrain of pushing democratic politics. This introduces the question of strategies and tactics. There has also been no shortage of attempts to revitalize the cultural traditions that have been dominant for so long and democracy is one of the greatest projects of the modern world. But the project has become somewhat disorientated and there is a feeling that the established forms of politics simply do not work anymore. However, critical social movements recognize that democracy does not have to be defined by party-political institutions but as a constantly worked theme, teasing open spaces to think and act. Walker argued that:

> democracy does not have a single defining characteristic. It is not to be equated with particular forms of government, with parliaments, representative institutions, party hierachies or national wills. Again the practices of movements are informed by a readiness to pursue different strategies of deepening democracy depending on circumstance (1988, p. 140).

The practice of *radical* democracy can both include a reforming of existing political institutions and the development of a richer and direct form of participatory democracy. Thus, Walker argued that:

> the importance of enhancing democratic processes within economic systems...leads to a recognition that democratisation is not the equivalent of voting in periodic elections. It requires an ongoing insinuation of peoples participation into all aspects of public life...constant vigilance about the preservation of substantial rights, about how the basic investment conditions of a society are made, about how production is organised and goods distributed, about how cultures, values and ideas are constructed (1988, p. 140).

Theme 3: Strategies and Tactics

Revolutionary theories and practices located in Marxist perspectives are conceptually and strategically constrained, and critical movements offer a new way of organizing resistance and offering a new kind of political engagement. The strategies used require a rethinking of the nature and site of political *power* as critical social movements both intellectually and politically refuse a transcendental politics of critique wedded to the practice of sovereign and revolutionary actors. The refusal of the taking of state power and the promotion of nonviolence/legality represents a distinctive rethinking as to the site and nature of political power, whilst the people engaged in such struggles also recognize, that although the broader economic/political structures of globalization may seem remote, infact they are only manifeted, articulated, interpreted and impact concretely on the 'everyday' or *specifically* on where they live and work. Indeed, the recognition that global structures are only manifested through various practices at the concrete, and that the local/global relationship is becoming increasingly fluid, is a recognition that opens out a key terrain for agency (Amoore et al., 2000). The movements recognize how the large scale structures are in fact connected to the myriad of local and 'minor' injustices that clearly crop up every day. Unlike the appoaches of the old left, there is no abstract and ironic privileging of structures *per se*. Walker argued that if:

> global struggles are inescapable, and if a just world peace must therefore be a struggle for One World, it must also be remembered that both *present structures and future aspirations are encountered and articulated on the basis of many different experiences, many different histories*. The pursuit of a just

world peace and new forms of solidarity must be rooted in an equal respect for the claims of both diversity and unity (1988, p. 5, my emphasis).

This is envisaging a global struggle but a struggle that is based upon connections rather than the ebulliant desire for new world orders (Cox, 1999; Spegele, 1997). Walker suggested that:

> the suspicion of universalism is not the same as a rejection of commonality. On the contrary it arises from movements that are able to understand fairly well the interconnected nature of contemporary life and the potentiality it offers. An openness to difference and to the great variety of experiences and histories that lead people to respond to global processes in highly localised circumstances occurs simultaneously with a sensitivity to the reality of connections (1988, p. 109).

For instance, the EZLN make a point of inviting *all* political views into their inclusive dialogue by deliberately disrupting conventional understandings of what it is to be 'leftist' and 'rightist'. Thus, rather than simply intensifying and reinforcing this artificial dualism it is now necessary to insist that critical social movements do not 'think globally and act locally' because this reproduces the false opposition between the general and particular and an understanding of politics as contained within the system of state-sovereignty. Thus, despite their celebration of diversity the local, critical social movements exhibit a clear awareness that without closer connections and greater solidarity they can only remain potentially 'weak'. This is a recognition that behind the insistence on acting locally is a challenge to rework the meaning of political community in an age which our vulnerabilities are indeed global in scale and have to be grasped as a dialectical moment, as a sense of participation both in large scale global processes and in particular circumstances.

Any critical enquiry on the antiglobalization movements must recognize that neither the character of this interconnectedness nor what some analysts have begun calling a 'world system' or a 'global economy' can be captured in a single conceptual account. There is also a sensitivity to building global networks and transcontinental connections. Critical social movements are elusive to categorize intellectually and politically by provoking a different understanding of the nature and site of political power. This should not be construed as a problem for activating protest as there was, and is, always a danger of imposing premature classifications onto political processes that have not yet run their course.

For instance, in Mexico the recent National Consulta organized by the EZLN sought to mobilize groups throughout Mexican civil society. An EZLN Communique (NCDM, 15 December, 1998) stated:

> a new form of doing politics was necessary, a politics created with all, by all, and for all making it possible for all Mexicans, regardless of color, religion, language, culture, social position, sexual preference or political conviction to have their voices heard and to have their weight felt in the important national decisions.

The building of tentative connections was evident in the *Encuentros for Humanity Against Neoliberalism* held in Mexico in 1996, and more recently, in August 2000, at the second conference of *People's Global Action against Free Trade* which took place at Bangalore, India. This inclusive struggle recognized that different economic, cultural and political groups are affected by neoliberalism differently but with a common purpose. This commonality of individuals from diverse backgrounds and yet with similar concerns that transcends the assumptions of social movement theory is not a universalized counter neoliberal doctrine. On the contrary, there was this implicit celebration of, and respect for 'many worlds' affected by neoliberalism, and concrete worlds which may collide and forge solidarity at times and which may see themselves as belligerents and protagonists at other times, with an awareness of the dangers of a right wing and regressive appropriation of struggles against free trade globalization. But critical movements, by challenging the theoretical and political schematics of the left, do forge a politics which the state does not quite understand at this stage.

Indeed, one major intellectual and political criticism from the orthodox left has been of this endeavour, is this really the time and place for such exploration, reflection and creativity? The answer is straightforward. Yes, on the contrary, time is in fact pressing for investigation because:

> it is quite clear that the visions of the future that are now offered by postindustrial statists, neoconservatives, unreconstructed social democrats, technocratic modernisers, self-righteous fundamentalists, and disruptive violence prone groups can only produce two responses, both unsatisfactory (Walker, 1988, p. 109).

In this increasingly turbulent world, constructing alternatives seems to be a necessity rather than a normative luxury. The first option would seem to be continuing clashes and chaos, and yet the other option may be essentially a 'managed order that excludes the poor and marginal from participation, and, over time, widens and hardens gaps separating those who are saved and those who are damned' (Walker 1988, p. 110). Consequently, the new forms of dialogue without dogma, are necessary *exactly because* the world is just so excruciatingly complex, in part, the result of failed ideological fundamentalism, with emerging patterns of convergence and divergence. Indeed, dogmatic responses are partly to blame for lives of the millions so precariously situated around the world. Critical movements explore and connect people and issues over time and space and they cannot be ideologically and dogmatically categorized or understood as activating on the basis of a singular logic. The development of capitalism cannot be ignored but its significance can be traced back to the transition from feudalism and to the emergence of the state system in early modern Europe. However, from this alternative critical perspective, there is no teleological reading of history and capitalism is not abstracted and 'reified' as a systemic process. Consequently, this gesture is *coterminious* with a rejection of Marxism as a political project. Yet, because the transition to capitalism has had such profound consequences almost everywhere, it is often wrongly and ironically privileged as it:

> monopolizes our modern historical consciousness. It can easily appear as the only point of origin, the beginning of all modern chronologies, the ground on which to demarcate between ancient and modern, primitive and civilized, developing and developed (Walker, 1988, p. 11).

The monopolization is clearly problematic and can occur when intellectual analyses are 'prone to treat these structures as cold, remote, and abstract, as huge determining forces beyond the reach of ordinary people' (Walker, 1988, p. 34). This manoeuvre leads to a dangerous expunging of human reflection, creativity and agency (Amoore et al., 2000). It follows that critical social movements cannot be limited to a critical enquiry based on the reassuring search for some kind of an underlying historical logic whilst there is concern with imposing artificial 'disciplinary divisions' as the movements 'are more likely to be open to the unexpected, to see what remains hidden by the categories and codes of conventional ways of thinking' (Walker, 1988, p. 98). Therefore the critical enquiry must recognize:

> people going about their normal everyday tasks. They absorb muscle and sweat, contemplation, emotion, creativity, and corruption. People may be caught up in huge structural transformations over which they have little direct control. But

structures are reproduced by the practices and rituals of everyday life (Walker, 1988, p. 34).

By implication, this perspective has established:

the capacity to interpret connections that gives certain kinds of movements a vitality and significance that goes beyond the claims of scholars and politicians, claims that are in any case often rooted in relatively limited interests and assumptions (Walker, 1988, p. 62).

As a consequence, the critical enquiry must recognize that it is no longer possible to take a single view, privileging the perspective of any particular group, class or people. Similarly, French philosopher Michel Foucault engaged in a specific and 'intellectual position which is different from technocratic or progressive uses of history for institutional reform and from Marxist uses of history for ideological criticism or some global alternative' (Hindess, 1998, p. 47). Contrary to intellectual Marxist approaches in critical IPE this perspective rejects a sovereign or privileged subject of history, because there is:

an emerging sense that attempts to bring grand designs down to earth in this century have often involved the kind of violence that makes the creation of the envisaged world simply impossible (Walker, 1988, p. 77).

Foucault was also sceptical of the radical intellectualism of the left and that of 1968 and Sartre said of the older intellectuals that 'They are always the same, even in my time-people who have written a dissertation they keep on reciting for the rest of their lives. But they fiercely cling to the little power they have, that of imposing, in the name of knowledge, their own personal ideas on others without allowing them the right to question them' (quoted in Cohen-Solal, 1991, p. 461). As Sawicki explained:

Foucault brings to our attention historical transformation in practices of self formation in order to reveal their contingency and so free us for new possibilities of self understanding, new modes of experience, new forms of subjectivity, authority and political identity...what he shares with the Enlightenment is the call to criticism (1994, p. 288).

Foucault refused a politics of critique that could be 'fitted into a single program'. Indeed he made this elusiveness 'a virtue and obligation of doing so' (Rachjman, 1985, p. 1). Foucault aimed to 'avoid single methods' and often held 'divergent and mutually inconsistent' views (Rachjman, 1985, p. 2). This deliberate conceptual and strategic elusiveness fed into the distinctive form of politics and critique envisaged by Foucault. Foucault developed an intellectual politics of resistance that accepted the ubiquitous and complex nature of power and where power was not sited in a sovereign and repressive entity but it was more relational and transmitting through a network of strategies or as Foucault explained 'we find ourselves here in a kind of blind alley: it is not through recourse to sovereignty against discipline that the effects of power can be limited, because sovereignty and disciplinary mechanisms are two absolutely integral components of the general mechanism of power in our society' (Foucault, 1983, p. 108). Thus for Foucault, political resistance must not be conceived as *external* to power because 'one is dealing with mobile and transitory points of resistance, producing cleavages in a society that shift about, fracturing unities and effecting regroupings, furrowing across individuals themselves' (Foucault, 1976, p. 96). Foucault explained:

> I am not looking for an alternative. You see what I want to do is not the history of solutions and that's the reason why I don't accept the word alternative. I would like to do a genealogy of problems, of problematiques. My point is that not everything is bad but that everything is dangerous...my position leads not to apathy but to a hyper and pessimistic activism (1983, p. 231).

From this intellectual perspective, Foucault was critical of intellectuals who made it a *cause celebre* to 'set emancipatory agendas' where the 'writing intellectual tries to become a conscience for everyone' (Rachjman, 1985, p. 9). Foucault recognized that it could 'no longer be taken for granted that the engaged intellectual is automatically *de gauche*' or where the enemies are automatically *reduced* to capitalism, the state and/or US foreign policy (Rachjman, 1985, p. 23). Foucault refused all claims to 'bureaucratic or charismatic authority' (Rachjman, 1985, p. 43). Foucault rejected the ideological self righteousness of Marxist colleagues who were intent on 'ferreting' a demystification of ideology (Hindess, 1998, p. 80). Foucault duly celebrated a certain incoherence as to the role of the intellectual and worked his way round to a position that was largely disabused of those old fashioned ideas about truth, knowledge, emancipatory critique because he cut these pretensions down to size. Norris wrote that Foucault's rejection of revolutionary politics was not surprising given that:

this was the heady period before and after the evenments of 1968, when French dissident or leftist intellectuals were required to take their stand on numerous issues and to choose between a range of competing positions, Marxist, Trotskyists, Marxist Leninist, Marxist-Leninist Maoist, anarchist, insipient post-Marxist etc (1994, p. 187).

Rather than *imposing* ideological/conceptual categories and strategical advice, it is now increasingly necessary to listen carefully to the way that people in these diverse and yet connected circumstances struggle with dangers and quite different historical experiences. Evidently, critical social movements can compete neither in analytical sophistication nor in overt power with which to respond to pressing problems but the movements are very sensitive to economic, political, social and cultural connections that may be invisible both to those with refined ideological and analytical categories and those who wield the instruments of power. This 'invisibility' or this sense of 'chipping at the margins' gives empowerment and although critical social movements struggle in specific and local situations it is clear that strategically many are able to look beyond the immediacy and specifity of their struggle to understand at least some of the wider connections in which they are caught as follows.

Firstly, the struggles discover new ways to act politically and to rethink what is meant by being political due to their marginality and their scepticism with existing political institutions and existing revolutionary politics of resistance. Secondly, they innovate new ways of acting within existing institutions and in these new spaces. Thirdly, they articulate new conceptions of knowing and being. Fourthly, they explore connections that may be achieved between seemingly different movements struggling in different situations and explore the concrete connections that may be made with other more familiar forms of political actions and this gives a critical space for reinventing and reworking the revolutionary tradition. Unlike either the great revolutionary movements of the past or the fundamentalists of the present, many contemporary movements seem to consciously refuse the false comfort of knowing exactly where they are going. With the critical social movements:

> there are no untarnished models, saints or heroes that can be singled out for reverent emulation. Movements struggle in difficult and dangerous places, and their potential is often crushed by force, inertia, or lack of imagination. Nevertheless there is also no doubt that some movements, in some places, at some times, in some struggles, have been able to demonstrate a striking capacity for a creative politics (Walker, 1988, p. 146).

Strategies, Power and the Political

Foucault once asked, 'why do we think that when we say yes to liberation we say no to power'. This alternative way of thinking about the relationship between micro forms of resistance and power offers a new way of thinking about the issue of power, and what it means to be powerful. Foucault's response was:

> in power relations there is necessarily the possibility of resistance because if there were no possibility of resistance (of violent resistance, flight deception, strategies capable of reversing the situation), there would be no power relations at all. This being the general form I refuse to reply to the question that I am sometimes asked: 'but if power is everywhere there is no freedom'. I answer that if there are relations of power in every social field, this is because there is freedom everywhere (1983).

The aim here then, was to abandon a tradition of a politics of revolutionary 'alternatives' that allowed and allows us to imagine that knowledge and 'utopia' can exist 'outside' and only where the power relations are suspended. So for Foucault, maintaining a practice of intellectual/political liberty becomes a constant strategic endeavour that is maintained at concrete sites because the political agent *must already be* conceived as an attribute of power and therefore of a site for resistance. Without the maxims of Marxism and socialism, resistance therefore, does not and need not, fall into the grip of postmodern nihilism, a nihilism which is itself merely the end product of the age and the road of revolutionary Enlightenment. Instead, as the doctrine of 'resistance is futile' seems to characterize the old revolutionary left more and more. And in an age when the revolutionary blueprints and certainties are under so much incredulity and suspicion, this is a politics of resistance that requires more and more thought, an intensification of political sensibilities and responsibilities, with no abrogation of such responsibility to privileged logics and dialectics, this time, that strange apathy borne of the *dogmatic* rather than the *reflexive* and historically in tune Enlightenment.

Foucault had said that he had been compared to Hitler by the socialists whilst other critics had complained that he was a crypto Marxist, a KGB agent or that he was a closet conservative. Such difficulties with the traditional political spectrum of left/right borne of the Enlightenment indicates his challenge to some of the wider ranging assumptions of what it means to be political and to be radical. Foucault maintained that his was a concrete political engagement which tore into the Enlightenment's philosophical quest but without maintaining an easy and relaxed assumption of its universal ideals. For Foucault the most radical feature of the Enlightenment was a Kant questioning and critically investigating the status of his own historical position, his reflection and his own philosophical enterprise concretely situated in time/space. Foucault argued that his historical investigations were not the search for formal structures with universal value but a more refined historical investigation into the events that have led us to recognize ourselves as political subjects of where we are, what we are doing, thinking, acting and saying. This was a more discreet investigation into the limits of freedom. Inevitably, Foucault preferred the specific transformations that proved to be possible in the last twenty years in a certain number of areas, that concern ways of being and thinking. These partial transformations are a rejection of the programs that the worst ideological political systems have repeated throughout the twentieth century. Such a perspective has implications for the kind of theory and practice of critical social movements in their struggles.

For over six years the Zapatistas have against great adversity demanded a fairer and *inclusive* modern Mexico as a sovereign national state based upon demands for better land, incomes, housing, education, democracy, liberty and justice. This is a profound mix and reflection of economic, social and political issues. It might be surprising that such interest would be shown in a resistance from a relatively remote corner of Latin America. The key to this ambiguity lies in the very nature of the Zapatista struggle itself. Marcos has said to revolutionary movements in Mexico:

> I know you will say this is utopian and unorthodox, but this is the way of the Zapatistas. Too bad. Go on with your path, and let us follow ours. Do not save or rescue us. No matter our fate, we want it to be ours. Do not worry about us. We will not attack you (1996, p. 4).

Marcos has stated that the EZLN:

> Don't believe that the result of this revolution that we are proposing will be a new world, a new country, it will only be a first step...(I)f there is a Trotskyite proposal, a Maoist proposal, an anarchist proposal, or the proposals from the Guevarists, the Castrists, the Existentialists or whatever ists that you may think of, they shouldn't be eliminated (Blixen and Fazio, 1995).

Here, Marcos is offering an inclusive dialogue that goes beyond party politics and the revolutionary doctrines (isms) of the *axiomatic* Enlightenment (on the left and right). Whilst eschewing the reductionist accounts it is also recognized that struggles are connected, generating a sense of interconnectedness through an experiment of possibilities. Let me quote Foucault (1991, p. 44) who had suggested that:

> if we are not to settle for the affirmation or the empty dream of freedom, it seems to me that this historico/critical attitude must also be an experimental one...open up a realm of historical inquiry and on the other, put itself to the test of reality, of contemporary reality, both to grasp the points where change is possible and desirable and to determine the precise form this change should take. This means that the historical ontology of ourselves must turn away from all projects that claim to be global or radical...we know from experience that the claim to escape from the system of contemporary reality so as to produce the overall programs of another society or another way of thinking, another culture, another vision of the world, has only led to the return of the most dangerous traditions.

It is suggested that social movements are *critical* in the sense that their participants rethink the meaning and nature of political power and refuse the ideological and teleological doctrines of the ahistorical left. The temporal and spatial site of struggle conceived by state-sovereignty have historically restricted the strategies and objectives of the internationalist left. Consequently, critical social movements offer a new *re-organization* and *re-representation* of political space. Given the near enmity thrown at global capitalism in Seattle and Prague, it would be fair to say that the globalization of capitalism and its institutions has paradoxically sown the seeds for the globalization of protest. The idea of cultivating a socialist/worker internationalist is key to contemporary Marxist theory and practice.

These micro spaces are constructing and rearticulating distinctive representations of an inclusive political space and rearticulating the strategic relationship between the local, national and global as found in the Marxist accounts. Firstly, critical social movements recognize how political space is both materially created and represented discursively by the sovereign mechanisms of the state *and* by the act of resistance to the dominant/repressive practice of the state itself. Secondly, critical social movements endeavour, from their micro spaces or space of 'otherness', to challenge the material exclusionary political space based upon the authority of state-sovereignty *and* the ideas and institutions of global capitalism. Thirdly, the strategies used by critical social movements represent a deterritorialization of political space. By using new technologies critical movements represent a new form of local *and* global politics of resistance. Fourthly, critical social movements cultivate a politics of inclusion by challenging the exclusionary practices of modern state sovereignty and neoliberalism, through a politics of national identity that can incorporate 'many worlds' and yet remain tied to an alternative national vision. As mentioned the:

> founding and specification of the state as a national community is a geopolitical act. This involves making one national identity out of many, establishing a boundary with an outside and converting diverse places into a unitary internal space. It also involves forging scattered and heterogenous histories into a transcendent and providential duration. These practices of nation-hood involve ensembles of acts to create nation-space and nation-time (Tuathail and Dalby, 1998, p. 3).

Critical social movements such as the Zapatista movement in the rural state of Chiapas, Mexico, are now acting within and creating these alternative and once silenced political spaces, creating their own histories. The Zapatistas have cultivated a unique juxtaposition of historical imagery in their desire to create a multicultural modern Mexico inclusive of 'many worlds'. Thus it is necessary to consider the conflicting representation of Mexican identity and Mexican political space/sovereignty used by the Mexican government and the Zapatista movement. But critical social movements do not simply glorify the future and they are engaged in a rethinking of what it means to live in a world in which the certainties of modernity have been shattered.

Conclusion

The chapter has shown that the Marxist/postmodern debates have coalesced on who and what movements represent, the nature of objectives, strategies, tactics and the normative justification of these struggles. The chapter has argued that the old/new social movement literature and its assumptions of political resistance engaged within critical IPE is conceptually and strategically limited. The chapter has argued that these perspectives have a tendency to miss the conceptual and strategic complexity of critical social movements, which provide the basis for a more politically and strategically creative and sensitive exploration of the kind of resistances to globalization that are now occurring, both in theory and practice.

Chapter 5

Globalization and its Real Discontents

Introduction

> That the cold war had ended seemed to mean nothing to the hundreds of insurgents who stunned their countrymen on Saturday by announcing themselves as the Zapatista Army of National Liberation and declaring war on the government. The struggle they describe is the timeless one of poor Indians against the rich, the new world they envision being one where things would be simply better...the rebels sway seemed a product less of any considered support than of confusion and fear (Golden, 1994, p. 1).

The purpose of this chapter is to outline the economic and political results of the neoliberal experiment within a wider-ranging global/regional context. The chapter is concerned with the restructuring of the developed and developing world, and specifically, the Latin American experience which seems to be so symbolic of the costs and benefits of the neoliberal enterprise.

Development and Neoliberalism in Latin America

During the Cold War, the term 'Third World' became synonymous with those states 'other than' the First World states (US and Western Europe) and the 'Eastern bloc'. The term was semantic *and* strategic, being used by many developing states to generate solidarity against the dominant geopolitical *and* development discourses of the Cold War. This was the era of the non-aligned movement and Third World solidarity movements during the 1950s, 1960s and 1970s (Dickson, 1996; Hoogvelt, 1996). Marxists and neoMarxists advanced a variety of theories and strategies for cultivating 'Third World development' which became known as state led import substitution policies (ISI), particularly fervent in Latin America. Such a policy cultivated a distinctive nationalization of industry, public spending and business protection under a strong and fervent banner of nationalism.

On the other hand, the liberalist export orientated strategies were based on free market enterprises, in theory, and were mostly used by the so-called East Asian Tigers. However, empirical studies showed how states such as South Korea and Taiwan, the supposed paragons of free trade and liberal virtues, also developed through unique conglomerates of state/family/business relationships, and often practices of political and military repression.

During the 1970s, many states were developing almost exponentially fast, becoming threats to a First World now hitting its own economic and political crises of capitalist hegemony. The alluring and relatively stable era of Third World development however, was also to come to an ignominious end, and by the early 1980s the experiments for many, were going horribly wrong. The ensuing crisis and its repercussions, were now manifested by a growing spectre of debt defaulting, whilst the optimism with a New International Economic Order (NIEO) evaporated very fast.

Mexico, was one of the first countries to default on its repayments in 1982, a country over-spending and bankrupt. Immediately the inquisitions started, and all representing a fundamental aspect of the debate on the politics of globalization. Who was to blame? Was the debt crisis a result of individual mismanagement, individual errors of judgement? Or was there something more *structural* going on, structures that limited the politics of the possible?

Indeed, the continents of Latin America, along with Africa, were branded as risky investment zones and it became very apparent that the *image* of a variety of states would prove to be just as important as the *reality*. In Mexico, it was the image of debt and chaos that the governments of Salinas (1988-1994) and Zedillo (1994-2000) tried so desperately to dispel. The defaulting crisis of 1982 (as with the implosion of Argentina in 2001) caused an unprecedented anxiety throughout the world's financial markets. As a consequence, the *Brandt Report* of 1980 called for more primary commodity price stabilization, as it was feared that more financial borrowing by developing states was going to be a key factor in the practical and psychological management of future economic crises (Dickson, 1996; Hoogvelt, 1996).

By 1985, the *Baker Plan* had been finalized. Its aim was to financially assist with the repayments as the burden of debt was further accelerated by the hike in global interest rates following the shift to monetarism in the US and the UK during the early 1980s. By this time, Argentina owed $47 billion, Brazil owed $102 billion and Mexico owed $95 billion (Gill and Law, 1988, p. 185). The World Bank helped out, but the US Congress then refused to donate the necessary cash *unless* there were certain conditions. These 'conditionalities' were part and parcel, with hindsight, of a broader based program of neoliberal economic rationalization through restructuring, public service and wage cutbacks and the rollback of the state. They were known as the infamous structural adjustment programs (SAPs).

The question of blame was still key to the politics of debt debate. The orthodox/liberal position was that the debt crisis was the inevitable result of both corrupt and inefficient Third World governments who were misusing state funds and using vast amounts of wealth for military expenditure, the bolstering of personal bank accounts and fashionable wardrobes all festooned with the latest fabrics from *Beverley Hills* and *Bond Street*, along with rather strange investment projects (such as the Brazilian government's ill-fated *TransAmazonia Highway Project*) and conspicuous consumption. Liberals blamed the earlier import substitution policies which, it was reasoned, had so wrongly protected inefficient national industry from the necessary vagaries of international competition. They also blamed the Western banks for loaning out money so readily and with such haste. This criticism was perhaps a little unfair as the banks were awash with billions of so-called 'petrodollars' deposited by the oil states and the oil sheiks who had been so richly benefitting from their OPEC price rises of 1973. After all, the business of banks is to make money.

The revisionist perspective was, and is as ever, more conspirational in accent and approach (Chomsky, 1993). The revisionist perspective puts the debt crisis into a Cold War framework and argues that the debt crisis was manufactured by a malign monetarist strategy so that the groundwork be laid for the imposition of a harsh and future 'disciplining' of a precocious periphery which was seen to have had an auspicious nerve to want to challenge the hegemony of the West and its transnational classes. In other words, the developing states had to be brought back into colonial line, if not simply for maintaining the geopolitical status quo but for defending the interests of global capital, a return to neocolonial status, a veritable dumping ground as Marxists put it, for overaccumulating core capitalism and the place to find an abundance of cheap labour. Dependency or neoMarxist writers who had earlier praised the nationalistic (even bourgeoise *and* proletariat) revolutions for breaking the bonds of exploitation, argued that that the West was concerned not only with socialist nationalism *a la* Castro's Cuba but also with a new and radical Third World bourgeoise (yet authoritarian) state which under the rubric of bourgeoise nationalism, diversified their economies and broke away from the bonds of core capital exploitation (Halliday, 1983). Such states had long since reasoned that a reliance upon its main exporting commodities was, in contrast to the theory of *comparative advantage*, unlikely to reap the rewards for future development, especially when the odds were stacked against them in the form of the unequal exchange of goods, wage levels and prices, which the theories of the Europeans such as Ricardo and Smith had not assumed. Then, during the early 1970s, US Secretary of State Henry Kissinger, using the 'carrot and stick' approach to international diplomacy, tried to forge a policy of divide and rule in order to break Third World solidarity (Hoogvelt, 1996).

Reagan's Foreign Policy

The perfunctory critiques of US foreign policy from the left as we have heard so much about since September 11 2001 bear little resemblance to the *concrete* complexities of foreign policy making in the US. Yes, there is an underlying and unsaid agenda that favours a liberally democratic *capitalist* state. The inexorable animosity thrown at the US in fact shows a distinctive, alarming and worrying lack of awareness of the many *real* factions within US foreign policy establishments which do make a *real* difference in the short *and* long term direction of International Politics. The revisionist view tends to ironically *abstract* the 'United States' as arch global imperialist, a country that seemingly cannot win, both challenged according to the convention, for its globality and then chastized for its isolationalism, seemingly only to intervene in matters of national interest. Of course, most states *do* intervene for national interests and the protection of oil. Development does *require* energy and oil and we are *all* complicit.

The allegation that the US has too many allies engaging with human rights abuses *is* a justifiable criticism. It is a criticism of the realist mindset, that old 'means justifies the ends' and 'he's a bastard but at least he's our bastard' philosophy of national interest. This is where the revisionist critiques of course, make most sense, if being directed at the politics of International relations because they bring in again, the intriguing issue of distance and *responsibility*.

The election of the Republican Governor of California, Ronald Reagan, to the US Presidency in 1980, brought about a whole new wave of thinking about the US' position and role in the world. Opposed to incumbent democrat President Carter's more pragmatic approach to International Relations, Reagan saw a battle of good versus evil and the Third World was a pawn in a (literally) Armageddon conflict between the morally pure US and the morally defunct and crumbling Soviet regime. Reagan's foreign policy was justified on the basis of moral superiority and fairness. His obsession was with the communist influence in Central and Latin America. Reagan saw the revolts of the Sandinistas in Nicaragua and the leftist revolts in El Salvador during the early 1980s as managed and directed by the machinations of an imperialistic Moscow still tediously but dangerously working in accordance with the doctrines of Lenin and the supposed 'inevitability' of world socialism. As in Vietnam, there was an executive concern with the 'domino effect' of collapsing states succumbing to 'commie influence' on the very hallowed boundaries of America itself. The activity of revolutionary socialist groups was seen as an obvious expression of the expansionist tentacles of the Kremlin which had maliciously taken advantage of the Nixon years of 'detente' during the early 1970s and the Strategic Arms Limitation Talks (SALT).

President Nixon's foreign policy was based on the percieved *and* real loss of US hegemony. The foreign policy objective was how to manage this decline and rise of Third World solidarity, whilst there was also a concern that the Soviets were 'on the move' particularly after the Soviet crackdown on Alexander Dubcek and the Czech dissidents on the streets of Prague in 1968. Nixon had been very suspicious of Cold War idealism and the policy of ideological containment which it was reasoned, would inevitably lead to imperial 'overreach' as witnessed in Vietnam, where Nixon vied for a noble American exit from South East Asia through the so-called 'Vietnamization' of the war. Nixon reintroduced realist statecraft back into US foreign policy, a world view based not upon ideological conflict but international negotiation built upon the cultivating of friends and shifting allies (no matter what the internal moral politics of the state were). For Nixon, the Soviets were to be integrated into a legitimate international order, under the assumption that all states, even the Soviets, had similar 'realpolitik' concerns in International affairs, namely security, rather than ideological desires. On 25 July 1969 the Nixon administration had announced that their Nixon doctrine was to be based upon the realization that greater burden sharing was required because the US could no longer maintain its once unchallengable lead in the arms race. Lyndon Johnson's earlier vision of the 'Great Society' was beginning to have serious and detrimental repercussions on the US along with detrimental effects on the value of the dollar, accelerated by a creeping inflation rate and a reduction in US gold supplies due to the policy of convertability established at Bretton Woods in 1944 (Wachtel, 1990). Indeed, Nixon had broken the Bretton Woods Agreement by 1971. The main strategies of Nixon's foreign policy were detente and linkage through peaceful coexistence. Reagan rejected all this even though like Nixon he was a Republican. But Reagan was a product and a supporter of the new ideological shift in established Republican and conservative thinking, a shift to the 'new right' which moved away from the policy of detente, and in domestic affairs, moved away from an economic policy of Keynesianism to one of less government, lower taxes and more responsibility. Reagan disliked Nixons' politics of realist nihilism.

For Reagan, it was assumed that economic and geopolitical instability in the Central American region had led to Soviet incursions. Reagan's foreign policy doctrine consisted of a low intensity counter insurgency program based upon economic and military aid, finance and military proxies such as the Contra freedom fighters in Nicaragua and a new and interventionist role for the Central Intelligence Agency (CIA). The US at this time also made strategic *and* ethical distinctions between friendly Cold War states which were domestically 'authoritarian' but allegedly open to change, and on the other hand, the unseemly communist totalitarian states (Gills et al., 1993). Leftist critics of US foreign policy (particularly during the Vietnam War) saw the directors of this policy as exaggerating the Soviet threat as a justification for US intervention in Europe and around the world which was working solely for the parochial interests of *American capitalism* and for keeping the public disciplined at home.[1]

Reagan's huge state spending on defence seemed rather anachronistic to his economic policy of less government, and as a consequence, led to a massive budget deficit with his administrations relaxing of tax burdens. Critiques of US foreign policy at this time, argued that 'socialist' revolts were not directed against the US *per se* but were inevitable reactions to the neoliberal structural reforms (Chomsky, 1993).

Neoliberalism, Mexico and Chiapas

One area of the globe that has attracted particular attention because the mobilization of one of the first revolts against neoliberal globalization took place there, is the Latin American state of Chiapas, southern Mexico (Krishnan, 1996). This has been an area of much US interest. Chiapas, one of 31 federal region/states of the United States of Mexico is located in the

Southern corner of Mexico. Chiapas was annexed by Mexico in 1824 from Guatemala following Mexican Independence from Spain in 1821. The annexation of Chiapas was justified on the basis that it would be better for the kingdom of Chiapas 'to be the tail of the dog rather than the head of the mouse'. Chiapas is noted for its areas of outstanding natural beauty.

From the sweeping highland plateaus swathed in the early morning mists, to the luscious vegetation of the Lacandon jungle rich in colourful species, flora and fauna, Chiapas has been a magnet for tourists, backpackers, anthropologists and natural scientists over the years. Chiapas remains a very Central American state with a very archetypical landscape, both natural and economic/political. The ripe tropical vegetation of the expansive Lacandon Jungle conjurs up indelible images of helicopter gunships, characteristic of the terrain in Guatemala, El Salvador and Nicaragua. Chiapas is geographically divided into the Southwestern region, the Southeast low lands of the Lacandon Jungle and the high central plateaus. It is in the Lacandon Jungle where the descendents of the early Mayan Indians still reside and it is here, where the most vulnerable inhabitants of Chiapas live. The Southwest low lands are agriculturally fertile. The Central Highlands, steep and rugged, considered to be the extension North of the Altiplano of Guatemala, are not so fertile because of the inadequate soils. To the east, towards Guatemala, the expanse of Lacandon whilst pleasant to the eye, is in fact mostly useless for agriculture. The state of Chiapas is the volcanic isthmus of the southern most frontier of the indigenous cultures of North America.

The early inhabitants of Chiapas were the Mayan peoples. The Mayan people had a rich culture, with their own Gods, knowledge, being, spirits, stories, philosophies and ways of thinking and being. The Mayan people developed their own systems of economic and political development, with emphasis on art, language, land, ancestory and heritage. Indeed, Mexico itself, is regarded as the most Indian country in Latin America. The original peoples and civilizations were represented by the Zoque, related to the Mixpopulaca, and the Mayans.

Chiapas is a microcosm of the impact of European colonialism and the disruption of the Mayan ways of life. According to Green (1995, p. 54) Indian life in the highlands changed 'with the arrival of the Spanish in the 16th century'. Main towns still show the cultural contrasts between the Spanish *conquistadores* and the indigenous populations. This former era is still evident in religion and the quaint architecture of churches and zocalos (squares) in the main sun-baked Chiapas municipalities such as San Cristobel de Las Casas and Ocosingo. During the early days of European colonialism as elsewhere in what became known as Latin America it was very easy to distinguish between the Indians and the European non-Indians. Andres Puig suggested that particular historical tensions in Mexico still derive from the original colonization of the Americas which in the years after Columbus' 1492 adventure, had:

> produced a blunt interruption of native histories, in which the whole social and ideological order of its original inhabitants and cultures was radically transformed, and a whole cultural heritage was denied. The colonial order imposed its own views bludgeoned local intellectual patterns placed an interdiction on art and science and refused to recognize the culture of peoples, who though new to European eyes had lived in these lands for thousands of years. Identities were badly bruised in their encounter with the new culture and they were especially affected by the harsh laws against the use of native languages and herbal medicine (1995, p. 25).

Indigenous peoples were peoples who were assumed to exist in self contained and isolated areas. What was also occurring was a gradual penetration of new capitalist relations and a break up of old economic, political, social and cultural relations. During the 19th century tensions began to grow between the Mayan Indians of the lowlands and the non-Indians of the highlands. Capital accumulation accelerated with the growing influence of scientific management. The non-Indians took advantage of the new liberal laws and therefore held the right to buy and sell land and property. This was an economic organization anethema to Mayan Indian culture. The liberal doctrine was maintained, again paradoxically, by an increasing political centralization. The arrival of the Spanish ushered in a period during which Mexico's indigenous peoples were progressively pushed off these lands and cultural/ancestral heritage, by the expansion of plantations owned by Spanish speaking Ladinos (Rosset and Cunningham, 1994). The Mayan Indians from the West were pushed back into the highland regions and on to the Lacandon Jungle by the expansion of colonial plantations. Anthropological studies of the region have noted a marked pattern of internal migration and agricultural land use (Nash, 1994).

Many Indians survived wage labouring in the large coffee plantations and were encouraged to move further East. There was an Indian and peasant migration into Chiapas, credited as the last Southern frontier (Deneuve and Reeve, 1995). This created a new and culturally mixed Mexican 'mestizio' through interaction with the original Mayan communities. The migrants were also given the poorest lands, leaving subcommandante Marcos of the Zapatistas, to state in 1994, that 'there are the rich men in Mexico, the medium men in Mexico, the poor men in Mexico, the very poor men in Mexico and at last, but not least, the Indian Mexico' (Ovetz, 1994). Marcos wrote that the kingdom of Chiapas:

> which willingly annexed itself to the young independent republic in 1824, appeared in national geography when the petroleum boom reminded the country that there was a southeast...Chiapas' experience of exploitation goes back for centuries. In times past wood, fruits, animals and men went to the metropolis through the veins of exploitation, just as they do today. Like the banana republics but at the peak of neoliberalism and libertarian revolutions the Southeast continues to export raw materials just as it did 500 years ago. It continues to import capitalism's principal products, death and misery...in obedience to the dictates of the neoliberal economic revolution, masterminded from outside and ruthlessly enforced by the government (1992, p. 5).

Historically, the Indian 'question' and the relationship between the Indian and capitalist modernity/development became part of a heated political debate throughout the American and Australasian continents. In Mexico, President Cardenas (1934-1940) developed the policy of *Indigenismo* in line with the positivist doctrine of society as an evolving organism. Indians were now to be assimilated and Cardenas' ideal was a Mexico inhabited in the near future, by the Mexican mestizio. This became an issue not of culture *per se* but one of class, as new cleavages of economic development occurred within and between the Indian communities themselves. The tension between cultural authenticity and an embracing of modernity accelerated. Could one embrace both, *simultaneously*? The sense of Indian identity and heritage began to assume rather less importance for those politically sanguine Indians benefitting from the rich plunderings of capital and 'using the system'.

In Chiapas, as elsewhere in Latin America, the 1950s and 1960s witnessed a rapid modernization of agricultural production (the so-called Green Revolution) financed by institutions such as the World Bank. Such initiatives also helped the rural areas to supply cheap staple food substances to the growing proletariats of the Northern cities. Yet during the 1970s new dynamics of Indigenous unrest were emerging across Mexico. Two movements specifically attending to Indian issues and concerns were the National Front of Indian Peoples (FIPI) and the National Coordination of Indigenous Workers (CNPI). The Etcheverra administration set up the National Indigenous Congress in 1974 and yet only served to unleash a forum for coalescing radical indigenous forces. Trujillo noted that:

> in October, 1974, the First Indigenous Congress was organized in Chiapas at first by the State government...from 1974, there began a very selective repression, a process that today completes a 20 year cycle with the explosion in January. The cycle can be divided basically into three periods. The first was that of 1974-1980 with the great highlight of the Independent Campesino Movement which began in a climate of great repression on the part of the state government...this period concluded in the month of July, 1980, with the assault on the community of Gololehan...commanded by General Dominguez who later became state governor (1994, p. 1-2).

In 1971 the World Council of Churches met in Barbados to consider the economic and social conditions of the indigenous situation in a number of developing states. In 1977 the United Nations (UN) set up the 'Inter Non-Governmental Organization Conference on Discrimination against Indigenous Peoples' which was followed in 1982 by the UN sponsored 'Working Group on Indigenous Peoples'. During the 1970s, agricultural production in Chiapas was mostly based on cattle ranching, sugar, coffee and cocoa on plantations/haciendas. Chiapas has been and still is the principle source of Mexico's coffee production (Burbach and Rosset, 1994). New economic and social relations were generated as both non-Indian peasants and Indian peasants left to work in the more lucrative oil regions opened up by the National Oil Company (PEMEX) (Ross, 1996). They returned in the early 1980s, having experienced the apparent joys of capitalist wage labour, and bringing back with them a tide of accentuated class differences and more capitalist penetration through new intensive agricultural technologies. Having sold their labour power on the market, and unwilling to return to a world of subsistence and what could be disingenuously termed 'noble poverty' many returning workers (some Indian) now had the available working capital to be able to purchase the modern machinery and hire additional Indian labour. This was hardly a climate for an ecumenical Indian consciousness as these migrants became local enforcers or the so-called caciques, controlling agricultural production in the highlands through money lending, land rental and sharecropping, with the occasional accusation of heavy handedness. Many had political ties to the Partido Revolucion Institucional (PRI) and would later benefit greatly from the neoliberal reform of Constitutional Article 27. Subsistence farmers and Indians in the East and in the Lacandon region were worse off because they had no access to the new technology which was now being used for intensive agricultural production on the plateaus and to the West.

Studies of the region have suggested that it was not a question of land ownership *per se* but a question of access to rich agricultural land, finance, new technology and the instruments of capitalization. The break up of the large latifundios was pushed (relatively late in Chiapas) by President Cardenas in the 1930s. This was a time when Article 27 was most acknowledged by the Mexican government. A large scale project of construction, dams, irrigation, roads and large scale commerical production ensued in the 1940s. The Mexican state was to provide the appropriated latifundio land for communal ownership and production by the Chiapas peasants and this was to be implemented by Mexican Constitutional Article 27.

But over time, the caciques began to manipulate credit and gained control of key properties and assets with the aid of the PRI and its affiliated Official Peasant Union (CNC). Their wealth was increased through the Green Revolution and the rise in international commodity prices. During the 1970s, the Chiapas economy grew by 10.5 per cent, but the cattle industry boom had also created a monopolization of land due to the required extensive farming and the displacement of traditional farming. Credit also reinforced the power of the cattle barons. It was the *skewing* of land concentration/ownership in the hands of the caciques/cattle ranchers that caused increasing frustrations in Chiapas.

Thus, as a response to the debt crisis, neoliberal reform during the 1980s, enforced cuts in state credit and cuts in agricultural subsidies hit the small commercial producers the hardest. The production of maize fell by 20 per cent from 1982 to 1987 and the government, through military enforcers such as General Dominiguez and the White Guards (hired gunmen of the caciques), began to undermine the rising plethora of militant and *autonomous* peasant organizations such as the Emiliano Zapata Organization of Peasants (OPEZ). The production of beans dropped by 18 per cent but the large scale production of cash crops still boomed with the devaluation of the peso during the 1980s. However, the price of coffee still fell from $120 per hundred weight in 1989 to $60 in 1994 which led to a 65 per cent drop in income for Chiapas coffee producers. There were also concerns with the environmental implications of neoliberal globalization and organizations such as the Maquila Solidarity Network and the Mexican Action Network on Free Trade (RMALC) showed their concern (Magdoff, Bellamy-Foster and Duttel, 1998).

Mexico's Economic and Political Development

Mexico is the world's largest Spanish speaking country. Geographically, most of Mexico is highland and plateaus, criss-crossed by a multitude of valleys and canyons. The only low land is the long desert peninsular of Baja California. Mexico has a population of 78 million, a density of 40 persons per square km. The population is made up of Mestizio, 55 per cent, Amerindian, 30 per cent, and European, 15 per cent. Mexico, a country of contrasts and of shadows (Oppenheimer, 1997). The often overwhelming, seething and sprawling metropolis of modern day Mexico City with an estimated population of around 25 million, contrasts to the Southern and sparsely populated highland and rural regions of Chiapas. The seductive opulence of the new and glittering modern buildings that now adorn the shimmering skyline of Mexico City contrasts spectacularly to the arid bleakness of the Chiapas highlands and the tropical swampy jungles to the South which almost lie in another time. Mexico etches an intriguing engraving on the fabric of world history, from the exotic riches of the Aztec and Mayan Empires to the conquest of Columbus.

The United States of Mexico became independent from Spain in 1821. From 1861-1867 the French invaded leaving Maximilian until 1867, when Benito Juaraz became President who was succeeded in 1876 by Porfirio Diaz. Throughout the early 20th century Mexico developed through intensive capitalization and industrialization organized by the dictatorship of Porfirio Diaz. This was a modernization based on capitalism focusing upon attracting foreign investment and particularly that of the US.

By 1910 the industrial-finance sector led by Madero and supported by Villa and Zapata were challenging the General Huerta dictatorship 1913-1914. Zapata led the Zapatistas, the peasants in the South, whilst Villa led the industrial petit bourgeoise, the Constitutionalists, the proletariats and the socialists in the North as a broad based movement. Ricardo Magon with his communist and anarchist aspirations for a political and social revolution organized strikes through the Mexican Liberal Party (PLM) and orchestrated seizures of the means of production.

In 1917 the Mexican revolution had succeeded in creating a nationalist, anti-imperialist and socialist populism. But the revolutionary state was creating a role for the powerful Mexican bourgeoise and produced the enslavement of the working class by the expansion of the petit bourgeois, due to a defeated peasantry. The revolutionary state was a conglomerate of the military, bureaucrats and technocrats. Gradually, through a series of contests and assassinations, the revolutionary state/party system was cemented. Mexico's society and economy have since functioned, until 2000, under the shadow of this one party/state monolith. In 1929 the National Revolutionary Party (PNR) was founded by Plutarco Calle, leading to the Mexican Revolutionary Party (PRM) which later became the PRI in 1946. Plutarco Elias Calle established an authoritarian state through forms of patronage, coercion and the institutionalization of class struggle. The post-revolutionary state carried on as a system of interest representation by hierachally organized and non-competitive groups recognized and regulated (if not created) by the state. President Cardenas (1934-1940) broke Mexico down into the major economic sectors on this basis, labour, peasant and popular. The revolutionary state tried to keep the Mexican bourgeois out and yet the power of the business sector could not be overcome.

From 1934-1940, President Cardenas developed a 'new deal' program of state regulated capitalism. This was ideologically cemented through consensus and a new found Mexican populism. Cardenas took a gamble. There were contradictions in the Revolutionary Constitution. The revolution swept away feudal relations but a socialist state was not formed *per se*. Despite its centralized government each state in the federation has its own governor and legislature. Both houses of National Congress are directly elected with 64 members of Senate with two from each confederation as a member for six years. The national Presidential elections take place every six years and yet the President is forbidden to take more than one term in office. Every three years there are mid-term elections. These federal elections take place annually and are focused on the re-election of members of the state Congress and the re-elections of local mayors in the municipalities. Ostensibly with efforts to maintain order the idea of succession in Presidential elections was and is meant to enforce a sense of continuity. Incumbent Presidents committed themselves to their PRI successor by supporting them through what is known as 'the pointing finger' (Zinser, 1987). The PRI justified presidential dominance on three main counts. Firstly, that a strong president is required for a strong national consensus. Secondly, that a strong executive and president is able to provide interests to all groups. Finally, that a strong president and executive is part of Mexico's distinctive historical tradition. Essentially the balance for the PRI has been one of maintaining its legitimacy consensually and the sometimes necessary stick of coercion and military intervention.

Like many Third World states in the post-war era in Latin America, Mexico developed through the import substitution policy. In contrast to the export orientation policies of the East Asian tigers which focused upon accessing the global markets (but with a pretty blunt interventionist policy of the state to curb union power), ISI was internally and statist orientated. This had political connotations for the West. During the 1950s and 1960s Mexico developed through a *developmentalism* strategy and the state was to play a major part by providing adequate production/consumption trade offs.

Throughout Latin America, this nationalist orientated development was influenced by the theoretical work of Raul Prebisch. Prebisch had convened the 1964 United National Conference and Trade and Development (UNCTAD) which had demanded fairer world trade for products exported from the developing world. The planned and centralized import substitution strategies, meant that developing countries could grow without concerning themselves too much with the relative uncertainties of internationalism. Middlebrook (1988) noted that the import substitution strategy was secured by the implementation in the post-war era of a Mexican 'alliance for growth'. As such, the ISI policy was an economic and political consolidation of economic and political sovereignty.[2]

The Etcheverra administration (1970-1976) responded to economic slowdown during the 1970s through a Keynesian inspired developmentalist strategy by increasing public expenditure and generating a diversification of Mexico's exports. This desultory strategy continued to fuel a climate of excessive public expenditure, stagflation, a lack of investor confidence and pronounced economic and political instability. This was a global concern.[3]

Through neoliberal structural adjustment, the margin between rich and poor was to become greater. Western *and* developing governments continued to perceive the economic stagnation of the 1970s in terms of the crisis of the 1930s or as one of a mass global overproduction. The response, higher wages and more public spending, mischievously castigated as simply 'throwing money at the problem' merely accelerated an inflationary spiral and nearly bankrupted many states, including the UK, where the Chancellor, Denis Healey had to go, cap in hand, to the IMF for a bail out loan. This was the era where stagnation and inflation went together as *stagflation*. This new phenomenon went against the grain of all existing Keynesian economic theory, the mainstay of the post-war compromise. Whilst Prime Minister Jim Callaghan returned to the UK in the late 1970s and asked, 'crisis, what crisis?' before the so-called 1978-1979 'Winter of Discontent,' the problem identified by political economists was one of *supply* and a lack of productivity and profit in an overaccumulating and inefficient economy. For the party political left, the newly proposed solutions to the crisis had to be a shift to neoliberal reform (put in place before Thatcherism) and therefore a betrayal of the Left's traditional political support. For Labour parties around the world, electoral defeat seemed inevitable. In the UK, unions refused to accept the new compromise and strikes galore ensued, as unions were then seen to be holding the democratically elected government to ransom. Not only did this play into the hands of the Thatcherite party, now waiting in the wings, creating a more aggressive conservativism than that of the Heath and Macmillan eras but it also played a part in the splits in the Labour party and inexorably, to the disciplinarian and anxious New Labour of Tony Blair. The shift to Thatcherism in the UK was almost a structural certainty. Thus, developed *and* developing states began realizing that globalization, the power of business and the market, was emerging and that all development strategies had now to be tuned in to the beat of foreign investment. In order to attract this investment a new market orientated development was required. Many Third World countries used the comparative advantage of low wages to attract TNC's where the new export processing zones proliferated (Mittelman, 1996). Mexico went through similar restructuring. It was stated:

Article 27 of the Mexican Constitution which in 1917 had established land redistribution and the ejido as the building blocks of agrarian reform in the countryside, was basically gutted by Salinas in 1992. The new legislation enacted by the PRI dominated Congress ended land redistribution and made it possible for private and foreign investors to invest in or buy existing ejido lands. Certain limits were placed on the move to privatization, such as the requirement that two thirds of ejidatories on a given ejido have to agree to any privatization scheme, and the setting of limits on the size (12.500 hectares) and number of shareholders (25) that could turn a former ejido into a commercial corporation (Burbach and Rosset, 1994, p. 12).

This is a world of symbols and images, of fashions, branding and waste. Any *hint* (the perceptions of countries by the investment community are so crucial in this world of mirrors and self-fulfilling prophecies and fragile speculations) of re-claiming state intervention was a concern of the De La Madrid (1982-1988) administration. De La Madrid did however, given domestic political pressure, increase public services in Chiapas and provided aid for the construction of a new highway along the Guatemalan border to secure the integration of Chiapas into Mexico as a sovereign *and* neoliberal state (Harvey, 1998). Indeed, the paradox was that this consolidation of state-sovereignty and emphasis on interventionist 'law and order' occurred at a time when neoliberalism demanded the continuing rollback of the state. It seems that the balance for any government at this time, was between short term political pressures, traditions and expediency, and long term economic rationalization which, according to the neoliberal maxim, would benefit everybody in the long term. The dominant view now was that 'the failure to keep inflation under control would raise questions about the continuity of political stability in Mexico and about continuing progress on a path of political opening' (Roxborough, 1992, p. 641). Neoliberal austerity seemed to work. Whilst inflation hit 200 per cent in 1982, by 1988 and into the 1990s inflation was controlled at around 14 per cent. The view was that this would inspire investor confidence, economic 'trickle down' and political liberalization.

Growing and Real Discontent in Mexico and Chiapas

Throughout the 1980s and 1990s there crystallized discontent with the general freezing of wages and welfare cuts. Burbach noted that:

> the IMF in many cases agreed to help the countries restructure their debt loads but only if they carried out neoliberal economic programmes. Social spending was severely curtailed and many state enterprises were sold off...these policies have failed. They have not induced growth in Latin America only more suffering and economic deprivation (1997a).

In 1973, the Program of Rural Development and Investment was forged with implementation of the National Plan for Repressed Zones and Marginal Groups (COPLNMAR). The National Basic Foods Company (CONASUPA) aimed to provide staple food prices for the rural areas. But Burbach also pointed out that:

> three aspects of globalization are particularly devastating for agriculture. First market liberalization which discriminates against small farmers...secondly as part of the globalization process, agribusiness corporations are acquring ever increasing control over all aspects of the world agro food provisioning system. And third the restructuring of many national economies often under the auspices of structural adjustment or stabilization programs has driven a new export orientated emphasis in agriculture, often at the expense of local food crops and internal consumption...an international conference of over 100 peasant and farmer organizations from 45 countries held in Mexico in 1996

similarly declared that trade liberalization is destroying the small farmers and peasants means of subsistence (1997a).

The PRI was now dominated by a new posse of sharp suited neoliberal technocrats. Indeed, many in Zedillo's administration had acquired their economic degrees from a variety of top American Universities. The development of neoliberalism was termed 'Salinastroika' in Mexico.[4] The controversial privatization was initiated by State Governor Garrido with the privatization of the Chiapas Forestry Corporation (COREO). In 1989, economic help for coffee growers was disbanded and state subsidies were reduced and an overvalued peso due to high interest rates plus an influx of cheaper grain now affected the economic effectiveness of agricultural exports. The Rural Association of Collective Interests (ARIC) offered to buy land for the benefit of the campesinos but this move was rejected by the PRI. Phillips (1991) noted that the PRI were already engaging in full scale economic transformation.

The North American Free Trade Agreement (NAFTA)

According to US President Clinton (1993) NAFTA, 'promotes market reform and the benefits of them to both countries' in the 'best interest of both countries'. NAFTA is representative of a new regional cartography of the political economy of the globe with more and more demands for free trade zones (Clapham, 1992, p. 1998). The US House of Representatives passed NAFTA on November 17 1993, the US Senate passed it on November 20 1993 and President Clinton signed NAFTA on December 8 1993. With the implementation of NAFTA, financial funds were set aside for Import Relief for businesses in the United States affected *in the short term* by the free market agreement. Assistance to workers was to be provided along with anti-dumping legislation. The influx of investment into the Chiapas region promoted by NAFTA was supplemented by the concern for the subsistence farmers who had produced the staple crop of maize for local markets and who required state assistance in order to maintain this function.

NAFTA is undoubtedly symptomatic of the changing pattern of international economic relations and in particular, the shift to a new form of economic regionalization. Such debates also echo around Europe on the issue of further European integration and the 'Euro zone' represented by the new single currency in 12 of the 15 member states and put into effect in January 2002. It remains to be seen of course, whether a single currency will prove to be sustainable and beneficial for the peoples of Europe, despite the obvious practical advantages. However, as in the US, many on the left *and the* right are sceptical as to the European Union, the former regarding the Union as a ruse of big business bringing about the end of the democratic institutions of the sovereign state, the latter, regarding the Union, as a bureaucratic threat to small businesses and the 'giving away' of sovereign cultures and customs. The balance which will be played out during a possible 2003 referendum, seems to be on whether involvement in the European Union from a UK position for instance, will negate or *increase* UK sovereign powers in a variety of forms, whether it be political, matters of security, cultural matters and economic concerns.[5] After all, a look at the history books shows how Winston Churchill himself was very much a 'European' in recognizing the inexorable historical links with the continent.

For the critics of the single currency now at work in the rather fun 'Eurozone' as it is now termed, bolstering the 'No campaign' does have an historical and logical problem in its view that the UK does not need Europe as it is already the world's fourth biggest economy whose trade is mostly with the 'rest of the world'. Moreover, it is said that UK taxpayers do not want the extra burden of subsidizing Spanish farmers or development projects in Belgium. The view however, takes a very static perspective on the changes occurring and the shifting to regional blocs. The UK is safe *at the moment* but historical shifts make this defence very shaky and even perhaps, more and more implausible.

The NAFTA treaty provided opportunities for other Latin American countries to benefit from free trade. There are groups such as the Mexican Action Network on Free Trade (RMALC) organizing trade unions and small farmers. One observer of the Zapatista rebellion was reported to have said 'I thought Mexico was peaceful, but apparently this state is different' (Garcia, 1994, p. 1). NAFTA was passed through the American Congressional Executive agreement, a way of passing a treaty without requiring the two-thirds majority in Congress usually required. NAFTA required just a simple majority because NAFTA was regarded as a revenue measure because it dealt with trade and taxes. However US President Clinton stated:

> keep in mind this is not simply a trade agreement, this is also an investment attractive for the United States to invest in Mexico...to promote market reforms and the benefits of them to both countries (1993).

It was estimated that three million families or 15 million people would be expelled from the countryside as the grain market collapsed. Tarleton argued that:

> a neoliberal economic regime is currently being imposed around the world. Sponsored by leading bankers, industrialists, compliant national governments and international agencies like the International Monetary Fund (IMF) and the World Bank, the neoliberal program is similar from one country to the next. So are the consequences...more unjust, authoritarian societies (1996, p. 4).

With the implementation of NAFTA, Nobel Prize winner Jose Saramago wrote that:

> six years ago in obedience to the dictates of the neoliberal economic revolution masterminded from outside and ruthlessly enforced by the government, the amendments to the Mexican Constitution put an end to the distribution of land and to any hope the landless peasants may have cherished of having their own patch of ground (1998, p. 2).

Saramago also noted:

> The native peoples believed they could defend their historic rights (or customery rights if you think Indian communities have no place in Mexican history...as a last resort they often had to flee to the mountains or take refuge in the forest and it was there, in the deep mists of the hills and valleys, that the rebellion was to take root (1998, p. 2).

From all over Mexico, Indian and nonIndian migrants now make their way Northwards to the US/Mexico border to what has become known as the 'Tortilla Curtain'. Burbach argued that in his view:

> particularly important...are global and regional trade pacts such as NAFTA which contain specific clauses dealing with the liberalization of trade in agricultural products...as part of the globalization process, agribusiness corporations are acquiring ever increasing control...a dark and adverse impact. It spawns new economic and social inequalities, uproots the peasantry as it accelerates the historic migration from the countryside to the megacities, retains a rural workforce employed on modern agricultural estates at less than subsistence wages (1997a, p. 2-4).

The large landowners saw the 1992 reform to Article 27 and NAFTA as the 'nod of approval' from the government to continue their 'punitive actions' on campesinos who were now seen as illegally and unconstitutionally soliciting privately owned land. The scepticism with neoliberalism was reported by a major NCDM report stipulating that:

> Mexico remains a country with severe street crime and business corruption, desperate poverty in the countryside, a major insurgency in the Chiapas province, a falling currency and stock market, a dependence on a sinking export, oil, and a political system fiercely resistant to Mr Zedillo's scheme to strengthen the country's fragile banking system (NCDM 10 September 1998).

One American journalist, who had worked in the region, John Ross (1994, p. 1-2), had wondered why so many leading American journalists, particularly Tim Golden and Anthony dePalma of the *New York Times,* were taken by surprise when the EZLN mobilization finally erupted in Chiapas on New Years Day 1994. The timing was of course carefully rehearsed, deliberate, and it hurt the government (Routledge, 1998). Ultimately, the problem for the PRI was its image, maintaining its congenial respectability for the global investment community because any sign of political disquiet and these selfsame and once cordial investors would forget their supercilious allegiances and jump from peso assets to dollar assets. Indeed, foreign investors quickly withdrew much needed dollars later on that year due to fresh allegations of drug related political assassinations and the Indian rebellion in Chiapas. The *Economist* (January 7 1995) considered the view that the Zapatista movement represented a 'Mexican volcano' whilst Ross argued:

> before the European invasion of 1519, South Eastern Mexico was covered with a densely wooded canopy extending from the Yucatan Peninsular to the Lacandon Jungle and Guatemala. Today these woods are a museum piece in enclaves such as Los Montes Azules (Blue Mountains) a biosphere reserve protected by the United Nations with the Zapatista community nearby...the plans for transnational planters for South Eastern Mexico are imperial...Pulsar has with close ties to the government (Pedro Aspe former treasury secretary heads the Stock Exchange) has planted almost a million hectares in Tabasco and Veracruz to produce cellulose for the next 25 years...the scheme to convert Maya Mexico into a vast eucalyptus plantation is a direct consequence of the reform of Article 27 of the Constitution (1998, p. 2).

The Chiapas air carries with it the light odour of petroleum production. The free market agreement crowds out local producers and local markets and NAFTA has contrived to reduce the local economic sustenance and self-sufficiency of more than two million maize producers in the Chiapas region (Nash and Kovic, 1996). The liberal argument is still maintaining that everyone will reap the benefits and rewards for disciplined waiting, 'in the long term'. Burbach concluded that:

> the restructuring of many national economies often under the auspices of structural adjustment or stabilization programs has driven a new export orientated emphasis in agriculture, often at the expense of local food crops and internal consumption (1997a).

The development of the neoliberal doctrine has enthused many activists with a passion to reclaim the political, to state that this is not 'inevitable'. Indeed, the sheer enormity of neoliberal influence over states and institutions is clear (Durbin, 1998). The *Economist* (12 November 1995) reported that many in Mexico had been critical of California's punitive laws towards migrants flooding the US/Mexico border since the implementation of NAFTA. The *Economist* (December 10 1994) also asked us, in protectionist mood, to 'listen carefully, can you hear a giant sucking sound of jobs and investment disappearing from the US to the Rio Grande in Mexico'. Protectionist and reactionary responses to neoliberal globalization from the right and from the likes of the 2000 *Reform Party* US Presidential candidate Pat Buchanan, are symptomatic of a new kind of conservative and even 'regressive' kind of resistance to neoliberal globalization (Murphy, 2000). But liberal elite optimism with free trade has continued unabated in many parts of the world. The *Economist* (July 23 1994) had earlier reported that President Salinas had rightly liberalized the economy, making 18 banks independent and more commercial. The Mexican government was split as to the costs and long term benefits of neoliberalism.

The opulence of downtown Mexico City, the crowded and sun drenched beaches of Acapulco and Cancun indicate that Mexico's rich have benefitted enormously, by pushing for an end to the protectionist policies and by integrating themselves more and more into the fierce talons of the volatile global economy. Today, Mexico has 23 billionaires. Meanwhile, lurking behind the cinematic paradise of Mexico's tropical landscapes and cocktail bars downtown, similar to other South American (and North American) metropolis', resides the underclass, the poor and the indigenous sectors, the new 'third world within', all continuing to suffer ignominiously from the readjustment policies imposed on their lives by the international finance community.

The quaint constructions of Indian life are suffocated by the gaudy global advertisments protruding from crumbling white plaster. The sights and sounds of the other provincial cities give this intriguing cacophony of the past, present and future all melded together. In the South, ethnic peasants and Indians alike, sacrilegiously uprooted from their ancient dwellings, mingle in the squalor of the inner urban areas where private property was defended by high voltage fences and privately sponsored armed guards. The hills of Chiapas are criss crossed by security fences disfiguring the tropical paradise with their rolling twisted metal and cheap, corrugated iron. The lines of conflict are being drawn and all it takes was just something small, infintisimile. Indeed, eleven months after the EZLN mobilization the PRI floated the peso on December 22, 1994 and put up interest rates to stave of inflation. This restrictive monetary policy and wage freeze invoked recessionary conditions.

In a speech, Michel Camdessus (1995), the Director of the IMF, had said that there had been profound and positive changes in the global financial economy. From 1990-1994 he said, the developing countries had experienced an increase in capital inflows of up to $130 billion per year. Between 1986 and 1987, the public deficit in Mexico was measured at a worrying 15 per cent of GDP yet between 1992 and 1993 this, in contrast, was being measured as a credible surplus of one per cent of GDP. Inflation also, due to monetary stringency, fell from its peak of 160 per cent in 1987, to ten per cent in 1993 and as a consequence, between 1990 and 1993, private and foreign capital inflows were being measured at around a healthy six per cent of GDP. Camdessus (1995) argued that the IMF had been right to provide financial support in the aftermath of peso devaluation in 1994 in order to keep Mexico on neoliberal track and in accordance with IMF member country guidelines. Yet by 3 January 1995, Mexico had hit a further liquidity crisis, and on 26 January the same year, the IMF and the US had agreed on a stand by loan if the PRI went ahead with its plans to privatize state electricity, oil and introduce cuts of $13.7 billion in social spending. Facts and figures are also highly abstract, with their glossy league tables and their economic projections, where nothing is said about the concrete methods of distribution, power, authority, about work practices, the environment and so forth. Indeed, as former US President Clinton stated[6] many governments *are* realizing that wealth creation is only part of the story, and they are making the connections between a lack of adequate wealth distribution/institutional networks and the rise of inter and intra instability. Throughout Latin America there remains the threat of conversion from national currencies to dollars by alarmed investors, which has further fuelled domestic inflation by pushing down the value of the local currency. This inflationary spiral tends to crowd out foreign investment. But the alternative, a pegging of national currency to the dollar which was meant to (and did) aid economic success, has gone horribly wrong for Argentina. The threat of 'contagion' in the financial markets *a la* the collapse of the Russian rouble in 1998, seems unlikely. However, five Presidents in a fortnight at the end of 2001, and the threat of a middle class and a right wing backlash, do not bode well for investor confidence.

On May 31 1995, Mexican President Zedillo (1995) had presented his own future predictions for Mexico's further integration into the global economy (World Development Report, 1995). The National Development Plan was based on grassroots consultation which aimed for an annual growth of five per cent to be financed by raising domestic savings from 16 per cent to 22 per cent of GDP. By the first few months of 1995 foreign direct investment (FDI) was being recorded at around $3721 billion. This was a 300 per cent increase over the same two month period the previous year. Confidence was returning to the region and by 1996 (World Bank Development Report 1996) the banking crisis was said to be being effectively handled by the administration (Zedillo, 1996, 1996a). The main lesson to be learnt from the financial instability of 1994 and 1995, according to the economists, was that states need to foster and secure domestic savings (Sachs et al., 1995). Moreover, investor insecurity has led the Mexican Central Bank to further increase interest rates to stop further capital flight. This led to an overvalued peso and no exports. Expectations of future peso devaluation were also rife leading to further speculation during 1995-1996 of a serious inflationary problem. The World Bank Annual Report (1996) noted that the containment of the peso crisis to a relatively small group of countries was the major global economic issue in the region.

Mexico, along with nations such as Columbia and Peru, remains a state with severe street crime, alleged business corruption, desperate poverty in the countryside, major insurgencies, falling currencies and further dependence on fluctuating export markets.

Conclusion

The chapter has suggested that an important relationship can be identified between neoliberal development, the role of the state and its development strategies at a global, national, regional and local connection. The chapter has argued that modernization has become inextricably tied to neoliberal globalization and yet the dynamics involved are causing real discontents which have led to critical social responses to globalization.

Notes

1 During the tyranny of the McCarthy (named after Senator Joseph McCarthy of Wisonsin) witchhunts of the 1950s targeted apparent 'Soviet sympathizers' but which critical writers have argued was a means to root out left wing and *democratic* dissent. The US became a national security state in which the American population became climatized and socialized into political obedience/discipline on the supposition of future *potential* war and a state economically engineered by what became known as 'military Keynesianism'.

2 The earlier sense of post-war optimism in the developing world, for many, influenced by the work of Walt Rostow. Rostow's 'stages of growth model' had eurocentrically assumed that *all* states went through a series of historical and inevitable stages of development emerging triumphant from agricultural and subsistence societies, preconditions for growth and finally to high mass consumption industrial societies in the Western image of course. Classical Marxists, paradoxically, pointed to the long term benefits of economic and political exploitation through the transfer of surplus capital which was a *necessary* stage on the road to world communism and the collapse of the capitalist state.

3 In 1971 President Nixon announced that 'we are all Keynesians now'. The ensuing recession heralded the shift to *supply side* economics. New economic and social concerns with the environment were also identified. According to a World Bank *World Development Report*, GNP per capita in the West was, by 1980, $10, 444, whilst in the South it was a quite miserable $650 per head (Frieden, 1981).

4 *The Economist*, October 28 1995, 'Mexico: A Survey'.

5 Interview with Lord David Owen, former British Foreign Secretary and a Director of the *No* Campaign, *Insight*, CNN, January 2 2002.

6 During the 26th *Richard Dimbleby Lecture* broadcast BBC TV, Sunday 16 December 2001; *The Economist*, 23 July 1994 'Mexico's Currency Wobbles', p. 86; *The Economist*, 7 January 1995, 'Zedillo and Sovereignty'.

Chapter 6

Connecting Resistance:
The Encounters for Humanity

The 'Triumph of economic globalization has inspired a wave of techno-savvy investigative activists who are as globally minded as the corporations they track' (Klein, 2000, p. 327).

Introduction

Alex Callinicos (2001) wrote, 'the Seattle demonstrations at the end of November 1999 marked the beginning of awareness of anticapitalist protests' (Callinicos, 2001, p. 110). In this chapter I show how *critical* social movements and antiglobalization protests, have engaged with an alternative strategic debate on the meaning, nature and site of political power and what it means to be engaged with a politics of resistance to globalization.

Critical Social Responses to Globalization

In contrast to the above leftist critiques of globalization, critical social movements recognize that 'globalization' is not a *systematic* process or a reified entity of determining laws 'out there' but rather, a complex process manifested as an overlapping and often paradoxical series of economic, political, social and cultural networks which are interconnected and which affect people differently over time and space. Focus on the specific 'everyday' experiences of individuals and groups reacting to the practices and institutions of neoliberal globalization *does not* close off local struggles from global structures. On the contrary, localized activism is *simultaneously* connected to the global and this is the strategic essence of critical social movements who recognize that not only is the relationship between the local and the global (as articulated through the concept of state-sovereignty) becoming more problematic, but also, that the activity of these critical movements is rearticulating new forms of political space and political power.

In many respects then, the assumption that global processes are somehow disconnected from concrete political agency, has given the impression that the state and the individual are powerless amidst the swathe of global financial markets. For the pessimists, timorous citizens in a democratic society are now being reduced to a posse of mere economic market consumers and the practice of democracy is systematically reduced to a technical obligation as political parties tend towards a homogenization of their economic and political agendas. Citizen choice now, simply means consumer choice and the power of the bland. Globalization has therefore produced a complex ethical debate on the nature of the relationship between the *responsibility* of governments and their citizens. As Falk stated:

> The dominant modern idea of citizenship was definitely linked closely to the emergence of individuals endowed with entitlements or rights in relation to the governments of territorial sovereign states (1999, p. 153).

However, this bounded idea of political community on the 'inside' as opposed to the realm of the International on the 'outside' is under threat from globalization, generating not a progressive politics but a politics of apathy, alienation and despair. This is generating a number of backlashes, despite talk of the 'global citizenry' and the 'global pilgrimages' of the newly mobile (Falk, 1999).

Undoubtedly, a gradual and yet potent fear has arisen as to the *powerlessness* of citizens and a reduced ability for the citizen to have a key say in the direction of national and global politics. Political institutions are being bypassed and protests from the streets are emerging. This protest has no overarching revolutionary objective. In the UK for instance, the foundation for cultivating alternative forms of direct action is emerging. Proposed plans for urban development at Claremont Road in London caused widespread antipathy from local residents concerned with the possibility of a future displacement from their homes and the effects of highway construction on local wildlife so thriving in the primaeval Essex marshes. Indeed, similar protests against the ubiquity of regional urban redevelopment near Newbury, Berkshire, had in 1994, also attracted widespread local, national and global media attention. Such protests of direct action have confirmed a growing sense of concern with 'urbanization' and the lack of political accountability from the local, regional and national political institutions. Whilst protests are not necessarily new *per se*, it is the way that these local issues have simultaneously attracted such widespread and accelerating global solidarity through a recognition of empathy and strategic *connections* to other local environments around the world. This is the key strategic change and challenge to understand.

Paradoxically, the resurgence of new age environmental protests of the 'back to nature' persuasion was linked to the new electro dance cultures of the late 1980s, by drawing upon a unique juxtaposition of 1960s environmentalism (a revival of the Glastonbury music festival) and new technologies. Outdoor raves and dance culture inevitably became commercialized whilst musings for 'authentic' artists and 'authenticity' (whatever that is) became branded and self indulgent. However, the new emphasis on 'street culture' and 'street language' (despite the ironic send ups not always recognized by those following the brand) was important, and global street protest parties became a feature of inchoate struggles such as those during the G8 meeting of ministers in Birmingham, UK, held on May 16 1998. However, the dogmatic 'anticapitalists', those we see on the television and who would tend to see global capitalism as a systematic class enemy that infects every economic, social, cultural and political relationship; from environmental destruction to Islamic fundamentalism, are still powerful and miss the point. Is it really possible to resist with such a gleeming lack of self-awareness of the hypocrises and contradictions involved? From this conspirational perspective, everything then, boils down to the logic of the capitalist mode of production. This highly reductionist enterprise of course, ironically reifies a complex set of practices and paradoxically uses the same conceptual assumptions and language of the right.

Yet 'awareness' of the local and the connections to 'global issues' has galvanized widespread support for those groups for instance in the so-called 'export processing zones' around the developing worlds. However, whilst many talked about the 'third world within' Europe and the United States, the ghettoization of many of the major cities now divided between a high class financial district and an excluded territory for low cost labour, others reasoned that the brutal economic and political climates in Indonesia and Nigeria were far worse and that distinctions between the first and second world's could still be maintained. Critical social movements do not see their politics as a scenario of either/or and recognize that labour politics and so-called middle class politics are equally as significant, at given times and spaces. Throughout the streets of Europe and the United States, the recapturing of a new and democratic public space was shown in a *Reclaim the Streets* (RTS) Declaration which stipulated its concern with:

> privatization of space in the form of the car continues the erosion of the neighbourhood and community that defines the metropolis: road schemes, business parks, shopping developments, all add up to the disintegration of community and the flattening of locality - community becomes a commodity, a shopping village sedated and under constant surveillance. The desire for community is then filled from elsewhere - through spectacle sold to us in simulated form - a TV soap street or square mimicking the area that concrete and capitalism are destroying (AGP, 2000).

Zapatistas and Mexican/Global Civil Society

Recent antiglobalization protests in the UK and the US have been linked with antiglobalization protests and events right across the world. *People's Global Action* (AGP) is one such forum, connecting diverse groups and interests and the Zapatista movement in Chiapas, Mexico is representative of the struggle against the vicissitudes of neoliberal globalization. Antiglobalization protest in Prague on September 26th was classed by RTS as the 'Five days that shook the world'. The politics was satirical as participants debated the new politics of the White Overalls Movement Building Libertarian Effective Struggles (the WOMBLES).

From 23-28 February 1998 movements from all continents met in Geneva and conducted a worldwide coordination of resistance versus the institutions of the global market through a new alliance of struggles and mutual support called People's Global Action against Free Trade - a new platform to serve as an instrument for communication and coordination for all those fighting against the destruction of humanity by the global market and for building up local alternatives. A worldwide coordination of local struggles made during the WTO ministerial conference in Geneva was a huge success; with many different demonstrations and global street parties which had also taken place on all five continents from 16-29 May 1998. The so-called hallmarks of organization and strategy were, to reject the WTO, EU and NAFTA, to reject all forms of domination and discrimination, such as racism and patriachy, to forge a confrontational attitude, with no lobbying with those institutions which are so utterly undemocratic as they abstractly apply the rules and interests of transnational capital structures, to develop non-violent disobedience with a decentered autonomy in organization and to maintain no registered membership. This is a wide-ranging and *inclusive* political forum for debate and discussion concerning the impacts of neoliberal globalization which eschews rigid organization, favours direct democracy, civil disobedience and a proposal for change flowing through world communication channels. AGP have organized a network of coordinated demonstrations by peoples with and experiencing different social, economic and cultural backgrounds but joined by a common purpose against the often diverse and local effects of the ideas and institutions of corporate globalization. June 18 1999 described as a 'jornada' ('day') of global action aimed at the heart of the ideas and institutions of the global economy. Actions and demonstrations were simultaneously mobilized in the major financial centers, markets and institutions around the world.

Indeed, the emphasis on the politics of the 'jornada' implies a sense that globalization is not an abstract entity measured by abstract economic market indicators but rather a structuration of ideas and institutions affecting peoples 'quotidien' or everyday existences. This is a global and yet non-unified and non-Marxist network of direct action which seeks the rediscovery and the liberation of city streets and public spaces that arose from the British anti-highway movement of the early 1990s. There is no blueprint of 'what is to be done' but in their 'manifesto' the AGP have stated:

> Today capital is deploying a new strategy to assert its power and neutralise people's resistance. Its name is economic globalization and it consists in the dismantling of national limitations to trade and to the free movement of capital: a gigantic system aimed at the extraction of profit and the control of people and nature. Words like globalization, liberalization and deregulation just disguise the growing disparities in living conditions between the elites and the masses in both privileged and peripheral countries (2000).

The AGP also gives a 'southern' dimension to connecting resistances from Latin America, Africa and the West, and it recognizes that calls for free trade and the free movement of capital from privileged states to the under privileged countries *could be*, in specific circumstances, regarded as a positive contribution. But, in echoing the old dependency perspectives, they also make the case that the policies of the rich countries will enable *their business institutions* to continue exploiting their population. Indeed, talking about 'countries', a description premised on the geography of the sovereign state system, in fact neutralizes the different experiences of individuals *within* states whilst a measurement of country wealth via GDP and GNP completely ignores the *redistribution* of wealth within borders and over the sovereign territory.

For instance, are people in the West willing to forego low prices for solidarity with the workers of the south even if such moral benefits seem remote and indeed, paradoxically quite abstract themselves? Indeed, defenders of globalization often maintain the view that if there was no globalization then many, particularly in the south, would simply be worse off given the strangely liberalist and Marxist maxim that 'it is better to be exploited than not to be exploited'. However, such an assertion draws upon the assumption that globalization is *economically* inevitable.

The AGP act as a forum for diverse projects of global resistance to neoliberalism and a desire to build up local and specific alternatives as a network of communities at the grassroots (but accepting that local and national political institutions can be harnessed). The AGP organize their own conferences usually three months before the IMF and WTO meetings to discuss efforts at coordination, reflecting on manifesto's and goals, deciding which organizations can send delegates and where future resources will come from, interpreting the manifestos and a rotative secretariat with regional platforms. Indeed the EZLN have their own decentralized political forum (the Emiliano Zapata Front of National Liberation) and organizational direct democracy was also an idea taken from the Zapatista village communities. The essential strategy of the Zapatistas Encounters was based on the incorporation of 'many worlds' affected by neoliberal globalization based on

> a collective network of all our particular struggles and resistances...the intercontinental network of alternative communications is not an organizing structure, nor does it have a central head or decision maker (Cleaver, 1997).

This network will engender a space for democratic struggle in Mexico and as part of a worldwide struggle. This has induced increasing difficulties for the government to govern the Chiapas region effectively. Cleaver (1997) noted that: through their ability to extend their political reach via the modern computer networks the Zapatistas have woven a new electronic fabric of struggle to carry their revolution throughout Mexico and around the world. Participants in social conflicts have extended their struggles from other zones of human space into cyberspace and the net provides new spaces for new political discussions about democracy, revolution and self determination. This is a far cry from aspirations for national or global Marxist revolution and expands the spatial understanding of what it means to resist globalization. Instead, what emerges is a politics that refutes a project/counter project and instead recognizes a commonality of interests and the ambiguities of globalization.

Consequently there is a rejection of organic intellectuals, vanguard revolutionary 'careerists' and an open attitude to (considered by the old Left) conventional lifestyles, as well as 'politically motivated' groups, seen as a crucial and inclusive part of an organic movement whilst the movement is less fixed on single issues and rejects any hierachy of determining or privileged grievances.

Whilst the small protests do not *necessarily* show up as the big power struggles in a world conceived along the lines of the sovereign state system, critical movements are a new cultural explosion and creativity. These are not movements that are based upon a pitting of wits on a 'them and us' or even a 'left versus right' but movements which are willing to listen to their greatest protagonists. These struggles are for a 'one world' which implies the ultimate commonality that we all live in this one world precariously balanced. These connections are not always recognized but at specific economic, social, cultural and political sites a recognition of common purposes can lead to empowering alliances. The EZLN refute a politics of winners and losers, of abstract electoral polls and the machinations of the party political process, also shown by groups such as *AGP, Globalize Resistance* and *Reclaim the Streets*, not a counter hegemonic project but a 'politics in formation' which rethinks the nature of political space and political power. On this basis, Conger stated in the March of 1994 that:

> The Zapatista National Liberation army is unlike any other Latin American guerrilla movement, and in its short public life has shown a flexibility and moderation previously unknown in the hemisphere. The Zapatistas distinguish their movement with their ready willingness to engage in peace talks. Only one week after taking up arms, the guerrilla leadership responded favourably to government offers to hold a dialogue to debate the EZLN agenda of social and economic demands, a ceasefire, and political participation for indigenous and other citizens (1994, p. 3).

After the uprising on New Year's Day 1994, the EZLN in their First Declaration of the Lacandon Jungle stated the following:

> We are a product of 500 years of struggle; first against slavery, then during the War of Independence against Spain led by insurgents, then to avoid being absorbed by North American imperialism, then to promulgate our constitution and expel the French empire from our soil, and later the dictatorship of Porfirio Diaz denied us the just application of the Reform laws and the people rebelled and leaders like Villa and Zapata emerged, poor men like us. We have been

denied the most elemental preparation so they can use us as canon fodder and pillage the wealth of our country. They don't care that we have nothing, absolutely nothing, not even a roof over our heads, no land, no work, no health care, no food nor education. Nor are we able to freely and democratically elect our political represntatives, nor is there independence from foreigners, nor is there peace or justice for ourselves and our children (1994).

In the First Declaration, the words imperialism, dictatorship and 'poor men' seemed to suggest that the EZLN was Marxist. Rodriguez (1994, p. 2) wrote that '(C)lass war has started in Mexico, that is not doubted even by the PRI (the ruling party). Its causes are well known secrets'. Indeed, US journalist John Ross (1994) noted that many of his fellow journalists interpreted the EZLN as a group of 'reds' who wanted to build a socialist Mexican state in the mould of Castro's Cuba. Ross (1994, p. 2) noted that many journalists had been trained to 'look for a red in every hut' and 'had a hard time understanding the non-Marxist Zapatistas'. Gerlind Younts of NBC News noted that:

Zapatista rebels in Chiapas and the Popular Revolutionary Army in hills above Acapulco...come against a background of years of corruption, land abuse, religious conflict, crushing poverty and prejudice...regional supporters of the Zapatistas have set up 32 town councils independent of local government officials recognised by Mexico City. Most of these councils are symbolic in nature...Zapatista rebels officially declared war on the government of the then, Carlos Salinas and vowed to lead a Marxist uprising against the Mexican government (1998, p. 1).

Carrigan (1998, p. 12) noted that the Marxist interpretations, political and intellectual, were powerful, including 'the Mexican government of Carlos Salinas, which was then in power and which looked for a forcign conspiracy behind the revolution' along with 'many of the foreign press who went to Chiapas' and were 'looking for answers to the Indian rebellion through a rearview, a Central American rearview'. In an early report, one insurgent stated, that the military orders to the EZLN in relation to the state were 'to knock it down', words from a thin 20 year old who identified himself as Jesus and stated that '(O)ur thinking is that we have to build socialism' (Golden, 1994). The military command called for solidarity with the rebel soldiers (EZLN, 1994). The command stressed that the Chiapas population should feed and clothe them if required. Golden noted:

the guerrillas military weakness was obvious today along a 30 mile stretch of rural highway that remained more or less under their control. From quiet conversations with townspeoples and villagers, the rebels sway seemed a product less of any considered support than of confusion and fear (1994, p. 2).

Ovetz (1994) asked Marcos, 'do you seek the overthrow of the Mexican state?' Marcos replies 'What?' Ovetz (1994) asked 'do you seek a new government?', Marcos replies 'yes'. Ovetz asked, 'Is it continuing the unfinished revolution of Zapata?' and Marcos' reply was 'yes' and 'a counter revolution against Salinas'. Consequently, it was reported that:

> the world press snapped up the Zapatista rebel movement when its leaders wearing black ski masks surfaced in Mexico's remote and desperate Chiapas province, and thinking big demanded the removal of an elected president and the surrender of an undefeated army...Chiapas has come to mean a condition of disorder...found in many parts of the world...the insurgents have been able to maintain a local physical presence...the Zapatista leadership is devoted to a primitive Marxism at odds with what the rest of the world has learnt about changes in the 20th century (NCDM, 2 December 1998, p. 1).

Rodriguez (1994, p. 4) noted that the 'Maoists (in capitalist press coverage) shouted that Chiapas began the popular war and that this uprising obeyed the advanced Maoist international in the last minute of the centenary year' and 'for their part the Stalinist-Trotskyists baptized the Zapatistas as the revolution and predicted the start of a socialist state in Mexico' (Rodriguez, 1994, p. 4). The EZLN has its roots back in the Mexican radicalism of the 1960s and 1970s. During the late 1950s and early 1960s movements such as the Workers Clandestine Party of the People (PROCUP), the Workers and the Revolutionary Party of the People (PROCUP-PDLP) and the Party of the Poor (PP) had reacted strongly to economic discontent particularly in the urban areas and the Catholic Church began a 'rescue and resistance' strategy by focusing on the centrality of political mobilizing.

As elsewhere during this heady time, the student protests of 1968 were politically decisive and in Mexico were arranged in part, by Professor Adolfo Orive, an organic intellectual, of Mexico City's Autonomous National University (UCAM) and ended violently even as the world media centered on Mexico for the 1968 Olympic Games. Federal troops ended the protests on October 2 1968 with the massacre of 200 students on the Three Cultures Plaza in Tlatelolco. Urban leftist and maoist groups such as Linea Proletaria (Proletarian Line) began linking their efforts to the radical libertarian priests in the rural areas. Contacts were being made. Professor Orive provoked a mass line of non violent socialism (Harvey, 1998). The spirit of revolutionary resistance in the 1970s was manifested by urban movements such as Proletarian Line and the Politica Popular, the latter being a maoist cell/group. Other revolutionary groups mobilizing were the National Liberation Forces (FLN) which had allegedly attracted a young Subcommandante Marcos in the late 1970s (Harvey, 1998). These groups were influenced by Marxist and Maoist ideals and these ideals were still particularly attractive to revolutionary romantic students at the time.

By 1977 Politica Popular had emerged as a potent forum in Mexico City. Various cells of the movement cropped up throughout the Northern city of Monterrey. Its participants were middle class intellectuals. Flood (1994) noted that radical campesino groups such as the Emiliano Zapata Peasant Organization (OPEZ) in Chiapas were now forging solidarity with these individuals. Various collective projects organized to solve smaller problems and on a number of issues, began linking the local concerns to the broader national picture. Local movements were infiltrated by urban revolutionaries who were thinking big and wanting to stake their claim in Mexico's revolutionary history. Various autonomous National Coordinating Bodies began to emerge and these became known under the term the 'coordinadoras'. A number of issues were in focus.

The National Coordination of Education Workers (CNTE) called for more local and national democracy. The National Coordination Plan of Agyala (CNPA) forged civilian resistances whilst the National Coordination of Urban Popular Movements (CONAMUP) was set up in 1980 with the express aim to coordinate radical actions and agendas in the larger city neighbourhoods. The National Union of Regional Peasant Organizations (UNORCA) aimed to open up new critical spaces in rural areas on issues of land and democracy and in 1979, the National Front of Womens Rights and Liberty (FNALIDUM) was also formed (Stephen, 1996). Proletarian Line helped organize campesinos during the late 1970s along with groups such as the People United, the Independent Organization of Agricultural Workers (CIOAC) and The Peasant-Mexican Communist Party (CIOAC-PWM). The Politica Popular proved to be a major forum for mobilizing, recruiting and bringing together future members of what was later to become the EZLN. Politica Popular became linked to a number of radical peasant groups such as the Union of Ejidos and the Independent Campesino Movement. The Union of Ejidos worked primarily in the Lacandon Jungle to the East, the Northern part of the state and the Sierra Madre Mountains. The Independent Campesino Movement bases its resistance on organizing the seasonal and permanent workers on Chiapas coffee farms and cattle ranches in the towns of Simojevel, Huitiupa'l and El Bosque. And OPEZ grew out of the community of Venustiano Caranza. It struggled for land and against repression primarily by confronting the state through direct and violent action.

According to Stephens (1996), the Ejido Union United was set up in Ocosingo around the mid-1970s whilst the organization, Ejido Union Land and Liberty (Tierra y libertad) was set up in Las Margaritas. The aim of these groups was 'to go to the people'. These campesino movements along with the Ejido Union of Peasant Struggle came together under the Union of Unions (UU) or the Ejido Union and Solidarity of Peasant Groups. The UU was set up in 1980 in the Lacandon Jungle (Harvey, 1998). Campesino groups were enhanced by the National Coordinating Committee (CNPA) which was formed in 1979. Concerns were levelled at the indelible corruption of the agricultural PRI bodies such as the Department of Agarian Affairs and Colonization (PAAC) and the CNC.

By the early 1980s, Proletarian Line was recognized as a solidarity between the PP and the Union of Peoples (UP). Proletarian Line and Professor Orive sent their recruits and organizers to each of these campesino groups. Campesino movements had by now tied together the fight for land with the question of appropriating the means of production (Harvey, 1996). By 1985 this solidarity had been consolidated through the UNORCA. The PRI had during the 1980s allegedly stepped up its repression with, in 1988 the joint assassinations of Nunez of the CIOAC and Valasco of OPEZ. According to Constitutional Articles 129-135 the PRI could justify the crushing of protests stipulating that unarmed mass demonstrations were a threat to public order. The Rural Collective Interest Association (ARIC) now primarily focused on credit issues. By 1988 two strategies/objectives were present. On the one hand there were those who had encouraged the formation of democratic organizations and the promotion of peasant self government. On the other hand there were those who believed that this was insufficient and that a more radical (Marxist) objective was required. The OPEZ maintained that only armed struggle could provide a real solution. The first vision gave rise to organizations such as the UU and the second to what became known as the Zapatista Army of National Liberation. Deneuve and Reeve pointed out that in post-1968

the Maoist-Marxist Politica Popular decide to leave the student milieu to concentrate its activities on 'the mass of the people'. So it establishes itself in the towns in the northern part of the country, where due to the drift from the land, large areas of shanty towns exist, a favourable terrain for militant leftists...(B)eing in competition for control of the same masses, Marxists and priests rapidly reach an understanding...(F)rom their miraculous cooperation 'torreonism'...the Mexican model for 'work on the masses'. In the middle for the 1970s the Mexican government, worried by the success of this tendency, begin a savage repression...the directors of the organization revise its positions, the 'masses lines' which puts its emphasis on political work in the urban areas is replaced by the Proletariat Line, giving their priority to the implementation amongst the poor peasantry (1995, p. 4).

The UU had split by 1988 into the ARIC and on the other hand, to the more radical Emiliano Zapata Independent Peasant Alliance (ACIEZ) which later became the Independent Peasant Nationale (ANCIEZ). This movement had gone underground by 1993 presumably to prepare for military operations (Stephen, 1996). The early rebels could collect arms little by little, without notice, a point of organization that urban struggles had not been able to do (Casteneda, 1994). This sense of isolation was to change dramatically in the subsequent years whilst the main participants and Commandantes of the EZLN such as Marcos and Commandante Tacho of the Clandestine Revolutionary Committee General Command (CCRI-GC) had 'been preparing themselves militarily for at least 12 years' with Subcommandante Marcos describing himself 'as one of a group of several Mexican leftists who came to the Lacandon Jungle in the early 1980s to organize Indians and wound up leading a revolt' (Parfitt, 1996, p. 121).

In March 1993, the Mexican army accidently stumbled across EZLN guerrillas in the area of Farrabundo. By this time the Zapatista Army of National Liberation (EZLN) although as yet unnamed was now thought to have emerged as an organizational synthesis of the OPEZ and the ANCIEZ. On New Year's Eve EZLN guerrillas took a rickety bus through military barricades which were being manned by Federal border guards who in turn, failed to notice anything particularly unusual. The Mexican Ministry of the Interior stipulated in 1993 that there were 'no guerrillas' in Chiapas and warned that 'to say that there are causes grave danger to the states development' (Ouweneel, 1996, p. 80). This is not however, simply a localized and historic Mexican issue.

Mexico joined NAFTA at a time when the US-Canada Free Trade Agreement was already in place. Thus Mexico had no time or ability to call for any deferential treatment, an episode which was consummately taken in the right way by the administration, as it gave a clear signal to Salinas from the US, that Mexico had finally joined the status of the First World. To open this alternative space Marcos used the terms *mask* and *mirror* to indicate a different Mexico ready to blossom, whilst the Nation cries out '(T)hey have treated me like a piece of injured land, full of scars, of wounds that do not heal, from healings and downfalls. They have treated me like a never ending curse, like a home left in ruins and bitterness. How heavy is history!'. Marcos reported that:

> There exists on this planet called 'Earth' and in the continent called 'America' a country whose shape appears to have had a big bite taken out of it of its west side, and which threw out an arm deep into the Pacific Ocean so that hurricanes don't blow it far away from its history. This country is known by both natives and foreigners by the name of Mexico. Its history is a long battle between its desire to be itself and the foreign desires to have it exist under another flag. This country is ours...(A)nd they said globalization and then we knew that this was how this absurd order was called, an order in which money is the only country which is served and borders erased (1998, p. 1).

Routledge noted that:

> armed guerrillas occupying Chiapan towns, then disappearing back into the Lacandon Jungle was a visually arresting event-action with a deep cultural and political resonance throughout the Americas...such event actions are specifically symbolic and media orientated, attempting to create spectacular images that attract the attention of a variety of public's in order to catalyse political efforts (1998).

In the First Declaration they reiterated their concern with the years of poverty and injustice, and hoped the Mexican peoples understood:

> To the people of Mexico. We, the men and women, full and free, are conscious that the war that we have declared is our last resort, but always a just one. The dictators are applying an undeclared genocidal war against our peoples for many years. Therefore we ask for your participation, your decision to support this plan that struggles for work, land, housing, food, health care, education, independence, freedom, democracy, justice and peace. We declare that we will not stop fighting until the basic demands of our people have been met by forming a government of our country that is free and democratic understood (EZLN, 1994).

The neoGramscian interpretation of the Zapatista movement (Gill, 2000) suggests that the movement still represents an emancipatory pocket of resistance of global struggle given that there are 'colliding forces at work' (Wagar, 1996, p. 2; Shaw, 1994). Chase Dunn (1996) pointed out that the:

> future success of resistance movements to neoliberal globalisation may be brought a step closer if resistance organisations themselves highlight the close relationship between the state and globalisation...to be successful resistance to neoliberalisation must be conducted in a coordinated manner on a local, national, regional and global level (1996).

During 1995, there had been numerous consultations within the communities based on issues such as land, housing, jobs, education and health. The consultations were broad based involving citizen participation. But the consultations were not to be based around an inclusive political forum, organization or through the transformation of the EZLN into a political party. On August 27 1995, with 41 per cent of the votes counted from the transparent boxes left all over Mexico, 95 per cent indicated that the EZLN commitment to democracy was right and 56 per cent stated 'no' to the formation of the EZLN as a political party. According to the EZLN (NCDM, 13 March, 1999) the Consulta that took place on the 21 March 1999 was a national:

> Consultation for the Recognition of the Rights of Indian Peoples and the End to the War of Extermination will be carried out. In it we will ask four questions to the people of Mexico in order to know their opinion on four essential points of the National Agenda, the recognition of indigenous rights, the fulfillment of the San Andres Accords, demilitarization and the democratic transformation of Mexico...the EZLN has designated 5000 of its members (2,500 men, 2,500 women) to visit the municipalities of the 32 states of the Mexican Republic (Rodriguez, 1999, p. 1).

This was a struggle from many diverse, specific and yet connected locations, a struggle that refused revolutionary struggle. Thus:

> above all, the struggle for politics to be citizenized if you will. The struggle to find new ways to create spaces, to nurture initiatives which give voice and a place to those who make a nation, the workers of the field and the city, the indigenous, the squatters, the housewives, the teachers, students, retired and pensioned, small businessmen, professionals, employees, handicapped, HIV positives, intellectuals, artists, researchers, unemployed, homosexuals, lesbians, youth, women, children and elderly, the everyone who, under different names and faces, dress and name themselves, the people.

During 1998 and into 1999 this whole consultation procedure was stepped up to the national level. For the National Consulta many groups affected by economic neoliberalism were invited to participate in a nationwide referendum on the Indian question and more broadly about the state of Mexico. Marcos (1999) emphasized on the student population at the National University as well as international solidarity through the participation of coordinator's and affiliated groups of interest in the US, Asia and Europe. Consequently an EZLN Communique (NCDM 15 December, 1998) maintained that the thrust of resistance aimed to promote a situation of peace with democracy, liberty, justice and dignity. This was an open, all including and creative dialogue between all of Mexican society concerned with the neoliberal doctrine, the cuts in welfare, the power of capital and the lack of democratic accountability within the Mexican state, now seen as impersonal and abstracted from the needs of ordinary Mexicans that cuts across the usual suspects, traditional class, age, gender and ethnic lines to name just a few.

This was a popular and direct consultation that would recognize the right of all Mexicans to participate freely and voluntarily in all processes of the National Consulta. The National Consulta included a process of preparation, diffusion and realization of the consultation for an all inclusive mobilization on the character of municipalities, regions and states. From an initial Marxist rebellion, this was not defeat but a new way of practicing politics and negotiation. This was seen as a new dialogue which *simultaneously* asked for concrete policy changes and also cultivated a new mood of questioning and political dialogue, crucially, this was not revolutionary or reformist, very slippery terms as mentioned in chapter four. All men and women over 12 years of age could take part and the consultation would be national and simultaneous. A member of the CCRI remarked that:

for us the Zapatistas, indigenous rights and culture represent the idea that after achieving that, other demands will follow; that this will create an enduring precedent for the Mexican people; that the solution is that we all make demands, that we all participate in making demands...(T)he consultation will be one way for the government to comply with the demands of the people, and not only that, but a great democratic exercise (quoted in Bellinghausen, 1998).

Just prior to the 1999 National Consulta Marcos (1999) reported that the EZLN would 'greet and hope everything is going well in the tours of the Zapatista delegates' and the Delegation Coordinating Committees. Marcos (1999) concluded 'That's all, now we leave it to the people'. This was not a defeat but a new form of mass struggle for all those who felt *powerlessness*. Three million 'strong' took part in the National Consulta through small and thoughtful acts of organization. The true victory Marcos had said, was not all about the quantity of votes cast in the exploratory consultation or a matter of facts and figures to define the site and nature of radical political power but it was all about hope.

There were 15,000 voting tables and the result of the Consulta would be based on the demands for the constitutional recognition of indigenous rights at the forefront of the national dialogue in Mexico by organizing an international dialogue on Mexican indigenous rights, the Accords of San Andres and the legal initiative on indigenous rights developed by the Mexican Congressional Commission on Concord and Pacification (COCOPA). But this was a common aspiration, a desire to completely alter the paradigm of power which kept them from establishing a more just society (Marcos, 1999). This was a movement which:

> like the wind, spreads the seeds and pollinates the flowers of struggles locally, nationally and internationally binds us to a practice that aspires to self governance and to ask what is resistance to us wind from below a network, whispering hope to all who will listen (Marcos, 1999a).

The consulta succeeded in placing the demands for the constitutional recognition of Indigenous rights at the forefront of the national dialogue in Mexico, it organized an international dialogue on Mexican Indigenous Rights by breaking the military blockades and through organizing the mobilization of Mexican and global civil society in discussing direct democracy from the 'bottom up'. This was a popular and direct consultation that recognized the *concrete* sovereign Constitutional right of all Mexicans to participate freely and voluntarily in the National Consulta based on the following questions.

1. Do you agree that the indigenous peoples should be included with all their power and richness in the national project and that they take an active part in the construction of a new Mexico.
2. Do you agree that the rights of the indigenous people should be recognized in the Mexican Constitution in accordance with the San Andres Accords and the corresponding proposal by COCOPA.
3. Do you agree that we should reach the peace through the path of dialogue, demilitarizing the country with the return of the soldiers to their barracks as it is established in the Constitution and the law.

4. Do you agree that the country should organize the government to lead by obeying in all aspects of national life.

The galvanizing of the citizens was also aided by the formation of the Zapatista Front of National Liberation in September 1997. The EZLN did not regard their 'political power' as necessarily *quantifiable*. On September 14 1997 working groups had aided the National Organization Commission of the FZLN including Javier Ellorriaga, to set the agenda and to organize. It was based on a Principles and Program of Struggle for a new type of political force for a new, just constitution, a 'horizontal' and direct democracy, a defence of the environment, the rights of workers and campesinos as well as the creation of strategic alliances with other social and political organizations which called for a just and dignified peace.

The new Zapatista front was in 1997 created for those who could not find a place for themselves and their views in existing political organizations and parties. It did not believe in struggling to take state power and it did not bar EZLN 'militants'. This new way of making politics had no way of being fitted into the criteria to distinguish radical from reformist. In an interview with Blixen and Fazio (1995), Marcos maintained that the EZLN, through their short lived insurgency were in effect:

> planning a revolution which will make a revolution possible. (W)e are planning a pre-revolution. This is why they accuse us of being armed revisionists or reformists, as Jorge Castaneda says. We are talking about making a broad social movement, violent or peaceful, which will radically modify social relationships so that the final product might be a new space of political relationship.

As such, an archaic 'stages of transition' revolutionary model was revoked. This was not the model pursued, and it was also stated that the EZLN were not waiting for neoliberalism to collapse and for a new social system to miraculously be installed. It is not, in short, the struggle toward socialism manifested by the revolutionary zeal of the sixties and seventies in Latin America. But neither is this a repudiation of the modern themes of development and democracy. It is a 'rethinking' as to what these terms concretely mean in communities, without revolutionary and vanguard pretensions. Parfitt noted that:

> Marcos, like many Mexicans, combines a sense of the absurd with fateful views. He's invented fanciful pasts for himself. He told one journalist that he'd

worked as a waiter in San Francisco, and that he was gay. Tonight he was grim. He spoke about a dramatic shift in goals, changing the Zapatistas from an army into a national political movement. Then his speech took familiar flight, embracing the extravagant expectations of Chiapas and Mexico, death, darkness, glory, and redemption (1996, p. 128).

New Technologies and New Participation

The 1996 encounters reverberated through networks of local resistances by cultivating a global solidarity through non-hierachical critical social movements. Such a perspective operates outside the spatial site of Marxist internationalist struggle. The inclusive intercontinental forum that was organized in Chiapas and made up of various non-governmental organizations, 2,000 delegates representing 43 countries, all concerned with the concrete effects of neoliberal globalization in their particular locations but aware that these locations were connected (Ruggiero, 1998). During the Encuentros, some 5,000 people went to Chiapas representing varying interests and concerns discussed the nature of politics, economy, culture, media and civil society through a *mesasa* or network. Encounters were held in an area surrounded by the Chiapas hills and participants paid respect to the Indian marches, and for putting on the event. Whilst there was recognition of living in 'one world', it was also recognized that individuals and groups were telling of their diverse experiences of how they interpret neoliberal globalization in their specific and concrete encounters given that:

> Today thousands of different roads that come from the five continents meet here in the mountains of Mexico's southeast. Today thousands of small worlds...Welcome to the Zapatista R/reality. Welcome to the territory in struggle for humanity. Welcome to the territory in rebellion against neoliberalism...(T)he globalization of markets erases boundaries for speculation and crime, and multiplies them for human beings. Countries are obliged to erase their national borders for money to circulate but to multiply their internal borders. Neoliberalism won't turn many countries into one country, it turns each country into many countries (Ruggiero, 1998, p. 20).

Firstly, the internet provides ongoing and up to date information on democratic struggles. Secondly, the internet forms new networking communities and facilitates an efficient method of communication and consultation, which can then, through political agents, be used for whatever cause is deemed fit. Finally, the internet may provide a space for direct democracy and the widespread lobbying of national governments by movements from the grassroots. The democratic nature of the new global technologies, plays a part in discussing the strategies and objectives of the EZLN in their attempt to re-construct radical democracy in Mexico in two main ways. Firstly, it enables individuals and groups to lobby the Mexican government, and gives access to government information and speeches. Secondly, it enables the EZLN to communicate with its sympathizers, locally, nationally and globally. The use of the internet is facilitating the flow of values, knowledge, and ideas and in allowing like minded groups to organize across national boundaries (Froehling, 1997; Routledge, 1998).

The Zapatista Net on Autonomy (1995) pointed out that the movement was able to traverse many landscapes and terrains and that distance was becoming increasingly irrelevant as the movement was operating on an increasingly de-territorialized political space. The EZLN have used technological weapons to rally support and solidarity across the globe. Cleaver (1997, 1998) noted that what he termed the new 'electronic fabric of struggle' indicated that the net is now providing a coveted strategic opportunity to engender new spaces of resistance beyond the exclusionary fabric of state-sovereignty as restricted political space. Consequently, Arquilla and Ronfeld (1993) have argued that the use of the internet would in the future engender a problem for maintaining traditional state authority and governability. Indeed, the heaviest users of the internet were groups and political parties of the center and the left. Traditional hierachies and institutions that stem such protest politics could possibly be defeated. In this new cyberwar as US President George W. Bush puts it, the US Federal Bureau of Investigation (FBI) have aimed to expose, disrupt and misinform such groups using so-called 'clipper chips' to intercept EZLN information. However, the EZLN had already placed information about their struggle and news and reviews through various sites and discussion groups.

Froehling (1997) noted that the internet is a site of struggle rather than a tool of struggle *per se*. This is a non-hierachal, molecular and rhizomatic flow of ideas and debate. But only San Cristobel and Tuextla the state capital, have internet plugs and access. Chiapas is a region where in some places there is no network of electricity or telephones. Originally, the internet was used by academics providing information and background to the struggle and, particularly from the University of Texas and the websites of Professor Harry Cleaver. For instance, on the day of mobilization the EZLN brought a printed declaration of war. News of the declaration went out through a student's telephone call to CNN. But only the Declaration of War made it to the global audience and even this was censored and based on the media's ideological biases. Many found this situation intolerable and USEnet, and PEACEnet, e-mail, uploading and reproducing were instigated. Cleaver (1999) noted that the result for 'business, the state and the ruling class generally is a crisis of governability where virtually every historical mechanism of domination is being challenged. Capital's response is more surveillance and monitoring'. Indeed, the coining of the phrase a politics of cyberspace is lifted from the Greek *kybernan*, or to steer or govern.

In 1995, Jose Guru, the Mexican secretary of state had admitted that the PRI would have to recognize that the EZLN activated a war of ink, of the written word, and the war of the internet.This has had an explosive impact on the sites and strategies of resistances as a new rhizomatic spirit that cannot be tamed by fixed strategies and rational calculations emerges. The local may, as in critical geopolitics, be seen as a manifestation of larger struggles and may produce effects elsewhere. Thus, the space of the local, as delineated by the confines of state-sovereignty and the 'limits of the possible' can no longer be separated into the hierachical spatial/strategic domains of local, national and global as created by the exclusionary space of realism (Watson, 2001a).

The world of neoliberalism is a world of economic, political, cultural and social exclusion, and a world of increasing poverty wrought by the bellicose 'race to the bottom'. The gap between the rich and poor (*within* and *between* countries) is accelerating. For the dominant neoliberal institutions such developments will undoubtedly require the continued imposition of *more* neoliberalism and *more* structural adjustment because they reason, the *alternative* would be disastrous. There is a more than just a bitter irony in the way that classic Marxists and neoliberals muse that 'it is better to be exploited than not to be exploited' whilst those disenfranchized and not benefitting from the undoubted gluts of wealth created by economic globalization are now forging struggles by *simultaneously* using globalization. Whilst globally orientated, the Encounters were based on diversity and incorporation of 'many worlds' based on a collective network of all our particular struggles and resistances, an intercontinental network of resistance against neoliberalism and an intercontinental network of resistance for humanity which exists by:

> recognizing differences and acknowledging similarities, will strive to find itself in other resistances around the world...the intercontinental network of alternative communications is not an organising structure, nor does it have a

central head or decision maker...Brothers and Sisters, we continue to be awkward (Ruggiero, 1998, p. 56).

According to the Encuentros (1996), the new technologies will be a 'true space for democratic struggle' in a struggle for humanity against neoliberalism 'a new form of participation' in Mexico and part of a worldwide struggle'. From the beginning, Cleaver (1999, p. 2) noted that 'the most striking thing about the sequence of events set in motion on January 1 1994, has been the speed with which news of the struggle circulated and the rapidity of the mobilization of support which resulted'. He notes that there are important implications for the maintenance of PRI governance and authority over the region, because:

> during the peasant uprisings in Chiapas in 1994, it became clear that the government could no longer control information as it had done in 1968...(T)he press and domestic and international NGOs monitored the conflict closely, and electronic mail became one of the main mechanisms through which the EZLN communicated with the world (Cleaver, 1999, p. 2).

Even the capitalist organizations and the Central Intelligence Agency (CIA), have recognized the need for a more flexible counter organization and were carrying out multiple and particular missions against these kinds of democratic threats to governance. There were:

> new forms of self-activity which escape and undermine capitalist authority and control, on the shopfloor, in the community, in the village, across borders and many other previously sharp divisions among workers. Integral to these new organisational forms are new patterns of communication including new kinds of horizontal rhizomatic linkages (Cleaver, 1999, p. 2).

A recognition of plurality of, many worlds was linked *simultaneously* and *dialectically* with the problem of global structures. The EZLN stated this was an:

> echo that breaks barriers and reechoes. An echo of small magnitude the local and particular, reverberating in the echo of great magnitude, the intercontinental and galactic. An echo that takes its place and speaks its own voice yet speaks the voice of the other. An echo that reproduces its own sound yet opens itself to the sound of the other (Ruggiero, 1998, p. 43).

The EZLN stated that the Encuentros represented a:

network of voices that not only speak but also struggle and resist for humanity against neoliberalism...(A) pocket mirror of voices...humanity recognizing itself to be plural, different, inclusive, tolerant of itself in hope continues. The human and rebel voice consulted on the five continents in order to become a network of voices and resistance, continues (Ruggiero, 1998, p. 43).

Instead this was an exploration of connections and *networking* from the grassroots as an open and inclusive politics of resistance based upon the theme of *commonality* rather than *universality*. Carrigan (1998) set out the technology problematic as follows:

> how has an indigenous army that has no foreign military support, that has not taken up arms for four years, that has been contained in inaccessible mountain camps deep in the rain forest, isolated and encircled by 40,000 Mexican troops and tanks, with helicopters and surveillance aircraft overflying their territory, managed to inspire and sustain this growing support network at home and abroad?

Routledge and Simons (1995) argued that this has had an explosive impact on the sites and strategies of resistances as this was a new enchanted and rhizomatic spirit of resistance.

Future Impact?

Given that the EZLN had taken the initiative, it was asked, did the Zapatistas have a burden, did they feel a responsibility? (Bellinghausen, 1999). Marcos replied 'No', stating that 'Zapatismo discovered at the moment it went out into the world that it was not alone. Not just at a national level, like what happened on September 12 1997, when there had been the march of the 1,111 to Mexico City who shouted 'you are not alone' (Bellinghausen 1999, p. 3). Marcos noted:

> (T)here is a war here, an armed conflict between two armies, the government and the EZLN's: a suspended dialogue, which leaves all the spaces open for violent actions...the political proposal of zapatismo...points towards a political ethic, 'govern obeying'. We say that the people from below, the governed, should have the primary role in all political processes or governmental activity...(I)t is the people who should be given voice and the weight of opinion (Bellinghausen, 1999, p. 8).

Marcos stated:

First we announced that there would be a consulta, and what the consulta would be about.We called on the people to mobilize themselves for that. The next stage is that the zapatistas could meet with and dialogue with the people. It was no longer going to be through intermediaries or communiques. No longer through the press, or whether the news items say bad or good, close to or removed from what was really happening. The people are going to learn directly from the zapatistas, just as they are (Bellinghausen, 1999, p. 8).

The NCDM (13 March 1999) emphasized that the Consulta was a fourfold demand for an alternative Mexican national agenda, a recognition of indigenous rights, the San Andres Accords and the democratic transformation of Mexico. On 22 February 1999 the NCDM reported that the Consulta would be a mass mobilization ostensibly designed to encourage all Mexicans to organize a popular vote. Moguel (1999) noted that the Mexican consultation organized by the EZLN was like a breath of fresh air by 'revitalizing the space of civil and political participation'. But the EZLN were aware of the naked force of power. Coercive activity enflamed by neoliberalism was manifested through the ongoing low intensity conflict. Thousands of Indians were displaced and forced to retreat into the highlands. The question of alternatives is thereby based on the issue of cultivating a new form of decision making process in an alternative and inclusive national development plan, perhaps based upon a greater allocation and *redistribution* of economic, social and political resources, fairness and equality. The pattern of redistribution is based upon the social fabric of the local Indian communities. A leading representative of the EZLN stated:

During the last years the power of money has presented a new mask over its criminal face. Disregarding borders with no importance given to race or colors, the power of money humiliates dignities, insults honesties and assassinates hopes. Renamed as neoliberalism the historic crime is the concentration of privileges of wealth and impunities, democratises misery and hopelessness. A new world war is waged, but now against entire humanity...by the name of globalisation (CCRI-GC, 1998).

In the Northern city of Chihuahua the local radio phone in show 'Live and Direct' had given opportunity for many to find out about the Consulta and had been inundated with numerous calls. Solidarity had come from many sources: Jordan, Singapore, Hong Kong, Australia, the Canaries and Indonesia. Marcos notes the possibilities of the new global technology. He stated:

navigating the internet is like entering the waters of a great river where many boats are travelling and we discover we're going to the same place, a place where we will have space without having to cease being ourselves. This gives our word backing and support beyond what is stated. It is a movement on the five continents (1999a, p. 2).

As night follows day, popular myths have been cultivated by the EZLN, coalesced around the EZLN's use of the World Wide Web (WWW) as a network of interconnectedness. In fact computer networks are accessed from outside the militarized region and this requires the determination and dexterity of 'operatives' to get the communiques and information out of the area through the military encirclement and posted onto the net on computers outside the militarized region in a dangerous operation. However, the internet has provided an opportunity for organizing and connecting. According to Cleaver:

in the narrow terms of traditional military conflict the Zapatista uprising has been confined to a limited zone in Chiapas. However through their ability to extend their political reach via modern computer networks the Zapatistas have woven a new electronic fabric of struggle to carry their revolution throughout Mexico and around the world...participants in social conflicts in society have extended their struggles from other zones of human space into cyberspace...the net has dramatically speeded up this process...the net provides new spaces for new political discussions about democracy, revolution and self determination but it does not provide solutions to the differences that exist (1997, p. 1).

Many once isolated groups are now connecting their local grievances and struggles but without engaging with an ideological/revolutionary alternative. Participants in movements such as AGP come from a variety of backgrounds and with a variety of specific concerns. Clearly, the ideas and policies induced by a frugal and disciplining neoliberal globalization are still a cause for concern, and yet the manifest effects of neoliberal globalization and concomitant strategic responses still occur at concrete sites. In reacting to the legacy of the old revolutionary left, and even the postmodern(ists), Subcommandante Marcos stated that when the EZLN 'proposed a guerrilla war, an armed struggle, we broke with this tradition, a tradition that was very strong during that time...(W)e *broke with theoretical schema'* (my emphasis) (Devereux et al., 1994).

Conclusion

A key feature of these new dialogues is the recognition of an articulation between this one world and the many worlds. This has led to a distinctive commonality of concern on the reactivation of citizen empowerment and responsibility to their local and national communities *and* to the one world of humanity which transcends bounded territories and the state. The underlying theme of this new empowerment is a recognition of diversity and difference which can work *simultaneously* with the common (rather than universal) values of rights, citizenship and justice.

Chapter 7

New Visions of Globalization: A New Politics of Inclusion and Democracy

Introduction

In this chapter I show how groups engaged with the intercontinental struggle against global transformations have cultivated a new kind of economic, political and cultural politics of resistance. In this chapter I assess examples of new forms of local, national and global civic participation developing the themes of equality and *inclusivity*. The essence of the struggles lies in the *connections* made with other groups, individuals and NGOs resisting the exclusions and inequalities of neoliberalism.

Radicalizing an Inclusive Development and Democracy

The end of the Cold War provoked considerable optimism with the potential flourishing of democracy and the democratic project. The era of Cold War proxies and 'dodgy allies' could give way to a more pleasant period of democratic harmony in what Samuel Huntington called the 'third wave'. Optimists, usually the liberals, talked of 'the end of history' or 'the end of ideology' which Marxists have understood as ideological itself. The problem occurts however, whether Marxists can truly recognize when they themselves have 'escaped' the system of bourgeoise false consciousness/ideology. The sense of democratic optimism was backed up by the fall of dictators across Eastern Europe (symbolized by Ceaucescu's ignominious demise and the vitriolic cries from the Romanian crowd in 1989 Bucharest), democratic openings in South Korea and Mexico and a progression towards a global respect for human rights (such as the overthrow of Milosevic and war crimes indictments in 2001).

But the story goes on. The house arrest of Aung San Suu Kyi, Burmese Democratic leader and 1996 Nobel Prize winner demonstrates that around this globe, repression and violence are a daily reality for millions, elites and the poor. The situation in Burma represents a horribly predictable paradox of economic globalization and the seduction of the neoliberal argument which runs as follows. More investment, more liberalism, more trade, more democracy. Aung San Suus Kyi's argument is quite different, more investment, more money for the military dictatorship, more corporate forgetfulness and an abrogating of corporate responsibility for the continuing hardship of the Burmese people living a world away from corporate hospitality. This is the essence of globalization, distance, yet a concrete and brutal reality neutralized by optimistic and dry statistics. For the intrepid tourists in their millions, seeking a 'conventionally' alternative lifestyle, playing out the pages of the 'Lonely Planet' the harsh reality is sanitized, it is forgotten, the tourist is 'just passing through'. Globalization of the economic variety is causing multidisciplinary unrest (Bienefield, 1994, Castillo, 1996; Castillo and Nigh, 1998; Centero and Maxfield, 1992; Chapman, 1994; Chomsky, 1999; Clapham, 1992, 1998; Dominiguez, 1995; Garcia, 1994; Hines and Lang, 1996; Klein, 2001; Petras and Morley, 1983; Tarleton, 1996). Reactions are now assuming traditionally leftist responses, for instance in Latin America (Starn, 1995). Yet others are both refusing Marxism and the associated postmodernism, and even technocratic pragmatism.

There has also been considerable moral disquiet concerning seeming Western approval of 'giving' the Olympic Games to China. Confusion over the meaning of 'ethical foreign policy' particularly that of New Labour, has led to the inevitable retorts from the left of policy inconsistency and organized hypocrisy over the relationship between the state, business and the arms trade, in a world now awash with outdated weaponary left over from the failed and decaying states of the Cold War. The left's staunch view, that Britain and the West intervene in international matters that may only affect oil production, and for the propitious bastions of big business is beginning to sound somewhat perfunctory. The challenge from revisionists to the realist perspective (that relations between states must be and is based on 'national security') also sounds a little naive. It surely *must* be realized that institutions *are* perceived as (and in reality) larger than the moral foibles of individual agents. Yet this is not to deny that certain actors must (and do) accept responsibility and accountability for economic decisions of a more nefarious nature, whether intended and unintended. But it is to show that some revisionist responses, after a forty year sorte into rejecting everything that hints of capitalism and US imperialism, is beginning to sound just a little cliched and just what 'the establishment' (as they would term it) in effect would want.

For critiques of tyranny and other dissidents, there *is* hope. Who would have thought fifteen years ago, that Vaclev Havel and Nelson Mandela would become the Presidents of the Czech Republic and South Africa respectively? It takes time and patience. But for many dissidents, the continuing of human rights abuses are also linked to liberal economic globalization and to the development of a new kind of authoritarian state that is 'friendly to business' and will provide 'law and order' and the future security of capital (Weinberg, 1995, 1995a, 1996; Welker, 1994, 1995; Whalen, 1995; Wilson, 1995). The entrenchment of the neoliberal doctrine has also created a new and more subtle form of *economic* dictatorship which may distort the development of 'real' democracy and real empowerment/political choice across the world. This has become known as 'low intensity democracy' and a process skewed by the underlying economic/political structures of inequality and marginalization with increasing backlashes (Davison, 1998; Gills et al., 1993; Huntington, 1997; Serrill, 1994; Marcos, 1996a, 1998, 1999b; Oppenheimer, 1997; Rouse, 1996). There are also worrying backlashes by states concerned with their investment credentials (Dillon, 1998; Smith, 1995). For instance, a statement from the National Commission for Democracy in Mexico (NCDM) (10 Sept 1998) responded ot this vagaries and went as follows:

In his address Mr Zedillo who has two years to go on a six year term celebrated his historic contribution to multi party democracy in Mexico. He has conducted a conservative economic policy that has helped his country start recovering from the depths of recession. It is his intention to avoid the massive disruption that has accompanied every presidential transition since 1976. He can fairly claim to have made substantial delivery on reforms that were the Clinton administration's price for its $50 billion bailout of Mexico four years ago. Among the emerging market countries, Mexico is given a certain credit for its readiness to deal with the current global economic upheaval. With all of that, Mexico remains a country with severe street crime and business coruption, desperate poverty in the countryside, a major insurgency in Chiapas province, a falling currency and stock market, a dependence on a sinking export, oil, and a political system fiercely resistant to Mr Zedillos scheme to strenghen the countries fragile banking system.

The neoliberal doctrine of 'there is no alternative' seems to be intensifying a very concrete climate of unrest, exclusion and repression. Moreover, across the globe, specific attention has been given to the conflict in Chiapas (Cockburn and Silverstein, 1995), whilst an EZLN Communique stated that:

> In this Mexico there is a growing State criminality...the bloodiest is the daily crime of an economic model imposed with the irrefutable arguments of bayonets, jails and cemetries...a country of masks and silences...it is evident that the masks hide and the silences silence, but it is also true that the masks reveal and the silences speak (17 July, 1998).

One way of resisting these 'national nightmares' has been through strategically rethinking the site and nature of democracy through using and cultivating a *radicalization* of the existing political institutions of liberal democracy (Falcoff, 1997). The radical democracy thesis is important but, some suggest, refrains from adequately responding to the new challenges of monopoly capitalism, thus ending up as apologists for the global expansion of capitalism 'out there' (Fotopoulos, 1997, 2000). The spate of recent anticapitalist protests such as those at Seattle, Prague and Genoa however, must now decide whether to strategically develop a fairer and more humane 'global capitalism' or seek, as antisystemic movements, the revolutionary removal of the world-system itself. Indeed, antiglobalization protests have brought together a range of non-state actors who, in their many different ways, have commenced such a discussion about what an opposition to the more rapacious aspects of *neoliberal* globalization and globalization might look like.

Nevertheless, despite these qualms, rather than 'reforming' the existing political institutions that are structurally biased in favour of the ideas and institutions of global capital, a radical democracy will open up a space for extending the site and nature of citizenship, sovereignty, the site and meaning of 'the political' and empower a consultative democracy from the grassroots within the economic, political, social and cultural spheres by connecting these spheres. Indeed, the capturing of democratic politics into the space and institutions of the nation-state may be restricting the development of alternative forms of 'globalization from above' and 'globalization from below' (Falk, 1999). This means a synthesis of the democratic and socialist traditions of direct and economic democracy with other forms of indigenous, ecological and social/cultural democracy.

The conditions for a radical democratization of Mexico for instance, represents a liberatory project and implies a rethinking of the major ideologies for change that does not *buy into* the market ethos of 'there is no alternative' nor totally rejects the *ethos* or the *spirit* of the Enlightenment. Resuscitating a space to be political is a cultivating of a public space which:

> does not pass through a direct attack upon the state apparatus but involves the consolidation and democratic reform of the liberal state. The ensemble of its constitutive principles, the division of executive, legislative and judicial powers, universal suffrage, multiparty systems, civil rights etc, must be defended and consolidated (Laclau and Mouffe, 1985, p. 105).

All participatory groups, must defend the gains of the democratic revolution but be aware of spindoctors. Radical democracy has been linked to issues of spatiality and the generation of new sites of democratic struggle (Mouffe, 1995). Clearly, contemporary political debate is being dominated by the identities of individual and the sovereign state whilst the concepts of contract, rights and freedoms for example, are inevitably held within their gravity. Where modernity and globalization have not swept aside all else, other identities and perspectives on the nature of development and democracy are being expressed with great force. The relationship between individual citizens, ethnic identities, and groups, and their loyalty to the modern institutions of the (nation) state is the challenge of obligation, and whatever the holders of power may think, all claims to political obligation are in fact in serious trouble (Falk, 1999).

The question of the relationship between citizenship and the membership of a community coupled with issues of legal and ethical responsibility is key. To what extent for instance, should respect and tolerance for cultural and religious difference within a *secular* modern state, be accepted? Where are the boundaries when freedom of speech and expression become a threat to national security? What happens when what is understood as religious 'blasphemy' is taken too literally and when the right to critique and irony is sorely missed? Indeed, when does the *attitude* toward a respect for cultural diversity (as opposed to cultural homogenization and cultural imperialism) become seen as, quite paradoxically and even inevitably, repressive and universalist, as the postmodern 'metanarrative' of plurality?

There is also a key difference between the issue of 'minority' rights in say the UK, Germany, Italy and other European states and the relationship between the 'indigenous' and the colonial majority in the former colonial states. Indeed, the power language of 'indigenous' peoples is always dangerous, particularly in European states, because it incites right wing sympathies for those who rally against 'asylum seekers' and immigration. In Australia, Mexico, New Zealand and the US for instance, the indigenous peoples use the term 'indigenous' as a means of political power.

Marxists of course, simply see racism as beneficial to capital accumulation, through not only justifying the harsh treatement of low cost labour in the developing world and within the developed world, but also as a means for establishing a false consciousness, a 'national family' which obscures underlying economic power and class cleavages, and scapegoating economic downturns on minority groups and naturalizing the very historically specific mode of production that is capitalism.

In Mexico, the EZLN through the San Andres Accords have demanded their inclusion into the national project of Mexico, as modern citizens whilst simultaneously recognizing their rights as culturally different Indians. Here, the idea of citizenship is not taken as a political and universalizing abstract but seen as concrete. Mouffe (1992) argued that the radical democratic citizen will be a more concrete and politically active citizen rather than a technical and legal abstraction as embedded within abstract political Constitutions. Mouffe (1992) suggested that a more concrete form of modern citizenship should accommodate cultural diversity *and* the growth of citizen loyalty to the inclusive and multicultural modern state. This is a radical and concrete form of citizenship that is entirely adequate and appropriate for a multi-ethnic society and would be particularly prevalent given the various cultural and political amalgamations generated by the forces of globalization (Camilleri and Falk, 1992; Held and McGrew, 1998).

Rethinking Development in an Age of Neoliberalism

The modern state, as a large literature has reminded us, in its quest for order and certainty, for purity and secularism, has been built upon exclusion and violence (Giddens, 1985; Linklater, 1997). The age of neoliberalism and the paradoxes of the competition state (Cerny, 1990) have exacerbated a new form of state interventionism which has led to a multidisciplinary interest in the changing site and nature of political community and the site and nature of political space. In International Relations Theory (IRT) this is particularly significant given that the political cartography of state-sovereignty has framed and reified a very historically specific mode of political organization which has bounded a very specific (and exclusionary) understanding of what it means to be political. Critical social movements offer an historically specific account of what political life is (and should be) about, beyond the logocentrism of state sovereignty. What is interesting is the way that the site and nature of politics envisaged by critical social movements generates a widespread rethinking as to the moral direction of community. The subordinate groups seek legal, political, social, economic and cultural inclusion within a *different* Enlightenment and its institutions.

Debate now configures around themes such as, who has the power and ethical willingness, right/imperative to *define* the alternative nature and direction of political community and do organic intellectuals have the right to make these claims? Such a pertinent economic, political, social and cultural debate is being invoked in Mexico following the 1994 uprising of the Indian peoples of Chiapas which has connected to and galvanized a national debate, manifested more recently during the 1999 National Consulta. Thus, critical social movements may represent a *commonality* rather than a *universality* of issues and concerns which will simultaneously connect individuals and groups locally, nationally and globally. Consequently critical social movements redefine what is meant by 'national community' by rejecting claims for *abstract* sovereignty and 'imagined communities'. Instead, the movements engage with a more concrete understanding of rights, democracy and community by cultivating an *inclusive* political community/modernity. This perspective responds to the *concrete* demands of (and pressures on) *all* Mexican citizens by rekindling the original spirit of the polis and radical democracy by reinventing ideals of citizenship, rights, belonging and responsibility.

In rethinking the site and nature of politics within civil society, the EZLN has cultivated a rethinking of the nature of the relationship between 'the people' and the sovereign political institutions of the state. Through their strategies the EZLN also refute boundaries between 'the inside' and 'the outside' by harnessing a political space that eschews the political imagination of the state system. But nor does the EZLN cultivate a nostalgic recourse to an exotic Mayan Indian 'past' which is a time framework itself created by the boundaries of modernity and state-sovereignty. In fact throughout its struggle, the modern/traditional dichotomy has been fundamentally eschewed in favour of cultivating an inclusive modernity wrought by *fundamentally unhooking* the neoliberal doctrine from the site, nature and practices of contemporary and sovereign Mexico. Thus it is necessary to understand the meaning given to, and the *application* of, the practices of sovereignty, nationalism and modernization as part of the EZLN struggle and its connections.

The practicalities and in essence the 'politics' of this form of struggle are shown by the negotiations between the EZLN and the PRI in February 1996 in the Chiapas town of San Andres concerning the 'Accords on Indigenous Rights and Culture' (EZLN, 1996; Zedillo, 1998, 1998a, 1999). Critical work has consistently insisted that sovereign states are not morally exhaustative and that nationalism for instance was an historically produced ideology/myth, hiding and naturalizing an historically specific capitalism. The nation state as community, container and definer of 'all things political' is historically understood to have relied upon the exclusion of 'the other' in legal and economic, social, political and cultural terms and in contrast to the unity and purity of *modernity*.

One concern that has continuously attracted much interest has been the status of indigenous groups in modern 'fixed' states (Australian Aborigines, New Zealand Maoris and American Indians) and the recognition of the different rights (land, political representation, cultural recognition) of groups and identities which fall within the jurisdiction of the sovereign state but which suffer exclusion from the national community. Modern state sovereignty was a rejection of the medieval chaos of decentralized power, local rivalries, lords and barons, and was a legal expression of the political and spatial legitimacy of the state. This was in contrast to the medieval hierachies of high and low authority, from the supreme celestial God, his terrestial representatives here on Earth, down to the lowliest peasant. Instead, modernity ushered in a different form of sovereignty; impersonal and rational, this produced citizens who obeyed no superior but the state, which in turn, became an entity which had, as Max Weber showed, the sole monopoly and legitimate use of authority and force.

The state became the centered political community based upon an abstract general will and rationality whilst the concept of political community as state sovereignty was compatible with economic processes but underlying this was both coercive force and silences. The modern state sovereignty created the cultivation of a proper relationship between the finite and infinite and the claims of men/women in general and as citizens of particular states (Linklater, 1997). Thus, state sovereignty is in fact, in niches of critical IR, seen as a limitation on the possibility of constructing alternative and cosmopolitan political communites (extending moral community) rather than retaining the exclusionary political community of the sovereign state. Moreover, if there are both intellectual and practical challenges to the cultural and technological boundaries of the state then surely this induces a new concern with delineating what it means to confront 'the political' (Walker, 2000; Watson, 2001a).

The idea of the citizen of course, emerged with modernity and in the spirit of the French Revolution. Citizen rights for freedom of speech and thought represented a distinctive relationship between the individual and the state which during the late 19th century was in turn solidified by nationalism. Loyal and equal citizens had in turn, an obligation as individuals to the unity of the whole and for early social contract theorists the state was individually writ large. The government's duty was to protect (in liberal contract theory) the natural rights of the individual to life, liberty and property. It was the duty of the government to enact general laws and to collect tax. These developments did not remove the supreme power from the sovereign people because the sovereign people were seen as rational agents. Those not considered modern or rational peoples, were excluded from their entitlement to citizenship. The question now of course, is, why should there be any citizen loyalty to the state, when the state is seen to be selling its citizens economically and politically. Governments seem on the face of it, to be intent on courting, wining and dining, the agents of economic globalization?

The dividends of acquiring citizenship for the individual of course gave the ability to contest unjust arrangements, for imagining alternative forms of life, freedom, to have the right to make the law, to democratize the nation and to acquire the full ensemble, legal, political and ability to enact those rights. Again there were specific troubles for Indian groups in their relationship with the modernizing state as they were simultaneously excluded from the national political community but still had to act as responsible citizens or they would be regarded as a threat to the national family and national sovereignty (Long, 1999).

The concept of the modern citizen was based upon the maxim that all men are created equal and independent, will have a love of freedom which would bring about the advance of humanity and enfrachizement. The power of the citizen and the ability to have a political say is being increasingly restricted by the *seemingly* impersonal forces of globalization. Indeed this new fear over apathy and the lack of accountability and representation in politics, has led the UK government (and others) to repackage/rebrand the state and its identity, and to initiate a new 'touchy feely' kind of national inclusivity. In other words, to 'sell' the state to global investment through an apparently slick 'cool Britannia' under a 'Third Way' renewal of social democracy. This is based upon the ideals of equality, the protection of the vulnerable, freedom as autonomy, the idea of no authority without democracy, cosmopolitan pluralism and philosophic pragmatism. The so-called 'Third Way' program was designed upon a new radical political centre, a new democratic state without enemies, an active civil society with an emphasis on equality in the family, a new mixed economy and equality as positive welfare, a social investment state with a cosmopolitan nation and democracy. The new democratic state was to be based on a double democratization, a renewal of the public sphere and the government as risk manager for a world of global risk.

Undoubtedly the UK's political debate has turned its attention therefore to the overarching themes of 'rethinking' globalization and cultivating a different form of globalization/capitalism through new and more innovative policies and strategies. Such a rethinking of civic participation has implications for the conceptual and strategic understanding of where the site and nature of resistance to globalization might and should reside (Giddens, 1999, 1999a, 2000).

The EZLN maintains a commitment to Constitutional reforms on the indigenous question of rights as individual citizens but simultaneously remains obligated as members to Indian collective communities which desire a modernist discourse of self-determination and autonomy. Such investigations are based on grassroots dialogue and are not imposed through the primary structures of the state.

Undoubtedly the emphasis on ethnicity, tradition, culture, 'poetry' or 'jouissance' was contrasted to the exclusionary modernity of neoliberalism. Created by the new Harvard educated and 'problem solving' technocrats in the Partido Revolucion Institutional (PRI) the neoliberal era has inextricably forged a new rationality and represented for many, Mexico's ticket to First World status, as a disciplined sovereign state adaptable to the new world economy. Couched in these contested terms the Indian cultures were a reminder of Mexico's ancient past and represented the threat of ethnic secession from the Mexican state. Security was required in the South and militarization was stepped up. President Salinas (1988-1994) had stated at the time of NAFTA that 'Mexicans were living in a moment of history' which meant 'looking for new terms of reference'. President Salinas emphasized that neoliberalism was *the only* way for Mexican development and Mexican security. The intention was to 'eradicate any part of Mexico' (Hilbert, 1997) and to exclude those who were not wishing to be tied to this modern vision. Indian groups rejecting neoliberal modernization were presented as *the other* Mexico and out of step with Mexican sovereignty and the modern world. Parfitt gave a sense of this *dichotomy* saying:

the Road to Reality runs past a typical conglomeration of modern Mexico - fancy homes buried in bougainvilles, a Kentucky Fried Chicken franchise, new car show rooms, colonias of wood, and mud shacks. But then the pavement winds up into the rough piney mountains of the Chiapas highlands, mists adrift across the view, and suddenly there are Zinacantan Indian women walking beside the road like figures out of a time beyond memory, wearing their neon combination of magentas, oranges, pinks and flaming reds jumbled together with sparkling silver thread (1996, 116).

The concept of citizenship and the practice of democratic rights are meaningless as nation states either lack the means or the will to regulate capital, to legalize labor mobility and to provide access to a dignified and participatory life for greater portions of their populations. Thus, Marcos (1995) stated that the EZLN:

believe that it is possible to have the same Mexico with a different project, a project that recognizes not only that it is a multi-ethnic state - in fact multinational - but also that new concepts are needed in order to reform the constitution (Blizen and Fazio, 1995).

The San Andres Accords on Indigenous Rights and Culture

The San Andres Accords were meant to be a new modern start for the Indians of Chiapas that rejected grand ideological liberal and Marxist politics. The EZLN sought to make San Andres symbolic of a wider ranging malaise in Mexico riven by neoliberalism and called upon the peoples of Mexico in the 1999 Consultation of direct participation and dialogue to link the struggle in Chiapas with other individuals and groups at different economic, political and cultural sites. This civic participation was to be a new way of making politics from the grassroots as linked to the EZLN's desire for a radical democratization of Mexico that would go beyond party politics. The San Andres Accords proposed a radical rethinking of the direction of Mexican economic, political, social and cultural development. San Andres was conceived over a process of grassroots dialogue and incorporating the views and advice from intellectual worlds, anthropological worlds and the Indians. According to the EZLN's declarations from the Lacandon Jungle the San Andres Agreements were originally drafted for:

the basis of a new relationship between the state and the indigenous peoples it is necessary to recognize, insure and guarantee rights within an emended federalist framework. Such an objective implies the promotion of reforms and addenda to the Federal Constitution and the laws emerging from it, as well as to State Constitutions and local Judicial Dispositions, to further, on the one hand the establishment of general foundations that may ensure unity and national objectives, and, at the same time, allow the federative entities the true power to legislate and act in accordance to the particularities of the indigenous issues coming before them (EZLN, 1996).

This was heralding a rethinking of the relationship between the primary political structures of the modern state and the people, through a unique recognition of historical and contemporary economic, political and cultural diversity: It also had global implications for indigenous peoples around the world. San Andres defines autonomy as the:

concrete expression of the exercise of the right to self determination, within the framework of membership in the National State. The indigenous peoples shall be able, consequently, to decide their own form of internal government as well as decide their way of organising themselves, politically, socially, economically, and culturally. Within the new constitutional framework of autonomy, the exercise of self determination of indigenous peoples shall be respected in each of the domains and levels in which they are asserted, being able to encompass one or more indigenous groups, according to particular and specific circumstances in each federal entity. The exercise of autonomy of indigenous people will contribute to the unity and democratization of national life and will strengthen national sovereignty (EZLN, 1996).

This sense of interconnectedness and the refusal to distinguish a 'principal' actor became explicit in 1995. Under the title *A New Relationship between the Indigenous People and the Rest of the Nation* the Accords are summed up. Firstly, a pluralistic orientation of the nation of Mexico is demanded through a development with a definitive respect for difference. San Andres by linking to the 1994 Second Declaration of the Lacandon Jungle specified a concern with the democratization of Mexico. The EZLN (1994a) had called on the political institutions of Mexico to reflect this inclusivity and accountability to the different and the colorful worlds of Mexico.

Reaction to San Andres and Subsequent Debates on the Nature of Mexico as a Political Community

Brothers pointed out that the San Andres Agreements were plagued by immense controversy and by June 1996 the:

> talks broke down when the two sides could not agree on language that would enshrine the accords in law, while moves to give the Indians greater autonomy were seen as a sticking point. The rebels quit the negotiating table in September 1996 accusing the government of backtracking on its promises. Negotiations have been stalled ever since. In his statement Marcos insisted the government had to fulfill the San Andres Accords and said what the two parties had already agreed was not negotiable...the government assured that it wanted to find a legal form to express them (1998).

The PRI and the EZLN had had very different views on the meaning and nature of Mexican modernity. President Zedillo (1999) argued that the PRI had, in 1992, in accordance with Indian demands:

> amended Article 4 of the Constitution so as to guarantee the multicultural nature of the nation, based on the diversity of origin of the indigenous peoples, to guarantee them access under conditions of equality, to the jurisdiction of the state and to make additional effort to promote their full development...the bill of reforms to Articles 4, 18, 26, 53, 73, 115 and 116 of the Political Constitution of the United Mexican States to make effective the social, economic, cultural and political rights of Mexico's indigenous peoples (1999).

President Zedillo (1999) accepted that the question of cultural diversity was important to the development of Mexico:

> indigenous Mexicans may fully participate in national development and democratic coexistence with full respect for their identity...the exercise of autonomy will contribute to the nation's democracy, sovereignty and unity. Diversity is characteristic of Mexicos indigenous peoples. 56 indigenous tongues are spoken in this country...wealth, knowledge and a unique view of the universe, nature and society. *In our constitution the concept of people has a historical character but must fall under precise categories like nationality and citizenship...(R)ecognition of the rich diversity requires that the General Constitution of the Republic regulate general principles* (1999, my emphasis).

Then late in 1996, as various conciliationary negotiators (COCOPA) drafted alternative resolutions whilst the lack of willingness to concede on any of these issues (from both sides) and the definitional problematic over the meaning and nature of Mexico accelerated into stalemate. Rosset and Cunningham (1994) had argued that if the EZLN was an ethnic struggle then why had there been no substantial declaration of *ethnic nationalism* and further demands for autonomy and self-determination which are, in this argument, linked to an ethnic *secession* from the modern sovereign state. Instead, Carrigan noted that in Marcos:

> the Zapatistas had found a unique linguist whose mastery of the idioms of both Mexico's allowed him to interpret each to the other. Straddling the historic chasm between the two, Marcos showed there were bridges to build and maps to be drawn to make each accessible to the other (1998, p. 8).

The PRI used the tragic imagery of Shakespeare's *Hamlet* to invoke the ghostly wanderer from the beginning of the play, Hamlet's father, and have claimed that Marcos and the EZLN are betraying their modern Mexico and the legacy of the Mexican revolutionary, Emiliano Zapata, by waking up his revolutionary ghost (Long, 1999). The EZLN are seen to be the rotten element and rotten core in Mexico, in challenging the neoliberal project and, by implication, the sovereign integrity of the Mexican state. In turn, the EZLN have argued that it is the PRI themselves, who were betraying the legacy of Zapata, by selling off Mexico to the callous whims of foreign global capital and privatizing sacred land for the mighty dollar. The Zapatistas want a Mexican nationalism to be sure, but not one of cold neoliberal technocracy, but a nationalism that is injected with inclusivity and color. According to the non-government group *Global Exchange* the PRI had also legitimated funds through the counter drugs war and the debate on the indigenous struggle was framed in terms of *security*. During 1999 the EZLN organized a national referendum on San Andres and associated issues. A representative of the CCRI-GC had stated:

> for us the Zapatistas, indigenous rights and culture represent the idea that after achieving that, other demands will follow; that this will create an enduring precedent for the Mexican people; that the solution is that we all make demands, that we all participate in making demands...(T)he consultation will be one way for the government to comply with the demands of the people, and not only that, but a great democratic exercise (1995, p. 2).

According to Commandante David of the CCRI-GC (1998a) the Chilion region had been divided into three zones, war, neutral and conflict. Despite its position in the deep South, Chiapas has chimed of resonance in every Mexican across the economic, social, political and cultural board, that rings out, 'maybe, just maybe, something is wrong here'. Marcos opened the door to a possible and new Mexico 'opening space for something else' as the Consulta opened a space for and connected to those Mexican men and women allowing them to say 'We are interested in Mexico and we have an opportunity to make ourselves heard' (quoted in Bellinghausen, 1999). Thus, the NCDM stated that for:

> the year of 1999 the Zapatista Army of National Liberation has launched a new initiative of dialogue and peace calling for a mobilization, both in Mexico and the rest of the world, that aims to achieve the recognition of the rights of the indigenous people and an end to the war of extermination (NCDM, 9 Feb 1999).

Indeed, as the 1996 encuentros suggested, the Zapatistas have galvanized a larger discontent as shown in Seattle, Prague, Davos and Gothenburg. Such connections have altered the political practices and site of the local and the global because the Zapatistas are both a real *and* symbolic representation of both new spaces of discontent and the new modes of struggle. Their effort to push forward a politics of inclusivity and a willingness to dialogue and listen forms a key part of the worldwide struggle of inclusivity in the antiglobalization protests.

Radical Democracy in an Age of Globalization

With the end of the Cold War the developing world witnessed a shift from military dictatorships to multiparty democracy. This democratic opening was linked to economic liberalization.

Marxists have returned to their analytical and political concern with the disciplinary and political separation of the economic from the political by essentially *reifying* the wage relation through the legitimation and *naturalization* of private property. Such democratic deficits are enflamed by global capitalism and the relinquishing of economic and political sovereignty. In a world in which the most powerful forces are global in scale the promise of democracy to enhance the capacity of people to exercise control over their own lives is put into greater and greater doubt. Critical social movements aspire to a radical reformulation and rethinking of democracy on an institutional/electoral basis and a localized and grassroots *direct democracy*. Here direct participation was promoted through the construction of different political institutions from the grassroots as the bureaucratization of politics, the 'iron law of oligarchy' is challenged. Two months after the EZLNs mobilization in 1994, Conger wrote:

> On January 11, 10 days after guerrillas calling themselves the Zapatista National Liberation Army (EZLN) launched bold attacks on five towns and an army barracks in the Southern state of Chiapas, television newscaster Jorge Ramos fired a pointed question at a Mexican official 'Senor Consul, is the government concerned that in this election year people might want to vote for an opposition party because it might bring peace instead of staying with the ruling PRI that has brought war to the country?'. With that single question, Ramos put the PRI's much touted record of 65 years of social peace on the line. This sharply unorthodox approach reflects a keen reading of the political climate by the Zapatistas who maximise their impact by seizing the precise moment for striking, the 1994 election year and have now chosen to join the growing clamor for honest elections and democratization (1994, p. 1).

Emphasis was placed on using the existing legal and Constitutional frameworks to forge a politics of electoral accountability. This was just the beginning. Their Second Declaration stated of the PRI:

> a party that has kept the fruits of every Mexican labourer for itself...cannot be allowed to continue. Understand the corruption of the Presidential elections that sustain the party that impedes our freedom and should not be allowed to continue. We understand the callous fraud in the method with which this party imposes and impedes democracy (EZLN, 1994a).

The EZLN insisted that:

> the problem of power in Mexico isn't due just to a lacking of resources. Our fundamental understanding and position is that whatever efforts are made, will only postpone the problem if these efforts are not made within the context of new local, regional and national political relationships marked by democracy, freedom and justice. The problem of power is not a question of the rules, but of who exercises power (EZLN, 1994a, p. 3).

In explicitly rejecting protracted revolution and a Marxist politics, they stated:

> We are not proposing a New World, but an antechamber looking into a new Mexico. In this sense, the revolution will not end in a new class, faction of a class or group in power. It will end in a form of democratic spaces for political

struggle. These free and democratic spaces will be born on the federal cadaver of the state/party system and the traditions of fixed Presidential succession (EZLN, 1994a, p. 3).

During the 1999 Consultations the EZLN cultivated an inclusive dialogue. This would mean that:

political leadership will depend on the support of the social classes, and not on the mere exercise of power. In this new political relationship, different political proposals (socialism, capitalism, social democrats, liberalism, Christian Democrats etc) will have to convince a majority of the nation whether the proposal is best for the country (Marcos quoted in Devereux et al., 1994, p. 12).

Consequently the EZLN stated that:

groups in power will be watched by the people in such a way that they will be obligated to give a regular account of themselves and the people will be able to decide whether they remain in power or not. This plebiscite is a regulated form of consultation among the nation's political participants (1994a).

A few months earlier on February 5 1994, below the imposing arches of the monument to the Mexican revolution in Mexico City, Cardenas, leader of the Party of the Democratic Revolution (PRD) had already announced the creation of the National Democratic Alliance (ADN) as a pluralistic coalition that included parties ranging across the political spectrum along with scores of local civic and labour organizations, and the Citizens Movement for Democracy. This was a National Coalition of 150 urban community associations, peasant leagues and ecology and human rights groups. In its Charter for Democratic Change the ADN set as its goal an end to the 'corporatist and authoritarian system' and the election of a pluralistic Congress that would draft a new Constitution and promote an equitable social policy. In Guadaloupe Tepeyae, 5000 representatives of various interested peasant and Indian movements from all over Mexico met in Aguisclentes at the National Democratic Convention set up by the EZLN between August 6 and 9 1994. On August 21 1994, President Zedillo won the Presidential election.

Through the use of direct consultations the aim was to generate a new form of direct participatory democracy on a national scale that went beyond the party-political machine. This was to be discussed at the National Democratic Convention where the EZLN in the Second Declaration had invited participants from ejidos, schools, collectivities and factories to attend. By June 1994 plans had been set up by the EZLN for a National Democratic Convention (CND) which was to be held in Chiapas prior to the 1994 Presidential Elections and from the CND would 'come a transitional government and a new national law, a new Constitution that would guarantee the legal fulfillment of the peoples will'. But despite the CND, the 1994 presidential elections were also treated with scepticism by most Mexicans used to the cycle of electoral unaccountability, the lack of representation and post-electoral violence.

There are two facets to the radically democratic program of the EZLN. Firstly, a willingness to try *to legally* make the existing institutions accountable and transparent. Secondly, to forge a new participatory direct democracy from the grassroots through new channels of decision making so that people felt 'empowered' that they could in effect politically 'have a say' and 'make a genuine difference' through 'verguenza' or the impertinent asking of questions and the impolite seeking of answers. The model of the radical democratization is based on the way the democratic process is organized and conducted in the Indian communities, built upon direct consultation and direct participatory democracy. Marcos stated:

> I can't say when - its not something that's planned - the moment arrived in which the EZLN had to consult the communities in order to make a decision...(A) moment arrives in which you can't do anything without the approval of the people (quoted in Devereux et al., 1994).

Within each Zapatista community this council meets once a week. Overarching this local community is the Autonomous Municipal Council. This is an autonomous organization in the sense that it was removed from PRI affiliated political organizations and the local government structure. The assembly in each community is integral to each Zapatista community and is based on the equal participation of both women and men (Flood, 1997). Each assembly within the Zapatista indigenous communities selects its own officers and select delegates to participate in one of the six Clandestine Revolutionary Committees. Marcos said that the Indian organization:

> is another culture, another way of practising politics. They are not politically illiterate. They have another way of conducting politics. And what those in power want to do now is to teach them political literacy, that is to say, corrupt them within the current political system (Bellinghausen, 1999, p. 6).

This is not merely a demand for periodic elections, political parties and more ballot slips. Democracy, Marcos explained in this interview, should not simply be *accepted* as a corporate machine.

> There are many kinds of democracy. That's what I tell them (the Indians). I try to explain to them. You can do that (to solve by consensus) because you have a communal life. When they arrive at an assembly they know each other, they come to solve a common problem. But in other places it isn't so. I tell them. People live separate lives and they use the assembly for other things.

Changing Political Climate(s); The 1997 and 2000 Elections

In Mexico, the 2000 Presidential elections heralded a new era for Mexican politics with the defeat of PRI candidate Labastida ending 70 years of PRI power. For many this was a real political and democratic change as it signalled the end of dictatorial political continuity, the legacy of electoral coercion, patronage and the emergence of true multiparty politics with the accession of Vicente Fox of the National Coalition. There was a view that this was not so much a positive endorsement of Fox, but rather, a political weariness with the PRI, a desire for change however limited. The same could be said for the overwhelming victory of New Labour over the UK Conservative Party in 1997. It's as simple as that, weariness rather than apathy. Fox's campaign was aimed at the media.

Carlos Fuentes (1995) argued that there are five 'commandments' for real Mexican democracy. Firstly, electoral reform, the consecration of alternation in power, an independent electoral organism and clear rules to party funding. Fuentes stated that Mexico cannot go on bleeding itself through post-electoral conflict. He wanted a better political system. Secondly, Fuentes wanted four more articles of democracy implemented, a working federalism, a true division of powers, electoral statute for Mexico City and rule of law through reform of an allegedly corrupt judiciary. Thirdly, Fuentes wanted a reform of the media and its 'comedy of errors'. Fourthly, Fuentes wants a respect for human rights and NGOs, and finally a market economy but with a social dimension and balance between the public and private sectors. Is this enough for the EZLN? The EZLN want more than a simple reform of the *existing* and limited structure of the political system. What now concerns the EZLN is that the euphoria surrounding the 1997 mid-term elections and concomitant academic and political commentary, has given the impression that real democratization is occurring in Mexico. But Chiapas is undergoing an ongoing militarization campaign. Mexico's political system is still based on centralism and corporatism with a definitive symbiosis of party and state.

The 1997 elections in Mexico were held to elect 500 seats in Congress, 32 senators and governorships around the country and seemed to suggest that in contrast to a strong authoritarianism, Mexican democracy was finally occurring. As such, Lawson (1997) noted that in the Chamber of Deputies the PRI lost its majority control and the figures showed that the PRI had gained 29 per cent of the vote, with 239 seats, the National Action Party (PAN) achieved 27 per cent, gaining 121 seats, the PRD took 26 per cent of the votes with 125 seats, the Green Party four per cent gaining eight seats, and finally the Mexican Labour Party (PT) gaining three per cent of the national vote, having seven seats in Congress. President Zedillo had also allowed Mexican citizens to form part of the board that oversees the elections process, the Federal Electoral Tribunal (IFE).

Previously, the board had consisted of magistrates appointed by the legislature on the recommendation of the President. Zedillo remained committed to changing the system of party funding. Lawson argued that the electoral shift in 1997 represented a definite dissatisfaction with the PRI's economic record and its handling of the 1995 economic crisis. But was the democratic space these writers identified a profound shift to real democracy or a lack of PRI willingness to provide its patronage. Was it merely party political language used as a marketing device to attract the undecided voter or could it have been interpreted as a recognition by the PRI that it needed to take a competitive edge in a party political system of pluralism, the beginning of a more enriching democratic process? Klesner (1998) noted that the PRI lost control of Mexico City's local government in the local elections of 1997 and opposition parties now control City halls in 11 of Mexicos main municipalities. And in 1997 the PRD Presidential candidate Cardenas became the mayor of Mexico City.

Firstly, there was an international pressure that no longer tolerates electoral intimidation and vote rigging, particularly with the threat of economic sanctions. Secondly, the rise of NGOs and other actors within Mexican civil society with online (WWW) information and the National Democratic Front (FDN) was set up in 1988. There are anti-systemic elite groups headed by political parties such as the PRD. There are systemic progressives/neoliberal technocrats and there are systemic conservatives such as the PRI dinosaurs. It is said that the Mexican political system is not simply bedevilled by corruption but on the contrary, corruption *is* the political system. This will require much attention (Laurell, 1992; Morris, 1999; Stephen, 1996).

Groups such as the Anti-Corruption League and the Public Accounts Commission have aimed to make the political system fair and more accountable. Indeed, members of such groups feel that political accountability may be served up if the public begin sponsoring their own politicians to maintain political integrity and by keeping them away from the temptation of bribery and corruption. The EZLN recognized that this is important, it may be the start of further democratization. But tinkering with the existing political system, or making it better, means that the *structural* democratic deficiencies must remain whilst more radical challenges to the political system are construed as 'irrational' or marginal. Certainly, the PRD have begun to keep a distance from the EZLN.

EZLN and Democratic Revolution: Beyond Party Politics

Subcommandante Marcos still takes his cue from the Indian communities and stated:

> Try to place yourself on this side of the ski mask. On this side there are people who have lived twelve years in the Indigenous communities. Who have lived with them. He is an Indian, as they say 'Marcos is an Indian like us'. And he thinks like them. For them, what do the political parties do? A political party arrives to divide a community. The party's look for the people to back them up, and those who don't follow another party. The strongest ones win. Political parties divide the communities and fracture everything...(P)olitical parties prevent the community from agreeing, because a political party is out to win individuals, then it is necessary to build a political force which will not divide. Which will not confront (Bellinghausen, 1999, p. 6).

The Fifth Declaration of the Lacandon Jungle stipulated:

> Time and again, since the beginning of our uprising on January 1 1994, we have called on all the peoples of Mexico to struggle together, and by all means possible, for the rights which the powerful deny us...(A)long the path which you asked us to walk, we held talks with the powerful and we reached agreements which would mean the beginning of peace in our lands, justice for the indigenous of Mexico and hope for all honest men and women in the country...(S)ilence, dignity and resistance were our strengths and our best weapons (EZLN, 1998, p. 1).

The Fourth Declaration of the Lacandon Jungle indicated the EZLN's willingness to form the Emiliano Zapata Front of National Liberation

(FZLN). This would 'not evert nor aspire to hold elective positions or government office' but would aim to create a 'space for citizen political action'. On 2 September 1997, the Zapatista Army of National Liberation mobilizing against the militarization of the indigenous region and for the fulfillment of the San Andres Accords marched on Mexico City and inaugurated the FZLN. On September 12 the EZLN held a political event in Xochimilco with demonstrations in front of the palaces of the powerful. On September 13, the founding conference of the FZLN occurred after a wait of 20 months and it was reported that the FZLN was a new type of political organization inspired by Zapatista banners of not struggling for power but rather for a new relationship between those who govern and those who are governed. Marcos stated:

> in the political arena, we have two great realities; one is the real reality where the people are greatly disenchanted with politicians. But the oppositon forces have also had election victories. They are creating expectations in the people, sometimes justified, that things can change. That's good. But the economic problems are continuously overwhelming everything (Bellinghausen, 1999, p. 5).

But Marcos recognized the importance of the PRD. The NCDM reported that:

> Subcommandante Marcos states his conviction that there is still space in Mexico for dialogue and for the construction of new alternatives...he clarifies that this process will not come from the government nor with the government which has already made the decision to maintain the economic model without regard to the political cost...neither are they interested in resolving the transition to democracy (18 July 1998).

So party political changes *are* important, but not enough (Lascano, 2000). To this end, the consolidation of a real politically democratic culture in civil society is an important part of the process. The generation of a *civic culture* implies that citizens express support for particular issues and parties. Such a new political culture expresses the requirement for more economic, political and cultural inclusivity and tolerance towards political opponents and alternative political views. Before the more recent 2000 Presidential elections Marcos expressed this alternative vision of democracy by stating:

the real problems are left aside, the loss of sovereignty, the privatization of the electrical sector, the social and political deteroriation. No what is important is that Fernando de Cevallos fought with Fox, or whether or not Zedillo told the PRI he was going to be involved in the succession, in the most absurd speech I have ever heard. The Zapatistas aren't leaving to do election propaganda...(N)or are they going to be promoting a military solution...We are not going to fall in with any candidacy (Bellinghausen, 1999, p. 5).

Nevertheless, the EZLN do accept that despite the continuation of neoliberalism, a new culture of reconciliation is possible, stating (EZLN, 2000):

> as for the Zapatistas you are starting from scratch as far as credibility and trust are concerned; you won the election but you did not defeat the PRI. It was the citizens. And not just those who voted against the state party but also those from previous and current generations who, one way or another, resisted and fought the culture of authoritarianism, impunity and crime built by PRI governments throughout 71 years. Although there is a radical difference in the way you came to power, your political, social and economic program is the same we have been suffering under during the last administrations.

Given the victory of Fox, new strategies and possibilities for exploring democratic participation are being discussed whilst it it recognized that this relationship requires careful strategy and reflects the need for a greater communication and *autonomy* from the state and capital to reflect and act by critical social movements within the existing political institutions. The EZLN has demanded concrete signals from the new government such as the fulfillment of San Andres as a transformation into law and the demilitarization of Chiapas (not simply a withdrawal or a moving back a few meters). Once done the EZLN stated that they would deliver a letter to the federal government peace commisioner and to the public to propose the date and agenda for a first direct meeting. The CCRI-GC stated that a Zapatista Delegation would then travel to Mexico City with the following points.

1. That it is not possible to conceive of a dignified Mexico without a dignified place for the country's dignified peoples.
2. That the resolution of San Andres must not be deferred any longer.
3. That Mexican and global civil society was supportive and sensitive to Indian demands (EZLN, 2000). Such a widely publicized march onto Mexico City by Zapatistas did occur in March 2001 to a flurry of

interest where mass crowds in the central square of Mexico City gathered in support.

Since the infamous memos on the Zapatistas (the case that in order for the government to keep the confidence of the financial community it would have to 'eliminate' the Zapatistas) international solidarity for the movement has emerged (Cockburn and Silverstein, 1995). Such a democratic politics is not only established by strong socialist advocates, but created by peoples not willing to lose their jobs in the capitalist system and not wishing to overhaul 'the system' but *are* willing to act for a fairer economic and political setup. There is a predominant view that:

> Our national leaders tell us that top down corporate globalization is an inevitable, naturally occurring phenomenon. But the terms of globalization have been defined by a few powerful organisations that operate without transparency or democratic oversight (Global Exchange, 1999).

Recent elections in the US and across Europe, show that voter apathy is at an all time high. A politics of resistance recognizes that political institutions have to be made to work effectively, whilst at the same time, discussions over the site and nature of politics, power and 'political institutions' must be nourished.

Conclusion

This is not simply a struggle that requires the destruction of the existing political institutions but a struggle that reworks the meaning and nature of a political institution and democracy. This is a struggle that challenges the authoritarian state 'out there' and challenges the routines (conventional *and* radical) that make our understanding of politics even possible.

Chapter 8

Reassessing Power and Authority: Globalization with a Human Face?

Introduction

The chapter focuses upon the a new era of dialogue promoted through a globalization 'with a human face'. The chapter considers the conceptual and strategic implications of this consultation and dialogue for a politics of resistance to globalization. The chapter highlights debates and concerns over the issues of authority and power in the global system.

Globalization with a Human Face: A New Political Era?

In a famous aphorism, it is said that 'all politics is local' or to put it another way, all politics is kitchen table politics at the end of the day. However, dichotomies between the domestic and international are becoming more anarchronistic in an age of globalization, and national leaders find increasingly that local/national politics is tied into international affairs. So when President Bush (2002) in his 2002 State of the Union Address talks of national security, there is clear acceptance that the traditional parameters of what counts as internal and external threat/concern, is becoming problematic. Clearly, this is an age of unprecedented danger. The 1990s were meant to be a decade of prosperity and relaxation. They were nothing of the sort with continuing crises of famine and debt, new dangers and immorality in the form of chemical terrorism and urbicide, the callous destruction of dwellings as a psychological war on creating rootlessness. Indeed the very term terrorist must come under scrutiny now, boundaries have to be constructed, morals thought about in the relationship between legitmate sovereign state sanctioned violence and other forms of violence currently understood as non state or terrorist violence. Security now comes in many forms, military, environment and economic According to former President

Clinton (2002), we are living in a world, so globalized, that it is a world without walls. This is a view in stark contrast with Bauman (2000) who has argued that within and between classes, states, walls and security fences are being built at a great ferocity as the world becomes ever divided between the haves and the have nots. For Clinton and the negotiators at the WTO, globalization heralds great wealth opportunities. Yet Clinton (2002, 1) remarks, 'The great question of this century is whether the age of interdependence is going to be good or bad for humanity. The answer depends, on whether we, in the wealthy nations, are willing to spread the benefits and reduce the burdens of the modern world, and on whether the poor nations enact the changes necessary, to make progress possible...'. The elites in business and government are worried, not exactly quaking in their boots, but they are beginning to recognize potential security and social limitations to territory and future investment with continued structural adjustment that is generating protests that may begin to surreptitiously disturb traditional sovereign fabrics and sites of power and authority (Annan, 1999, 1999a, 2000; Giddens, 1999, 1999a; Schwab and Smadja, 1999). As Brazier (1999, p. 34) has noted, 'even the world's economic thought police, the World Bank and the IMF, are having to take stock'. In a world of economic and religious fundamentalism, more conciliation and transparency at an individual, national and global level seems naïve and even absurd at times. Indeed, as one major critic of economic globalization, John Pilger (2001, p. 15) also wrote recently, 'there is a view fashionable in the media that the world is being taken over by huge multinational corporations, accountable to no-one'. Yet, despite the seemingly unpenetrable power of the market, antiglobalization challenges have caught attention in critical IPE, particularly following the events at Seattle, Davos and Gothenburg. In this typically leftist response, Pilger wrote with some caution for readers of the *New Statesman*:

> The World Bank and IMF now under siege as never before, have devised their survival tactics in relation to this. Overnight, the IMF, the greatest of the loan sharks, has begun to sound like an institutional mother Teresa with 'a mission to defeat poverty'...(I)t now promotes dialogue with moderate non-governmental organizations opposed to globalization, anointing them as 'serious opponents' in contrast to the hooligans on the streets. Clare Short's Department for International Development employs this tactic, coopting leading NGOs for consultation, even commissioning them to contribute to government white papers. This collaboration should not be underestimated. Following the successful attack on the WTO at Seattle two years ago, more than 1,200 groups and organizations from 85 countries called for a moratorium

on further liberalization of trade and an audit of WTO policies as the first stage of reforming it. The WTO and its creators in Washington were delighted, for its legitimacy was not in question. Yet this secretive, entirely undemocratic body is the most rapacious predator devised by the imperial powers (2001, p. 15).

Awareness of the many contradictions and latent hypocrises in acting in a world of global transformations should surely mean a reduction in ideological ferment and belief in the old dogmas, political or religious? Yet, this does not have to mean a further step into the machinations of the new technocracy borne of real world pragmatism (Callinicos, 2001). On the contrary, the old politics of the Enlightenment, the separation of left versus right, (and even the middle/third way) becomes more and more difficult to sustain. In Seattle, the protestors who had jetted into town, then kicked out at a *McDonalds* windows with *Nike* trainers, is an almost absurd gesture against global capitalism, and a clearcut paradox (and probably unintentional manifestation) of the ambiguities involved in the act of resistance. The intricacies of the new global networks require an escape from the old categories.

Before the UK Labour landslide in 1997 Tony Blair, had made a point that cynicism only benefitted those in power. Given that New Labour only received a *positive* endorsement from 25 per cent of the total electorate in the 2001 elections (despite the disarray of the Conservative opposition), token participation, has certainly worried the political elite, despite their rather gallant efforts to hide their uneasiness with this social affront. Tony Blair (2001) wrote recently:

> The events in Genoa may give the political leaders room for thought, but they should also raise questions fundamental to modern politics: the way democracy works, the way issues are reported and the sense of disengagement from the political process...(T)hose protesting against globalisation are entitled to their view but, in truth, global trade and the opening up of the world economy are not the obstacles to, but the means of, advancing the interests of the poorer countries. Protectionism is their enemy (*The Sunday Times*, 22 July, p. 2).

Those 'in power' now recognize that their own security interests are beginning to be disrupted by the ensuing volatility of the *economic* order. Ethnic tensions in the former Yugoslavia and secessionist claims from disenchanted groups such as the Basques and the Indians of Chiapas are increasingly common and governments are even beginning to recognize the possible *connections* of national security threats with the accelerating social vicissitudes of neoliberal globalization (Clinton, 2000). Many governments are reacting to these concerns through what can best be described as 'regressive' right wing responses whilst even within progressive states, right wing tumult such as the UKs *British National Party* and the *Northern League* in Italy is stoked by more or less unreflective responses from those proud to 'tell it like it is' (Semler, 2001).

In many parts of the world, the neoliberal restructuring of the state and society has engendered a 'Third World within' where a 'global freedom of movement signalling social promotion, advancement and success' occurs side by side with 'the repugnant odour of defeat, failed life and being left behind' (Bauman, 2000, p. 121). Threats from within and across state boundaries manifested in the form of transnational terrorism, narcotic trafficking and the activities of far right groups, have engendered a new discourse on the site and nature of state security and the way issues and events are being connected (Rupert, 2000). Firstly, states are becoming increasingly aware of the continuing need to maintain an effective and secure investment climate in the face of global competition. Secondly, these policy responses are cultivating the need for a rethinking on the site and nature of state security. Thirdly, governments are rearticulating new responses to neoliberal globalization through a new emphasis on the politics of redistribution and the making of *connections* between increasing poverty and new internal threats to state security. This emphasis on inclusive dialogue as shown by the UK's International Development Program tied to New Labours 'third way politics' is a response to the real and perceived dynamics of *neoliberal* globalization (Giddens, 1999, 2000).

Four events are perhaps illustrative of this new mood swing. Firstly, the OECD not getting through the Multilateral Agreement on Investment (MAI). Secondly, the battles in Seattle which 'brought together that range of non-state actors who, in their many different ways over the previous decade, had commenced the discussion about what the nature of an opposition to the most rapacious aspects of globalization might look like' (Higgott, 2000, p. 136). Thirdly, a change of mood to a wider audience awareness that global income gaps are increasing. Fourthly, connections made between global poverty and concerns of security for capital and state sovereignty, all the more so since recent violence at G8 summitt in Genoa.

There are concerns from the grassroots/civil society and international organizations. The tension between the antiglobalization protestors and the elites is thus. Whilst the latter were convinced that 'more globalization' was the answer to global poverty the protests have maintained that poverty increases are daily occurring *exactly because* of more economic neoliberal globalization. Thus, distinctions are made between *neoliberal* globalization and globalization.

Paradoxically however, the free market ethos goes hand in hand with increasing authoritarianism and a new disciplined interventionism which is due to the new security pressures on and *within* states in the global market place. Zygmunt Bauman gave the following perspective on the *social* results of this:

> The walls built once around the city now criss cross the city itself, and in a multitude of directions. Watched neighbourhoods, closely surveilled public spaces with selective admission, heavily armed guards at the gate, and electronically operated doors are all now aimed against the unwanted co-citizens, rather than foreign armies or highway robbers (2000, p. 31).

The ideological basis of the neoliberal globalization doctrine is for all states to provide a restful investment climate and for states to bow to the demands of an equally restless foreign investment. This leads to the downward cycle of discontent and inexorably the need for state-sanctioned discipline (Gilbreth, 1997). Rather than the 'end of the state' then, it is only the states willingness to forego its *social and distributive* functions and its post-war historical responsibilities, that is the key and the conundrum.

Crucially, the Blair government in the UK has identified this relationship, and has also made a more nuanced and strategic distinction between globalization and *neoliberal* globalization. This is a response to economic globalization which results in the forging of a way between market forces and state-socialism. Such a national perspective on a 'globalization with a human face' has developed along with new initiatives from the United Nations such as the 1999 Global Compact announced at the World Economic Forum at Davos by Kofi Annan. Michael Camdessus (1999) also proposed a number of new principles for a reregulation of the global financial system including 1. good governance through increasing transparency and accountability, 2. for the private sector to be more accountable for its actions, risks and responsibilities, 3. a new commitment to social and human development and finally, a greater cooperation and stability amongst the developed/industrialized world.

During the 1960s, Labour's Barbara Castle committed the UK to providing a variety of resources (but with perhaps a little colonial paternalism) to the developing world under the Overseas Development Assistance Program (ODAP). During the 1980s, successive ministers most notably Lynda Chalker sought to lobby funds for developing nations during periods of war, natural disaster and famine.

With the success of New Labour in the 1997 election, came a revamping of the Overseas Development Agency which became the Department for International Development (DFID) under the leadership of the new Minister for International Development Clare Short. In line with 'third way politics', Short accepted globalization yet sought to rework the site and nature of globalization by rejecting both statist *and* neoliberal development theory and practice. This would require a new styled communication between departments in Whitehall. The aim of the first White Paper on International Development which was entitled 'Making Globalization Work for the Poor' published in 1997, was to eradicate *abject* global poverty by 2015. The economic, social, cultural and political exclusions identified within the developing world did not mean that the developed world was immune to similar such problems (Harris, 1987).

As a response to the economic and social fallibilities of neoliberal globalization, New Labour has, like Kofi Annan of the UN, accepted both the 'reality' of economic globalization and the undoubted wealth it creates, and yet at the same time, put increasing emphasis upon the national and global institutionalization of a recognition of worker rights, equality, fairness and a *redistribution* of wealth. But how is the state to do this, in an era of financial discipline? Previous crises were solved by Keynesian demand management: is it time for a new global fordist compromise? (Panitch, 1998).

The UK Governmental initiative mirrors the initiatives of global institutions such as the UN, World Bank and the International Monetary Fund (IMF). Consequently, despite the usual and disgruntled rumblings from the left and readers of *Socialist Worker*, the new rethinking of economic globalization has conceptual/strategic implications for the theory and practice of critical social responses to globalization.

Yet criticisms have also been levelled directly at Kofi Annan for the Global Compact initiative which has no actual mandate to legislate on the actions of Transnational Corporations even if they wish to invest in those states that are violating human rights, worker rights and environmental destruction (Annan, 2000). There is increasing concern from many non-governmental organizations (NGOs) that under the philanthropic flag of the UN many companies who sign up to the Global Compact merely use it as a dubious marketing strategy in order to attract more politically conscious customers. This is known as the phenomenon of 'bluewash'. The Washington consensus was powerful of course, but since the 1998 global financial crisis there has been considerable unease amongst the global financial community and the once harbingers of global capital because:

> the turmoil of the last 18 months reflects the first systemic crisis of the global economy of the 21st century dominated by financial capital. It shows how much we are lagging behind in managing the implications of the initial results of the globalization process. And it illustrates the urgency to put in place the structures and the processes that will allow us to manage this new reality of globalizing responsibility (Smadja, 1998, p. 12).

From a number of governments, there have emerged new initiatives and new recognition, given to the International Labour Organization (ILO) (Hughes and Wilkinson, 2000). There is also a new emphasis on an inclusive dialogue at a national and global level. The GATT once put issues of labour rights in the background until the Tokyo round of 1973-1979 whilst in 1996, at the WTO's first ministerial meeting held in Singapore, it was suggested that issues of labour rights should be incorporated into new national and global legal framework. These were to be based upon a new recognition of core labour standards, freedom of association, collective bargaining, the abolishing of child labour and forced labour. But there were concerns on who would actually 'enforce' these rules and whether such reforms would harm the developing world by eroding the comparative advantage, imposing culturally incongruous values on societies and increasing the likelihood of First world protectionism.

Nevertheless, since 1996, the 'WTO has committed itself to the principle of core labour standards but resisted pressure to share in the administration or enforcement of these standards' (Hughes and Wilkinson, 2000, p. 263). The IMF urgently wanted an 'engagement with civil society' but it also, as critics pointed out, narrowly defines civil society, it does not differentiate between business or other groups and it is selective with who it actually deals with (Hughes and Wilkinson, 2000). Nevertheless, the IMF's 'Poverty Reduction and Growth Facility' (PRGF) program wants concessional lending to be broadened to include an explicit focus on poverty reduction in the context of growth and the participation of civil society. There would also be a connecting of poverty reduction programs to macro economic growth/inflation projections and new subjects for public consultation through a bottom up approach based on good governance, sustainable growth and a willingness to listen to local and fresh ideas.

New demands from civil society include new forms of company monitoring. This is maintained through access to new global technologies and through powerful consumer boycotts of companies such as *Nike*. And the big companies *are* listening because their branded images and logos, despite what the left say, are actually quite fragile in this age of the global economy, perceptions and symbols and can be threatened by substantiated (and even unsubstantiated) allegations of human rights abuses in areas of their business investment. Many industries are now reacting to this new form of politically aware and questioning consumer with choice (Klein, 2001). The problem has been that many 'citizens have tried to reverse conservative economic trends over the last decade by electing liberal, labour or democratic socialist governments, only to find that economic policy remains the same' (Klein, 2000, p. 341).

The World Bank, IMF and WTO are beginning to move towards reengaging with relations between capital and labour which many in these institutions are suggesting are quite essential for a *sustainable* global capitalism. This links to new security concerns that are no longer restricted to realism but are now broadened to include environmental security, transborder terrorism and far right 'threats from within'. Although it is premature to identify the factors leading to the collapse of the neoliberal global system a recognition of this new dialogue must be introduced into the debates concerning the politics of resistance to globalization. On closer inspection, such movements now refuse ideological politics in favour of a more concrete engagement of dialogue with the existing local and national political institutions. Left and right have traditionally understood each other on basis that both utilized a well structured ideological argument. This is not the case now, as critical movements operate on a variety of 'spokes' and are multiheaded, a hydra, difficult for the 'power's that be' to eliminate, as the movements operate with different forms of power and persuasion. In other words they are not easily coopted. (Hertz, 2001; Klein, 2001; Watson, 2002a, 2002b). The movements represent a jumble of contradictions, in this 'worst of times, best of times' age of unelected global government and yet an era with scattered and non-linear resistances which are proving increasingly virulent in this potentially new and controversial era (George, 2001; Hopkins, 2002). However, for Mike Moore, the Director of the WTO, developing a dialogue and forging new legal frameworks for the maintenance of global capitalism at an institutional level are 'false' moves because with further economic liberalization, the lauded liberal ideals of justice and rights will follow *naturally* and automatically through what Adam Smith once called, the 'invisible hand'.

Given the practical difficulties of reconciling the inevitable power interests and agendas the *general* view is an awareness that globalization is not a bulldozing teleological force 'out there' but rather as the product of a process of structuration manifested at concrete sites by political agents. For instance, the World Bank has now called for an explicitly *inclusive* debate with NGOs but criticism has been that this has been cultivated purely for the future efficiency of the Bank rather than *necessarily* for altruistic purposes, although unintentional consequences may ensue. New forms of governance are based upon the enhancement of effectiveness and efficiency in the delivery of public goods and a normative enterprise to enhance democracy. Thus:

> even leading globalizers - that is, proponents of the continued liberalization of the global economic order occupying positions of influence in either the public or private domain - now concede that in its failure to deliver a more just global economic order, globalization may hold within it the seeds of its own demise. As James Wolfensohn, President of the World Bank, noted in an addres to the Board of Governors of the Bank in October 1998, '(i)f we do not have greater equity and social justice, there will be no political stability and without political stability no amount of money put together in financial packages will give us financial stability' (Higgott, 2000, p. 131).

This post-Washington consensus represents a mood swing, and 'a wider normative commitment to the creation of a global ethic of poverty alleviation via a commitment of redistribution' (Higgott, 2000, p. 148). The conclusion is that 'from these perceptions a world that sustains major magnitudes of inequality is likely to be unstable' (Higgott, 2000, p. 149). More demands for a new regulatory framework such as better macroeconomic and dialogue could produce a social dimension to the multilateral system (Wintour, 2001). At a recent debate on *BBC Newsnight* (July 30 2001) Guy Taylor from the group *Globalize Resistance* made the point that dialogues are unlikely to take place given the kind of security and police presence required, as witnessed at Genoa 2001. There is also a possibility of future WTO meetings and the G8 meetings inexorably forcing the issues behind barbed wire. It is also alleged that the summits represent a corporate program and that the leaders are not addressing the real issues.

Poverty and New Responses

There is a growing awareness of connections between what seem to be at first glance, quite diverse events of cause and effect. Thus, state splintering in Chechnya and Macedonia and the new problems of extreme nationalism, human rights abuses, human cloning and GM crops are all linked together, in a new risk society (Beck, 1992; Falk, 1999). However, we must be careful not to fall for the old 'conspirational' perspectives that many activists seem intent on doing, thereby falling into the trap of their most notorious protagonists.

These new pressures are hitting states and big business and a new awareness is emerging from individuals and groups concerned with 'shareholder activism'. In a recent interview, Niall Fitzgerald, Chairman of *Unilever* (BBC News 24 *Hardtalk* August 22 2001) talked of the new pressures on global companies coming from their shareholders and the need for new code of principles implemented by local discretion and local management. The buzzword is 'accountability'. Thus:

> focusing on the moral values of particular companies - or their immorality - invites a selfrighteous response among readers that is too easy and undeserved...Nike has concocted a particularly sick ideology to sell its shoes - glamorous images of superstar athletes concealing the human brutalities (Klein, 2000, p. 321).

There is also a belief that one can open up important doors through close public scrutiny. This means that the whole system is under the microscope. In many cases however, the codes of conduct are not translated into English or the local language (Pilger, 2001). Companies such as *Shell* and *Mattel* have also noted the need for new public relations and:

> It's difficult not to get swept away in the starry eyed idealism of it all - perfect ahistorical innocence...codes of conduct are awfully slippy. Unlike laws they are not enforceable. And unlike union contracts they were not drafted in cooperation with factory managers (Klein, 2000, p. 430).

Responses from state authority have also led to increasing concern with how Europe is policing its people. Such paradoxes were also reflected by Johnson (2001, p. 22) who suggested that 'the Anarchy on our streets' reflects our lack of liberty.

Global Compact and the Human Face of Globality

The Global Compact therefore, is a UN sponsored platform for encouraging and promoting good corporate practices in the areas of human rights, labour and the environment. It is an entry point for the business community to work in partnership with UN organizations in support of the principles and broader goals of the UN and a basis for dialogue between the UN, business, labour and civil society on improving corporate practices. It sets a frame of reference for corporate practices to address social problems, but it does not ask companies to take over responsibilities from governments The Compact now makes it incumbent upon businesses to give a clear statement of support and public advocacy of the compact and to post once a year on the website a concrete example of progress and lessons learnt from management to operations. The Compact also wants an input from the World Business Council on Sustainable Development and thereby wants corporations to promote and apply within their corporate domains, new principles to help strengthen and sustain social pillars within which any market, including the global market, must be *locally* embedded, if it is to survive and thrive in the short and long term. So far, the TNC's that have signed up include those large corporations representing the fields of banking, petroleum, software and footware which aim for responsible corporate citizenship by advocating the compact through their mission statements, annual reports and similar venues. Postings are placed on the internet site set up by the Office of the High Commissioner on Human Rights (OHCHR), ILO and UN Environmental Program executive office of Secretary General Annan, who stated that he required help from the private sector. TNCs are the first to benefit from free market policies of globalization so they must take their share of responsibility for coping with its effects. Firstly, recent concern has been that the activity of corporations threatens the integrity of the UN, as the corporations are still only responsible to their shareholders. That's the way it works. Secondly, that the corporations gain all the benefits of UN affiliation but without the responsibilities, and that the UN should serve as a counter balance to corporate globalization not simply to bolster it. Moreover, the compact monitoring is voluntary. Thirdly, that wrong companies *Nike* and *Shell* have joined in the relationship with the UN. Recently Kofi Annan (2001) stated at Davos on 28 January 2001 that 'if we cannot make globalization work for all, in the end it will work for none' and that 'it is not the case that most people would wish to reverse globalization. It is that they aspire to a different and better kind than we have today' whilst the 'Compact is a platform for learning and sharing lessons about what works and what doesn't'.

Nevertheless, economic neoliberalism has brought about an ultra nationalistic and neoconservative agenda and strangely bringing the left and right together. For instance in Mexico the PRI was split by a conservative group the 'breakfast club', a:

small off the record breakfast meeting of the ruling party faithful, or more precisely, about 50 current and former lawmakers faithful to one particular wing of the party, the old guard, autocratic faction known as the dinosaurs. Manuel Bartlett an urbane, charismatic state governor and key leader of the dinosaurs saying 'we are not going to commit suicide' (Anderson, 1998, p. 1).

In an interview at his governor's mansion in Puebla, capital of a state with the same name southeast of Mexico City, Bartlett reported:

I didn't call for a revolt in the PRI, because I believe the unity of our party is a fundamental principle...(B)ut maintaining that unity is not an easy task because our party has many currents in it...(W)e have lost our dynamism...(W)e have lost our creative thinking. The party has become very bureaucratised. It has just followed, without any discussion whatsoever, the lines of the government and it should be the other way around. The government should follow the lines of the party (Anderson, 1998, p. 1).

Undoubtedly the recent global financial crisis has added to governmental concern, in a country prone to capital flight and short term investment (*Economist*, May 25, 1996; Smith, 1995) whilst resistances such as those in South Korea against the 'Sekekwa' or 'total globalization' of the South Korean government, were carving a new critical space for dialogue *within* global financial institutions (Swift, 1997).

Ultra nationalists are emerging all over the world and the centre right finds it increasingly difficult to reinvent itself. Agendas of immigration and asylum seekers now dominating the Western bodypolitic paradoxically occur at a time of heavy liberalism. At the 1999 World Economic Forum at Davos, its President Klaus Schwab and managing director Claude Smadja (1999) stated:

We are confronted with what is becoming an explosive contradiction...with globalization and the power of the market. If we do not invent ways to make globalization more inclusive, we have to face the prospect of a resurgence of the acute social confrontations of the past, magnified at the international level.

During the late 1990s they were unable to construct a tripartite dialogue between the World Trade Organization (WTO), the International Labour Organization (ILO) and national governments. Moreover, the debates concerning the administration of core values such as the abolishment of child labour and the promotion of collective bargaining produced nothing concrete. For instance, the World Bank has now called for an *inclusive* debate with NGOs but criticism has been that this has been cultivated purely for the *efficiency* of the Bank rather than *necessarily* for altruistic purposes. Nevertheless UN General Secretary Kofi Annan (1999) stated, 'let's choose to unite the power of the markets with the authority of universal ideals' and *choose* to enact the 'Nine Principles' of the Global Compact in governing globalization divided into the three themes of Human rights, Labour and Environment and including demands for the freedom of association, the right to collective bargaining, a stance against forced and compulsory labour, sustainable development and the need for 'moral first movers' by global corporations.

At the 1999 meeting of G7 ministers at Davos Kofi Annan (1999) had stated that 'globalization should not be made a scapegoat for domestic policy failures'. Moreover the International Petroleum Industry Environmental Conservation Association (IPIECA) stipulated that as far back as 1974 in the aftermath of the oil crisis, the oil industry had recognized that the UN played a key role in specifying acceptable solutions to global environmental concern.

Manifestations of this new concern, have been for instance, with the partnership with the International Maritime Organization (IMO) for coordination with assisting the aftermath of oil spills and air quality such as the World Bank's Clean Air Initiative. To the World Economic Forum in Davos 1999, Annan also remarked:

> Globalization is a fact of life but I believe we have underestimated its fragility. The problem is this. The spread of markets outpaces the ability of societies and their political systems to adjust to them, let alone guide the course they take. History teaches us that such an imbalance between the economic, social, political realism can never be sustained for very long (Annan, 1999, p. 1).

Given this concern, Annan then turned to potential solutions which he said were possible if the Global Compact (and its implications for sustainable development) were to be explored, by stating:

> The challenge today to devise a similar compact on a global scale, to underpin the new global economy. If we succeed in that, we would lay the foundation for

an age of global prosperity, comparable, to that enjoyed by the industrialized countries in the decades after the second World War. Specifically I call on you individually through your firms and collectively through your business associations, to embrace, support and enact a set of core values in the areas of human rights, labour standards and environmental practices (1999, p. 1).

In 1999 the UN Secretariat launched the 'Global Sullivan Principles' where Pierre Sane of *Amnesty International* stated that 'human rights and business responsibility are now firmly on the international agenda as demonstrated also by the Global Compact initiatives' and Kofi Annan stated at Davos on 28 January 2001 that:

Two years ago I spoke here about the fragility of globalization. Some of you probably thought I was being too alarmist. Yet I believe events since then have shown that my concerns were justified. Our challenge is not the protests we have witnessed., but the public mood they reflect and help to spread (2001, p. 1).

Amnesty are adamant that the new initiatives for democratic and transparent global governance must debunk the 'postmodern' myth of cultural relativism (human rights are as African as they are Asian), the myth of economic determinism and the myth that global business must not interfere in issues of ethics and politics. In other words, ethics and morals can engage in reflective *commonality* rather than *universality*, as Michel Foucault noted. One accusation levelled at the UN has been that it reproduces the existing power structures of the international system. Yet demands for reforming the Security Council are becoming concrete. The World Bank's *World Development Report 2000/2001* entitled 'Attacking Poverty' emphasized these global issues. Nick Stern, Chief Economist at the World Bank, made the point that more than one billion people lived on less than one dollar a day but that the institution was listening to the 'Voices of the Poor'. The emphasis was placed on 'redistribution' and it was felt that the World Bank had been able to 'make real inroads' in accelerating the political empowerment and security of the world's poor. Recently US President Clinton (2000) in his final State of the Union Address accepted that 'Globalization is the central reality of our time. There is no turning back' and said to his fellow Americans to 'understand and act on reality'. Clinton (2000) said that government and business must now 'forge a new consensus' based on trade and open markets which are the 'best engines we know for reducing global poverty' stating that 'globalization is about more than economics' and has enabled a process 'to bring together the world' based on the ideals of 'freedom, democracy and peace'. US firms have followed Kofi Annan's lead to 'embrace and enact' this 'globalization with a human face' which is responding to the need for world business to support and respect the protection of international human rights within their sphere of influence and to make sure their own corporations are not complicit in human rights abuses. He also calls for the continuing the upholding of freedom of association, a recognition of the right to collective bargaining, the elimination of all forms of compulsory and forced labour, the elimination of discrimination of employment and occupation. The support is also there for a precautionary approach to environmental challenges aiming to promote greater environmental responsibility, development and diffusion of environmentally friendly technologies. The Compact more concretely, makes it incumbent upon businesses to post once a year on the UN website a concrete example of progress made and lessons learnt, from management to operations, and to further the broader goals of the Compact for a sustainable global system.

UK, Europe, Blair, Third Ways and the DCID

The vicissitudes of the global unequal exchange of goods and capital have been well documented. Much concern has understandably been to rethink the nature of the WTO and the market agenda in favour of a new protectionism based upon sustainable development and accent on local communities in contrast to the abstract theories of development of liberalism and Marxism. Tony Blair stated that it was his ambition to 'create an international consensus of the centre left for the twenty first century' with 'a policy framework to respond to change in the global order' (Blair, 1997)

Despite the end of real existing socialism in 1989 it has been increasingly clear that the left could not just put aside the values and ideals that drove them, for some remain intrinsic to the good life that it is the point of social and economic development to create because capitalism is economically inefficient, socially divisive, and unable to reproduce itself in the long term (Giddens, 1999). There were five new dilemmas for the state; globalization; the nature of individualism; the articulation of left and right; new forms of political agency and ecology. Giddens (1999, p. 9) had accepted that global processes 'pull away' from the nation state and pushes down on the state by creating 'new demands and also new possibilities for regenerating local identities'. Third Way politics pushes for an idea of 'no rights without responsibilities' at both an individual, state and global level. This development is to be based upon the ideals of equality, the protection of the vulnerable, freedom understood as autonomy, the idea of 'no authority without democracy', a global cosmopolitan pluralism and a philosophic kind of pragmatism. The issue of 'responsibility' is a key first stage of nurturing the new and active citizen.

There is also much emphasis upon the need to calm the excessive and economically/politically harming turbulence of the capital markets and neoliberal globalization under the assumption that the neoliberal response, to free up capital markets still further, is only a recipe for even greater social dislocation. Giddens (1998, p. 9) defends the Third Way from his critics on the left *and* right, (who suggest that it is all 'spin') by stating that 'a precept of successful advertising, however, is that image alone isn't alone'. UK Chancellor Gordon Brown (1999) whilst showing his legendary 'prudence' also recently stated that poor country debt was possibly 'the greatest single cause of poverty and injustice across the earth and potentially one of the greatest threats to peace'.

The *First White Paper* entitled 'Eliminating World Poverty: a challenge for the 21st Century' included the publication of a variety of international development targets endorsed by the World Bank, IMF and the European Union Development Assistance Committee of the OECD. The objectives were then reiterated by Clare Short (2001) in a speech to 'reduce the proportion of people living in poverty by a half in 2015' to include the provision of primary education, to ensure reproductive health services and to reverse environmental degredation. The assumption was that globalization is creating unprecedented new opportunity to achieve *International Development Targets* and yet the distribution of wealth was also creating a national and global society where many 'had nothing to lose' and this was being manifested as cultural rivalries, electoral apathy and far right allegiances (Rupert, 2000). New Labour, in reflecting the UN's Global Compact initiative, have claimed that it is only one *specific* type of globalization at fault, a *neoliberal* globalization, rather than globalization *per se*.

The DFID was created in May 1997 to provide a comprehensive UK response to global issues to incorporate a wider range of connected areas such as trade, debt and human rights which impact on international security and development. The *Second White Paper* entitled 'The Challenge of Globalization' was a policy agenda for better managing the economic, political, social and cultural processes of globalization by 'making globalization work for the world's poor'. The targets were endorsed by the World Bank, IMF, European Union and 77 African, Caribbean and Pacific countries and 149 countries whose representatives had gathered at the UN Millennium Summit in New York. This initiative of the UK was part of a new global security interest, given that:

> Many of the world's contemporary challenges, war and conflict, refugee movements, violation of human rights, international crime, terrorism and the illicit drugs trade, the spread of health pandemics, are caused and exacerbated by poverty and inequality (Short, 1999, p. 1).

Indeed, the backing of the World Bank was due to its own initiatives on 'attacking poverty' as Chief Economist Nick Stern (2000) pointed out:

> the World Bank's mission is about poverty. It's the commitment that brings all of us to work on development, and it is central to our work...(S)econdly it is the magnitude of the challenge. As we describe in this report, 1.2 billion people live on less than $1 a day. That's extreme poverty by anybody's standards...(T)he world's changed dramatically...(B)ut it's not just the circumstances that has changed. Our understanding has changed too.

There were also new policy initiatives dedicated to a strong and vibrant private sector to work alongside more effective government systems which aim to regulate and 'redistribute' wealth locally, nationally and globally, with both intended and unintended consequences for the politics of resistance. Is poverty a cause of new religious zealoting and cultural fundamentalism? Well it is to an extent, as long as it is not made as a 'deterministic excuse' for a lack of responsible behaviour. Yet it doesn't require much debate into the variations on a theme of cause and effect, to grasp this. Connections between issues were most starkly evident in September 2001. However, *Oxfam* have complained that the initiative is still anti poor because the White Paper still ignores the critical role of income *distribution*. The main emphasis behind both White Papers was summed up in the Prime Minister's *foreword* to the original document in 1997 when he stated that abject poverty affected one in five of the worlds population and he stated that these initiatives would crucially, be 'in the UK's national interest' as we were all 'affected by its consequences' and that such an internationalist orientated policy was 'consistent with our determination to tackle poverty and social exclusion in the UK' (Blair, 1997).

Clare Short (2001) reiterated Kofi Annan's view that 'history is moving under our feet' and that 'Globalization is generating great wealth'. She stated that the West had 'learned a lot about what works in development' and that this would be aided by a 'sound regulation of banks, action against corruption and proper enforcement of contracts'. In an interview in the *New Internationalist* Clare Short (1999) stated that with globalization 'I think talking about stopping it is like trying to stop the industrial revolution and keep feudalism. History is moving. The world economy is reordering'. Crucially, when asked whether the institutions of neoliberalism say the role of government is not to improve equity but to make markets work Short (1999) replied:

> No, the World Bank has changed. It's not advocating total liberalisation anymore. It's saying the state has a role: globalization and liberalisation are not the same thing.

The implication here of course, is that the state still has a negotiated role to play here and that globalization doesn't necessarily have to mean *neoliberal* globalization and that state resources *can be* tailored towards a stable global economic, political and cultural order which is in the UK's national interests, in a world in which whilst the richest 20 per cent of the world's countries have access to 85 per cent of the worlds GDP, whilst the poorest 20 per cent have access to only one per cent of the world's entire GDP. Such discrepancies in wealth allocation and creation, are a mere prelude to instability in an age where localized incidents have, exponentially, intended *and* unintended consequences for state security (internal *and* external) and economic development itself. It is this state of unease and vulnerability by the established sites of power that challenges to globalization must take seriously.

The Hansard Debates and the Aftermath of Davos and Seattle

The UK House of Commons Hansard Debates which took place on 9 December 1999 centered mainly upon identifying the many diverse costs and benefits of globalization. They also came in the light of the anti-globalization protests in Seattle. Clare Short (1999a) stated that 'Seattle was a wake up call' and she challenged her 'friends on the left' to look what happens with protectionism, more poverty and the threat of a closed and antagonistic nationalism. Mike Moore (2000) Director of the WTO, stated to a Parliamentary Select Commitee on International Development that his principle concern was how trade and development worked together because we are 'faced with some awesome challenges'. He stated that in contrast to the skewed perception of the WTO coming from antiglobalization protestors, in fact the:

> WTO is a small organization whose mandate is to assist sovereign governments to negotiate trade agreements and then to help police these agreements and handle the dispute system when the agreements freely entered into by governments do not quite work out. The WTO can make a major contribution to creating a more just and prosperous and equitable world (Moore, 2000).

In Copenhagen in 1995, ministers present at the World Summit for Social Development committed themselves to the protection of basic workers rights, vowing to stop forced and child labour, to allow for worker freedom of association and the right to organize. Such organizations would provide the basic structure for a 'globalization with a human face' which resistances have to take seriously, despite the accusations of 'reformism' from the orthodox left. There still of course, in the realm of debt relief, remain obstacles for development, in particular for states in sub-Saharan Africa, caught in the vicious circle, needing debt relief, developing in accordance with conditionalities, which in turn requires more debt relief. But institutions such as the World Bank do recognize the problem with 'conditionalities' and development 'imposed' from the top down (Adams, 2002). The WTO is now interested in furthering economic activity and trade to generate the necessary wealth, as well as the reduction of inequality so as to enable human security on a broad perspective inclusive of environmental security, economic security, job security, the securing of democracy and the securing of authentic and threatened cultures. Clare Short (1999) stated that there were 'many myths about the WTO partly because negotiations are so complicated that people can make up anything that they like'. Undoubtedly, there is also a distinctive uneasiness shown by the neoliberal elite as to the sustainable future and security of capital accumlation and the free market. Significantly, the ministerial participants at Davos 2001 invited the better behaved critics of globalization to engage in dialogue. Swiss professor Klaus Schwab set up Davos 31 years ago and said at the 2001 conference that business had a contribution to make but that it was going to be necessary to acknowledge the power of protest and rub shoulders with *Oxfam* and *Greenpeace*. It was stated that:

> criticisms of globalization used to be dismissed out of hand, largely because the protestors were (and are) ridiculously unfocused. Now, though, while being touchy feely does not come naturally to most businessmen, there is genuine

unease. Vicente Fox the impressive new President of Mexico, received more than polite applause when he said 'attempts to sugar coat the present form of globalization with compensatory policies are not enough' (Smith, 2001, p. 19).

The willingness to dialogue with the formal political institutions at the state and global level cultivates a politics that adapts to these changing circumstances for all those who feel a sense of *powerlessness*. There was an acceptance by the World Bank, IMF and WTO that positive relations between capital and labour are essential for a *sustainable* capitalism and state security. Clare Short (1999a) stated:

> It is striking how many lobbying groups and trade unions have come to Seattle. They understand that history is moving under our feet. Globalization is a new historical era. Capital now moves in vast quantities and at great speed across the world...(G)lobalization is generating great wealth. This could be used to massively reduce poverty worldwide and to reduce global inequality.

As Marxist historian Eric Hobsbawm (2000b) has explained, the 'idea that globalization is uncontrollable is mistaken. We know it could be controlled. Although some things are more difficult to control, we know that control is sometimes possible simply because governments have done so successfully'. Within many states, reactions to immigration and the free movement of people and culture is causing much discontent. Huntington's 'clash of civilizations' seems increasingly prescient as ethnic and cultural rivalries reach fever pitch. One reaction, not surprisingly perhaps, has been to literally 'shut up shop'. Isolationism, rethinking authority and security, law and order, all, paradoxically run hand in hand with global transformations, experienced differently and at different times and places.

One form of alternative, echoing the 'small is beautiful' thesis is through cultivating a politics of localization understood as a romantic and postmodern 'disengagement' from the modern world. However, on the contrary, this alternative perspective pushes and identifies the intrinsic connections from locality to the global issues. Nevertheless, Colin Hines (2001) of *Earthscan* is now pushing for more emphasis on making, buying and selling local products, or a return to the quaint cooperatives in response to the market envisaged by liberal economists of the Manchester/Chicago School persuasion, by using the argument, that we do not infact require international trade but we do need to push for more self sufficiency. This is possible through a unique juxtaposition, (maybe anachronistic relationship) of economic self sufficiency and the use of new technologies through which to achieve this. Here, the axiom states a *need* to compete for investment on the international market is rejected in favour of a local production that provides basic needs, which is, after all, the whole point of an economy. One sardonically wonders of course, whether GM crops and the like, i.e. very controversial technological innovations, can, without fear of contradiction, work with certain niches of the 'antiglobalization protests' or the 'greens' who axiomatically reject new scientific innovations in a risk society. However, Hines (2001) would like to see more monitoring of cross border activities, especially financial activities, and indeed since the events of September 11 2001, there is a new sense of unease amongst the once confident institutions of economic globalization. The emblems of global capitalism, profits, markets and consumerism (a world where shareholder activity is seen as a protection against one's old age, as state pensions are eroded) are rejected for a politics of an alternative economy *not based* on foregoing everyday social benefits or blindly following abstract economic theory through the 'trickle down' effect.

We still live in one world of increasing danger, of immeasurable exploitation, of repression and suffering. Modern living is itself based on the paradox of suffocating concerns and barren distances. Daily, images from around the world instantaneously forge their shock bringing the global into our localities in a flash and creating an unease with our security. We are in the one world and connected up and sometimes the connections are hard to face because they give unprecedented responsibility which, paradoxically, may give birth to immeasurable apathy and disengagement.

It is also quite clear that any indication of human beings living together in harmony, in one world, a global village is pretty unlikely in the foreseeable future. Too many interests benefit from 'the way it is' and the world is unlikely to move towards the 'way it ought to be'. Indeed, making such judgements is itself a risky business. Nevertheless it is a business worth pursuing. The rejection of the liberal rhetoric emanating from intellectual and political pronouncements about the New World Order or the End of History is depressing but necessary as cracks in the fabric of global security and order become ever more frequent.

Yet both resignation and parochialism *are* evident around the world and yet this seclusion is deceptive as the relationship between locality and globality is becoming ever more complex. Global structures are not abstract and impersonal although they may seem that way. Structures are experienced at concrete locations, *all* politics is still local yet various interconnected pressures and opportunities now impinge and affect our everyday lives. Such connections are the reason why a small band of insurgents in Southern Mexico for instance, produced such startling intellectual and political interest in the ensuing six years.

The halcyon images of a Panglossian globalization and the optimism inspired in Mexico by President Salinas to make the country 'feel good' and to inspire welcomed and much needed confidence in the global investment community during the early 1990s was shattered by the EZLN mobilization and the cries of 'Basta!, a cry reverberating from Seattle to Prague to Davos.

An awareness of the kinds of difficulties enveloping the majority of the world's population led to critical intellectual interest forged by a recognition that the glossy triumphalism of the end of the Cold War disguised a number of secrets which gave the impression that the reaction of problem solvers and policymakers was simply not good enough. Critical social movements struggle against the most obvious and reprehensible injustices and dangers in the one world (e.g. against nuclear arms and military repression in Africa and Central and South America). But these struggles whilst connected to a broader sense of radicalism will be articulated by an understanding derived not from some sovereign center but from the critical capacities of people learning about their world and through their own struggles.

Opposed to Marxist intellectualism and practice, the critical enquiry was self-conscious enough not to draw out new conceptual rigidity, however subtly. Through engaging, people are discovering that they are not powerless but capable of making enormous advances in the immediate situation and by connecting these sites. Marcos said:

Oh the macro economic achievements! But, where are they? Are they in the fortunes of the richest men of Mexico and is the place they occupy the Forbes list? You search, search and find what behind the macroeconomic mask is hidden, an economic model which has been imposed on the country since the beginning of the decade of the eighties (NCDM 18 July, 1998).

Do antiglobalization protests matter? Can one indeed speculate on how these protests will be integral to the formation of a fairer world and can one measure their effects? Indeed, one suspects that even the posing of such questions is based on dogmatic understandings of what it means to 'resist' and 'to be powerful' and critical social movements may not have come to, or indeed likely to want to come to any conclusions about this issue. What can be speculated upon however, is that critical social movements now empower new political spaces by directly appealing to those disenfranchized. The exploration of these political spaces means that the critical social movements will operate at the margins of conventional political institutions. Yet this space has the possibility of being an extremely important space for direct protest. The kind of 'elitist' revolutionary politics is eschewed because it uses the language of 'power' and 'force'. However, the multitude of connections between issues and people marks the need for a reappraisal of the critical politics of globalization which is both pragmatic and visionary. They do not talk about counter hegemomic blocs. This all forces a critical introspection which is important because it has questioned the role of critical enquiry on the process of conceptualization, interpretation and the strategic relationship between theory and practice. There are signs of unlikely possibilities here for an alternative politics, for everyone to communicate, to think and most importantly, to act with humility.

Conclusion

This changing economic, social and political cartography has enflamed a multitude of protests against globalization by people not succumbing to the 'there is no alternative' axiom as rigorously pursued by governments on the left and the right. The temptation for those in critical IPE is to create a 'them' versus 'us' scenario on the cultivation of alternative world orders. This temptation must of course be resisted. The response to the fallibilities of neoliberal globalization shown through the Global Compact and the UK's Development Initiative has implications for the way responses to globalization articulate their challenges and influence, directly and indirectly.

Bibliography

Adams, J. (2002), cited *File on Four*, BBC Radio 4, 29 January.

Aglietta, M. (1979), *A Theory of Capitalist Regulation*, London: New Left Books.

Agnew, J. (1998), *Geopolitics*, London: Routledge.

Agnew, J. and Corbridge, S. (1995), *Mastering Space: Hegemony, Territory and International Political Economy*, London: Routledge.

AGP. (2000), (http://www.agp.org).

Alexander, J. (1995), 'Mod, Anti, Post, Neo', *New Left Review*, No. 210, pp. 65-105.

Amoore, L., Dodgson, R., Gills, B., Langley, P., Marshall, D. and Watson, I. (1997), 'Overturning Globalisation, Resisting the Teleological, Reclaiming the Political', *New Political Economy*, Vol. 2, pp. 179-194.

Amoore, L., Dodgson, R., Gills, B., Langley, P., Marshall, D. and Watson, I. (2000), 'Overturning Globalization, Resisting the Teleological, Reclaiming Politics', in Gills, B. (ed.), *Globalization and The Politics of Resistance*, London: Macmillan.

Amoore, L., Dodgson, R., Germain, R., Gills, B., Langley, P. and Watson, I. (2000), 'Paths to an Historicized International Political Economy', *Review of International Political Economy*, Vol. 7, pp. 53-71.

Anderson, J. (1998), 'Dinosaurs Clash with Technocrats for Mexico's Soul', *Washington Post*, 6 April, p. AO1.

Annan, K. (1999), 'A Compact for a New Century' (http://www.unglobalcompact.org/partners/business/davos.html).

Annan, K. (1999a), 'Help the Third World Help Itself' (http://www.unglobalcompactoverview/SG/9911/3014.html).

Annan, K. (2000), 'Coalition says Global Compact Threatens UN Mission and Integrity' (http://www.corpwatch.org/trac/globalization/un/gcpr.html).

Annan, K. (2001), 'Address to the World Economic Forum' (http://www.unglobalcompact.com/gc/unweb.nsf/content/sgspeech.html).

Armstrong, D. (1998), 'Globalisation and the Social State', *Review of International Studies*, Vol. 24, pp. 461-479.

Arquilla, J. and Ronfeld, D. (1993), 'Cyberwar is Coming', *Journal of Comparative Strategy*, Vol. 12, pp. 141-165.

Ashley, R. (1988), 'Untying the Sovereign State: A Double Reading of the Anarchy Prolematique', *Millennium: Journal of International Studies*, Vol. 17, pp. 227-262.

Ashley, R. and Walker, R.B.J. (1990), 'Reading Dissidence/Writing the Discipline. Crisis and the Question of Sovereignty in International Studies', *International Studies Quarterly*, Vol. 34, pp. 367-416.

Barry-Jones, R. (1995), *Globalization and Interdependence in the International Political Economy: Reality and Rhetoric*, London: Pinter.

Barry-Jones, R. (1999), 'Globalization and Change in the International Political Economy', *International Affairs*, Vol. 75, pp. 357-369.

Bauman, Z. (2000), *Globalization: The Human Consequences*, Oxford: Blackwell.

Bayliss, J. and Smith, S. (eds) (1997), *The Globalization of World Politics*, London: Macmillan.

Beck, U. (1992), *Risk Society: Towards a New Modernity*, London: Sage.

Beck, U. (1999), 'The Cosmopolitan Manifesto', *New Statesman and Society*, 20 March, pp. 28-30.

Beck, U. (1999), *What is Globalization*, London: Polity.

Bellinghausen, H. (1998), 'Without Approval of Indigenous Rights. No Fear of Deal', *NCDM*, 25 November.

Bellinghausen, H. (1999), 'Bellinghausen Interviews Marcos about Consulta' (http://flag.blackened.net/revolt/mexico/ezln/1999/inter_marcos_consul_mar.ht ml).

Bienefield, M. (1994), 'New World Order: Echoes of a New Imperialism', *Third World Quarterly*, Vol. 15, pp. 31-49.

Blair, A. (1997), 'Foreword to the First White Paper on International Development' (http://www.globalisation.gov.uk/Forewords?ThePrimeMinister.html).

Blair, A. (2001), 'We Made Progress Despite the Violence', *The Sunday Times*, 22 July, p. 2.

Blixen, S. and Fazio, C. (1995), 'Interview with Marcos about Neoliberalism, the Nation State and Democracy' (http://flag.blackened.net/revolt/mexico/ezln/inter_marcos_aug95.html).

Booth, K. (1997), 'Discussion: A Reply to Wallace', *Review of International Studies*, Vol. 23, pp. 371-377.

Boyes, R. (1999), 'Blair Must Wait While Schroder Pays his Dues to the Left', *The Times*, 6 December, p. 12.

Brazier, C. (1999), 'Heaven, Hell and Spring Sunshine', *New Internationalist*, No. 309, January/February, pp. 33-34.

Brewer, A. (1982), *Marxist Theories of Imperialism*, London: Routledge.

Brothers, C. (1998), 'Mexico Denies Zapatista Claims for Clandestine Talks', *NCDM*, 3 February.

Brown, C. (1992), *International Relations Theory: New Normative Approaches*, London: Harvester Wheatsheaf.

Brown, C. (1995), 'The End of History', in Danchev, A. (ed.) (1995), *Fin de Siecle: The Meaning of the Twentieth Century*, Taris Academic Studies, pp. 1-20.

Brown, G. (2000), 'Crumbs of Comfort: The G8 Cologne Summit and the Chains of Debt' (http://www.jubilee.org).

Burbach, R. (1992), 'Ruptured Frontiers. The Transformation of the US/Latin American System', *Socialist Register*, pp. 239-250.

Burbach, R. (1994), 'The Roots of the Postmodern Rebellion in Chiapas', *New Left Review*, No. 205 (May/June), pp. 113-125.

Burbach, R. (1996), 'For a Zapatista Style Postmodern Perspective', *Monthly Review*, Vol. 48, pp. 34-41.

Burbach, R. (1997), 'Undefining Postmodern Marxism. On Smashing Modernization and Narrating New Social and Economic Actors', (paper sent to author).

Burbach, R. (1997a), 'Global Agribusiness and the Right to Food', paper presented at 'The Other Economic Summit', Denver, USA, 22 June 1997.

Burbach, R. (2001), *Globalization and Postmodern Politics: From Zapatistas to High Tech Robber Barons*, London: Pluto Press.

Burbach, R. and Rosset, P. (1994), 'Food and the Chiapas Rebellion', *Documents on Mexican Politics* (http://www.cs.unb.ca/~alopez/politics/chiapasagri.html).

Bush, G. (1990), 'State of the Union Address', *Keesings Diary of World Events*, Vol. 36.

Bush, George W. (2002), 'State of the Union Address', broadcast *BBC News 24*, 30 January.

Buzan, B., Held, D. and McGrew, A. (1998), 'Realism versus cosmopolitanism: a debate', *Review of International Studies*, Vol. 24, pp. 287-399.

Callinicos, A. (1985), 'Postmodernism, Poststructuralism and PostMarxism', *Theory, Culture and Society*, Vol. 2, pp. 85-101.

Callinicos, A. (2001), *The Third Way: A Critique*, London: Polity.

Camdessus, M. (1995), 'Speech: The IMF and the Challenges of Globalisation: The Funds Evolving Approach to a Constant Mission: The Case of Mexico' (http://www.imf.org/external/np/sec/mds/1995/MD59519/HTML).

Camdessus, M. (1999), 'Looking Beyond Todays Financial Crisis: Moving forward with International Financial Reform', *Remarks by Michael Camdessus, Managing Director of IMF to the Foreign Policy Association*, New York, 24 February, pp. 2-6 (http://www.imf.org).

Camilleri, J. and Falk, R. (1992), *The End of Sovereignty. The Politics of a Fragmented and Shrinking World*, Aldershot: Edward Elgar.

Carrigan, A. (1998), 'Why is the Zapatista Movement so Attractive to Mexican Civil Society?', *Civreports*, Vol. 2. (http://www.civnet.cvg/journal/issue6/repacatt.htm).

Castaneda, J. (1994), 'Interview with', *Documents on Mexican Politics* (http://www.cs.unb.ca/~alopez/politics/critique.html).

Castaneda, J. (1996), 'Who are the EPR?', (http://epn.org/castan/epren.html).

Castillo, G. (1996), 'NAFTA and Neoliberalism: Mexico's Elusive Quest for Ist World Status', Otero, G. (ed.) *Neoliberalism Revisited: The Economic Restructuring of Mexican Politics*, Boulder: Westview Press.

Castillo, R. and Nigh, R. (1998), 'Global Processes and Local Identity. Agricultural Mayan Coffee Growers in Chiapas', *American Anthropologist*, Vol. 100, pp. 136-147.

Cavorozzi, M. (1992), 'Beyond the Transition to Democracy in Latin America', *Journal of Latin American Studies*, Vol. 24, pp. 665-684.

Centeno, M. and Maxfield, S. (1992), 'Managing Finance and Order. Change in Mexico's Political Elite', *Journal of Latin American Studies*, Vol. 24, pp. 57-87.

Cerny, P. (1990), *The Changing Architecture of Politics: Structure, Agency and the Future of the State*, London: Sage.

Cerny, P. (1995), 'The Changing Logic of Collective Action', *International Organisation*, Vol. 49.

Cevallos, D. (1995), 'Understanding the Zapatistas' (http://www.nativenet-unl/9501/0017.html).

Chapman, G. (1996), 'Mexico: A Window on Technology and the Poor' (http://mexconnect.com/mex_/articlechapman.html).

Chase Dunn, C. (1996), 'Buchanas Right on New World Order', *World Systems Network* (WSN@csf.colorado 7 May, 1996).

Chomsky, N. (1969), *American Power and the New Mandarins*, London: Chatto and Windus.

Chomsky, N. (1993), *Deterring Democracy: With a New Afterword*, New York: Hill and Wang.

Chomsky, N. (1999), 'Notes on NAFTA. Masters of Mankind', *Directory on Mexican Politics* (http://www.cs.unb.ca/~alopez.o/politics/chomnafta.html).

Chore, R. (1999), 'Forum to Help Prevent Crisis Agreed', *Financial Times*, 22 February, p. 5.

Church, G. (1995), 'Raining in all Directions', *Time Magazine Online* (http://www.time.com/time/magazine/archive/1995/990227/990227.mexico.html).

Clandestine Revolutionary Committee Headquarters/General Command (CCRI-GC), (1994) 'February 21 Dialogue' (http://flag.blackened.net/revolt/mexico/ezln/crci_dialogue_feb94.html).

CCRI-GC (1995), '503 Years Later: The Generation Continues' (http://flag.blackened.net/revolt/mexico/ezln/ccri_503_years_oct95.html).

CCRI-GC (1998), 'Consultation for the Recognition of the Right for Indian Self Determination and the End to the War of Extermination' (http://flag.blackened.net/revolt/mexico/ezln/1998/ccri_procedure_dec98.html).

CCRI-GC (1998a), 'Communique from Commandante David of the Clandestine Indigenous Revolutionary Committee: General Command of the EZLN' (http://www.ezln.org/archive/ezln980103-eng.html).

Clapham, C. (1992), 'The Collapse of Socialist Development in the Third World', *Third World Quarterly*, Vol. 13, pp. 13-27.

Clapham, C. (1998), 'Degrees of Statehood', *Review of International Studies*, Vol. 24, pp. 143-159.

Clarke, I. (1997), *Globalisation and Fragmentation: International Relations in the Twentieth Century*, Oxford: Oxford University Press.

Clarke, I. (1998), 'Beyond the Great Divide. Globalisation and the Theory of International Relations', *Review of International Studies*, Vol. 24, pp. 479-499.

Cleaver, H. (1996), 'Reforming the CIA In the Image of the Zapatistas?'
(http://www.eco.utexas.edu/cleaver/homepage/faculty/chiapas95.html).

Cleaver, H. (1997), 'The Electronic Fabric of Struggle'
(http://www.ecoutexas.edu/faculty/cleaver/zapatistacyber.html).

Cleaver, H. (1998), 'The Zapatista Effect. The Internet and the Rise of an Alternative Political Fabric'
(http://www.eco.utexas.edu/~hmcleave/zapeffect.html).

Cleaver, H. (1999), 'Computer Linked Social Movements and the Global Threat to Capitalism' (http://www.utexas.edu/~hmcleave/polnet.html).

Clinton, W. (1993), President of The United States 'NAFTA: Press Conference by The President', *Office of Press Secretary*
(gopher://csf.colorado.edu;70/00/1...afia/nafta_speeches/clinton.nafta).

Clinton, W. (2000), 'State of the Union Address', Broadcast *BBC News 24*, 28 January.

Clinton, W. (2002), 'World Without Walls', *The Guardian: Saturday Review*, 26 January.

Cockburn, A. and Murray, K. (1994), 'A Fistful of Promises', *New Statesman and Society*, 18th March, pp. 20-23.

Cockburn, A. and Silverstein, K. (1995), 'Major US Bank Urges Zapatista Wipeout: A Litmus Test for Mexico's Stability', *Counterpunch*
(http://www.anatomy.su.oz.au/danny/anthropology/anthro1/archive/february195/0463.html).

Cohen, J. and Arato, A. (1981), 'Social Movements, Civil Society and the Problem of Sovereignty', *Praxis*, Vol. 4.

Conger, L. (1994), 'Zapatista Thunder', *Current History*
(http://www.indians.org/welker/thunder.htm).

Cooper, M. (1993), 'Starting from Chiapas: The Zapatistas fire the shot heard around the world', in Ruggiero, G. and Sahulka, S. (1993), *The New American Crisis: Radical Analyses of the Problems Facing America Today*, The New Press: New York, pp. 126-139.

Cooper, M. (1999), 'After Seattle'
(http://www.laweekly.com/ink.00/18/news.cooper.shtml).

Cox, R. (1981), 'Social Forces, States and World Order. Beyond International Theory', *Millennium: Journal of International Studies*, Vol. 10, pp. 126-155.

Cox, R. (1983), 'Gramsci, Hegemony and IR: An Essay in Method', *Millennium: Journal of International Studies*, Vol. 12, pp. 269-291.

Cox, R. (1999), 'Civil Society at the turn of the Millennium; Prospects for an Alternative World Order', *Review of International Studies*, Vol. 25, pp. 5-29.

Crook, C. (2000), 'The World Gets Remarkably more Prosperous', *The World in 2001*, The Economist.

Davison, P. (1998), 'Down trodden Indians Present Major Challenge', *Independent on Sunday*, 22 March, p. 21.

Deneuve, S. and Reeve, C. (1995), 'Behind the Balaclavas of South East Mexico'
(http://flag.blackened.net/revolt/mexico/comment/balaclava.html).

Der Derian, J. and Shapiro, M. (eds) (1989), *International/Intertextual Relations: Postmodern Readings of World Politics*, Lexington.

Devereux, P., Hernandez, A., Aguilera, E. and Rodriguez, G. (1994), 'Interview with Subcommandante Marcos' (http://flag.blackened.net/revolt/mexico/ezln/anmarin.html).

Dicken, P. (1992), *Global Shift: The Internationalisation of Economic Activity*, London: Chapman.

Dickson, A. (1996), *Development and International Relations*, Oxford: University Press.

Dillon, S. (1998), 'In Massacre Aftermath Zedillo Replaces Interior Minister', *New York Times Newsservice*.

Docherty, T. (ed.) (1993), *Postmodernism. A Reader*, London: Harvester Wheatsheaf.

Dominguez, R. (1995), 'Run for the Border. The Taco Bell War', *CTheory* (http://www.ctheory.com/c22-run_for_the_border.html).

Dominguez, R. (1998), 'Electronic Zapatismo', *CTheory* (http://www.ctheory.com/98/=Zapatistas.html).

Drolet, M. (1994), 'The Wild and the Sublime. Lyotard and Postmodern Politics', *Political Studies*, Vol. XLII, pp. 259-274.

Duran de Huerta, M. and Higgins, N. (1999), 'Interview With Zapatista Leader Subcommandante Marcos', *International Affairs*, Vol. 75, pp. 269-281.

Durbin, A. (1998), 'IMF and Their Ideal World Foreign Policy in Focus World Banks Private Sector Agenda', *NCDM*, 11 December.

Eagleton, T. (1985), 'Capitalism, Modernity and Postmodernity', *New Left Review*, No. 152, pp. 66-74.

Eagleton, T. (1995), 'Where do Postmodernists Come From?', *Monthly Review*, Vol. 47, pp. 59-71.

The Economist, 23 July 1994, 'Mexico's Currency Wobbles'.

The Economist, 6 August 1994, 'Mexico's Gentle Left'.

The Economist, 13 August 1994, 'Mexico on Election Eve'.

The Economist, 1 October 1994, 'Murder in Mexico'.

The Economist, 29 October 1994, 'Foreign Banks in Mexico'.

The Economist, 12 November 1994, 'Mexico Defies Proposition 187'.

The Economist, 10 December 1994, 'Happy Eve NAFTA'.

The Economist, 7 January 1995, 'Zedillo and Sovereignty'.

The Economist, 4 March 1995, 'PRI Devours its Children'.

The Economist, 7 October 1995, 'The Myth of the Powerless State'.

The Economist, 28 October 1995, 'Mexico: A Survey'.

Eder, K. (1993), *Class and New Social Movements*, London: Macmillan.

Eliorraga, J. (1996), 'The Significance of San Andres to Civil Society' (http://flag.blackened.net/revolt/mexico/comment/sig_san_andres.html).

Eliorraga, J. (1997), 'An Analysis of Evolving Zapatismo', *Inmotion Magazine Online* (http://www.inhousemagazine.com/chiapas1.html).

Elizonda, C. (1994), 'In Search of Revenue. Tax Reform in Mexico Under the Administrations of Etcheverra and Salinas', *Journal of Latin American Studies*, Vol. 26, pp. 159-191.

Elshstain, J. (1999), 'Really Existing Communities', *Review of International Studies*, Vol. 25, pp. 141-147.

Falcoff, M. (1997), 'Mexico Mid-term Elections a Major Turning Point', *Latin American Outlook* (http://www.aei.org/lao/lao7828.html).

Falk, R. (1995), *On Humane Governance: Towards a new Global Project*, Cambridge: Cambridge Polity Press.

Falk, R. (1996), 'An Enquiry into the Political Economy of World Order', *New Political Economy*, Vol. 1, pp. 13-27.

Falk, R. (1999), *Predatory Globalization: A Critique*, Polity Press.

Flood, A. (1997), 'The Zapatistas, Anarchists and Direct Democracy' (http://flag.blackened.net/revolt/andrew/zap_asr.html).

Foster, H. (ed.) (1983), *Postmodern Culture*, London: Pluto Press.

Fotopoulos, T. (1997), *Towards an Inclusive Democracy: The Crisis of the Growth Economy and the Need for a New Liberatory Project*, London: Cassell.

Fotopoulos, T. (2001), 'Globalisation, the Reformist Left and the Antiglobalisation Movement', *Democracy and Nature*, Vol. 7, pp. 233-281.

Foucault, M. (1976), *The History of Sexuality*, London: Penguin.

Foucault, M. (1983), 'On the Genealogy of Ethics: An Overview of a Work in Progress', in Dreyfus, H. and Rabinow, P. (eds), *Michel Foucault. Beyond Structuralism and Hermeneutics*, London: Minerva Press.

Foucault, M. (1991), 'What is Enlightenment', in Rabinow, P. (ed.) (1991), *A Foucault Reader*, London: Penguin.

Frieden, J. (1981), 'Third World Indebted Industrialisation. International Finance and State Capitalism in Brazil, Mexico, Algeria and South Korea', *International Organisation*, Vol. 35, pp. 407-431.

Froehling, O. (1997), 'A War of Ink on the Internet. Cyberspace and the Uprising in Chiapas, Mexico', *Geographical Review*, Vol. 87, pp. 291-307.

Fuentes, C. (1995), 'Mexico's Financial Crisis is Political, and the Remedy is Democracy', *Documents on Mexican Politics* (http://www.cs.unb.ca/~alopez/politics/fuentes.html).

Fukuyama, F. (1991), 'Liberal Democracy as a Global Phenomenon', *Political Studies*, Vol. 11.

Garcia, A. (1994), 'After NAFTA North and South Need a New Beginning' (http://garnet.berkeley.edu.3333/.mags/.cross/.38/.38art/.nafta.html).

George, J. (1994), *Discourses of Global Politics: A Critical (Re)introduction*, Boulder: Lynne Rienner.

George, J. and Campbell, D. (1990), 'Patterns of Dissent and the Celebration of Difference. Critical Social Theory and IR', *International Studies Quarterly*, Vol. 34, pp. 269-294.

George, S. (2001), 'How a Collective Insanity is Taking a Grip on the World', in Roddick, A. (2001), *Take it Personally: How Globalization Affects You and Powerful Ways to Change It*, London: Harpercollins, pp. 184-188.

Germain, R. and Kenny, M. (1998), 'International Relations Theory and the New Gramscians', *Review of International Studies*, Vol. 24, pp. 3-23.

Giddens, A. (1984), *The Constitution of Society*, Cambridge: Polity Press.

Giddens, A. (1985), *The Nation State and Violence*, Cambridge: Polity Press.

Giddens, A. (1990), *The Consequencs of Modernity*, Cambridge: Cambridge University Press.

Giddens, A. (1999), *The Third Way: The Renewal of Social Democracy*, Cambridge: Polity Press.

Giddens, A. (1999), 'The Reith Lectures; Globalisation' (http://www.bbc.co.uk/hi/english/static/events/reith_99/week1/week1.html).

Giddens, A. (2000), 'The Third Way Budget', *The Guardian*, 29 February, p. 15

Gilbreth, C. (1997), 'The Development of Low Intensity War in Chiapas' (http://flag.blackened.net/revolt/Mexico/comment/develop_/liw-feb97.html).

Gill, S. (ed.) (1993), *Gramsci, Historical Materialism and International Relations*, Cambridge: University Press.

Gill, S. (1995), 'Globalisation, Market Civilisation and Disciplinary Neoliberalism', *Millennium: Journal of International Studies*, Vol. 24, pp. 399-423.

Gill, S. (1996), 'The Global Panopticon? The Neoliberal State, Economic Life and Bentham's Surveillance', *Alternatives*, Vol. 20, pp. 1-47.

Gill, S. (2000), 'Towards a Postmodern Prince, the battles in Seattle as a moment in the new politics of globalisation', *Millennium: Journal of International Studies*, Vol. 29, pp. 131-140.

Gill, S. and Law, D. (1988), *The Global Political Economy*, London: Harvester Wheatsheaf.

Gills, Barry K. (ed.) (2000), *Globalization and the Politics of Resistance*, London: Macmillan.

Gills, Barry K., Rocamora J. and Wilson, R. (eds) (1993), *Low Intensity Democracy: Power in the New World Order*, London: Pluto Press.

Giordano, C. (1995), 'The Death Agony of Indigenous Mexican Textiles', *Voices of Mexico*, Vol. 34, pp. 20-24.

Gladwin, M. (1994), 'Theory and Practice of Contemporary Social Movements', *Politics*, Vol. 14, pp. 59-65.

Global Exchange (http://www.globalexchange.org/).

Golden, T. (1994), 'Rebels Determined to Build Socialism in Mexico' (http://nativenet.uthesca.edu/archive/nl/9401/0188.html).

Gordon, D. (1988), 'The Global Economy. New Foundation or Crumbling Edifice', *New Left Review*, No. 168, pp. 24-66.

Gramsci, A. (1971), *The Prison Notebooks*, London: Lawrence and Wishart.

Grant, I. (1998), 'Postmodernism and Politics', in Sims, S. (ed.) (1998), *Postmodern Thought*, London: Iconbooks.

Green, J. (1995), 'Threads of Life', *Mundo Maya/Chiapas.*

Habermas, J. (1981), 'Modernity An Incomplete Project', *New German Critique*, Vol. 22, pp. 3-15.

Halliday, F. (1983), *The Making of the Second Cold War*, London: Verso.

Harvey, N. (1995), The Rebellion in Chiapas: Rural Reform and Popular Struggle', *Third World Quarterly*, Vol. 16, pp. 39-75.

Harvey, N. (1998), *The Chiapas Rebellion: The Struggle for Land and Democracy*, Durham: Duke University Press.

Harris, N. (1987), *The End of The Third World*, London: Heinemann.

Haynes, J. (1997), *Democracy and Civil Society in the Third World: Politics and New Political Movements*, London: Polity Press.

Held, D. (1995), *Democracy and the Global Order: From the Modern State to Cosmopolitan Governance*, Cambridge: Polity Press.

Held, D. and McGrew, A. (1998), 'Globalisation and the End of the World Order', *Review of International Studies*, Vol. 24, pp. 219-245.

Held, D., Perraton, J., Goldblatt, D. and McGrew, A. (1999), *Global Transformations*, Stanford: Stanford University Press.

Hertz, N. (2001), *Global Capitalism and the Death of Democracy*, London: Heinemann.

Higgins, N. (1998), 'The IMF's New World Order. Uncle Sam Disturbs Asia's Dream', *The Observer*, 18 January, p. 14.

Higgott, R. (2000), 'Contested Globalization: the changing context and normative challenges', *Review of International Studies*, Vol. 26, pp. 131-153.

Hilbert, S. (1997), 'For Whom the Nation? Internationalisation, Zapatismo and the Struggle Over Mexican Modernity', *Antipode*, Vol. 29, pp. 115-148.

Hines, C. (2000), cited in *The World Tonight*, BBC Radio 4, 25 September.

Hines, C. (2001), cited in *Analysis*, BBC Radio 4, 15 November.

Hines, C. and Lang, T. (1996), 'Global Free Trade: The New Protectionism', *New Political Economy*, Vol. 1, pp. 111-115.

Hindess, B. (1998), 'Politics and Liberation', in Moss, J. (ed.) (1998), *Later Foucault*, London: Sage.

Hirst, P. and Thompson, G. (1996), *Globalization in Question*, Cambridge, Polity Press.

Hobsbawm, E. (1994), 'Barbarism. A Users Guide', *New Left Review*, No. 206, pp. 44-55.

Hobsbawm, E. (2000), *The Age of Revolutions*, London: Abacus.

Hobsbawm, E (2000a), *The Age of Empire*, London: Abacus.

Hobsbawm, E. (2000b), *The New Century*, London: Little, Brown and Company.

Hoffman, M. (1987), 'Critical Theory and the Interparadigm Debate', *Millennium: Journal of International Studies*, Vol. 16, pp. 231-249.

Hoffman, M. (1991), 'Restructuring, Reconstituting, Reinscripting, Rearticulating. Four Voices in Critical International Relations Theory', *Millennium. Journal of International Studies*, Vol. 20, pp. 169-189.

Hoffman, S. (1998), 'The Crisis of Liberal Internationalism', *Foreign Policy*, Vol. 98, pp. 159-176.

Hoogvelt, A. (1996), *Globalization and the Postcolonial World*, Oxford: Blackwell.

Hopkins, A. (2002), 'History of Globalization and the Globalization of History', in Hopkins, A. (ed.) (2002), *Globalization and World History*, London: Pimlico, p. 47.

Hughes, S. and Wilkinson, R. (2000), 'Labor Standards and Global Governance: Examining the Dimensions of Institutional Engagement', *Global Governance*, Vol. 6, pp. 259-277.

Huntington, S. (1997), 'After 20 years: The Future of the Third Wave', *Journal of Democracy*, Vol. 8, pp. 3-13.

Huntington, S. (1998), *The Clash of Civilizations: The Remaking of World Order*, London: Simon and Schuster.

Hutcheon, L. (1988), 'A Postmodern Problematics', in Merrill, R. (ed.) (1998), *Ethics/Aesetics: Postmodern Positions*, Washington, Maisonneuve Press.

Hutton, W. (1995), *The State We're In*, London: Jonathan Cape.

Ignatieff, M. (1996), *The Warrior's Honor: Ethnic War and the Modern Conscience*, London: Vintage.

James, H. (2001), cited in *Analysis*, BBC Radio 4, 15 November.

Johnson, D. (2001), 'The Anarchy on our streets reflects our lack of liberty', *The Daily Telegraph*, p. 22.

Jubilee (2000) (http://www.jubilee2000.org).

Kaldor, M. (1998), *Old Wars and New Wars: Organized Violence in a Global Era*, London: Pinter.

Kaldor, M. (2000), 'Civilising Globalisation: The Implications of the Battle of Seattle', *Millennium: Journal of International Studies*, Vol. 29, pp. 105-114.

Keohane, R. (1989), *International Institutions and State Power. Essays in International Relations Theory*, Boulder: Westview Press.

Keohane, R. (1998), 'International Institutions; Can Interdependence Work?', *Foreign Policy*, Vol. 110, pp. 82-96.

Keohane, R. and Nye, J. (1977), *Power and Interdependence. The Changing Nature of World Politics*, Boulder: Westview Press.

Klesner, K. (1998), 'The Electoral Route to Democracy. Mexico's Transition in Comparative Analysis', *Comparative Politics*, pp. 477-497.

Klein, N. (2000), *No Logo*, London: Flamingo.

Klein, N. (2001), 'Welcome to the Net Generation', in Roddick, A., *Take it Personally: How Globalization Affects You and Powerful Ways to Change It*, London: Harpercollins, pp. 32-38.

Krasner, S. (ed.) (1983), *International Regimes*, Cornwell Press.

Krishnan, R. (1996), 'December 1995: The First Revolt Against Globalisation', *Monthly Review*, Vol. 48, pp. 1-22.

Kundera, M. (1969), *Laughable Loves*, London: Faber and Faber.

Laclau, E. and Mouffe, C. (1985), *Hegemony and Socialist Strategy*, London: Verso.

Lapid, Y. (1989), 'Quo Vadis International Relations? Further Reflections on the Next Stage of International Theory', *Millennium: Journal of International Studies*, Vol. 18, pp. 77-88.

Lascano, S. (2000), '10 Theses Concerning the PRI Defeat' (http://flag.blackened.net/revolt/ezln/2000/fzln_10theses_july.html).

Laurell, A. (1992), 'Democracy in Mexico. Longer it Lasts the Better', *New Left Review*, No. 194, pp. 33-55.

Lawson, C. (1998), 'Mexico's New Politics. The Elections of 1997', *Journal of Democracy*, Vol. 8, pp. 3-28.

Leys, C. (1996), 'The Crisis in Development Theory', *New Political Economy*, Vol. 1, pp. 41-59.

Linklater, A. (1986), 'Realism, Marxism and Critical International Theory', *Review of International Studies*, Vol. 12, pp. 301-312.

Linklater, A. (1990), *Beyond Realism and Marxism: Critical Theory and International Relations*, London: Macmillan.

Linklater, A. (1997), 'The Transformation of Political Territory: E.H. Carr, Critical Theory and International Relations', *Review of International Studies*, Vol. 23, pp. 321-339.

Linklater, A. (1999), 'The Transformation of Political Community', *Review of International Studies*, Vol. 25, pp. 165-175.

Lipietz, A. (1989), *Mirages and Miracles, Towards a Global Fordism*, London: Verso.

Lloyd, J. (1997), 'Interview with Anthony Giddens', *New Statesman*, January, pp. 8-9.

Lloyd, J. (2001), 'How the Rich Rule Politics Again', *New Statesman*, 26 March, p. 9.

Long, R. (1999), 'Challenge to State Hegemony: Competing Nationalisms and the Staging of the Conflict in Chiapas', *Journal of Latin American Cultural Studies*, Vol. 8, pp. 91-115.

Lyotard, J. (1979), *The Postmodern Condition: A Report on Knowledge*, Minneapolis: Minnesota University Press.

Macewan, A. (1994), 'Globalisation and Stagnation', *Socialist Register*, pp. 130-144.

Maclean, J. (1988), 'Marxism and International Relations. A Strange Case of Mutual Neglect', *Millennium: Journal of International Studies*, Vol. 17, pp. 295-319.

Magdoff, F., Bellamy Foster, J. and Duttel, F. (1998), 'Editorial', *Monthly Review*, Vol. 50, pp. 1-11.

Magdoff, H. (1992), 'Globalisation to What End?', *Socialist Register*, pp. 44-76.

Mallon, F. (1994), 'Promise and Dilemmas of Subaltern Studies: Perspectives from Latin American History', *American Historical Review*, Vol. 9 , pp. 1491-1516.

Mandel, E. (1975), *Late Capitalism*, London: Humanities Press.

Maquila Network Update (1996), 'Favesa Workers Win Severance', Vol. 1, p. 1.
Maquila Network Update (1996a), 'Are Sweatshops a Northern Tradition?', Vol. l, p. 5.
Subcommandante Marcos. (1992), 'South East in Two Winds' (http://www.ezln.org/Se-in-two-winds.html).
Subcommandante Marcos. (1994), 'First Interview With' (http://flag.blackened.net/revolt/mexico/ezln/marcos_interview_jan94.html).
Subcommandante Marcos. (1995), 'Message to Zedillo' (http://flag.blackened.net/revolt/mexico/ezln/marcos_blood_/can_feb95.html).
Subcommandante Marcos. (1996), 'We know about the EPR' (http://flag.blackened.net/revolt/mexico/ezln/marcos_no_links_epr_july96.html).
Subcommandante Marcos. (1996a), '2nd Declaration of La Realidad: Closing Words of the EZLN at the Second Intercontinental Encuentro for Humanity and Against Neoliberalism' (http://flag.blackened.net/revolt/mexico/1996/marcos_2nddecl.html).
Subcommandante Marcos. (1998), 'Invitation for Dialogue Between EZLN and Civil Society' (http://flag.blackened.net/revolt/mexico/ezln/marcos_dialogue_sept98.html).
Subcommandante Marcos. (1999), 'Some Further Notes for the Consulta' (http://flag.blackened.net/revolt/mexico/ezln/1999/marcos_cons_notes_mar99.html).
Subcommandante Marcos. (1999a), 'The International Consulta and International Jornada for the Excluded of the World' (http://flag.blackened.net/revolt/mexico/ezln/1999/marcos_int_con_feb.html).
Subcommandante Marcos. (1999b), 'EZLN has no favorite for the 2000 Elections' (http://flag.blackened.net/revolt/mexico/ezln/1999/inter_marcos_elect_july99.html).
Subcommandante Marcos. (2000), 'Why do we all agree the global market is inevitable?' (http://flag.blackened.net/revolt/mexico/ezln/2000/marcos/why_agree_sept00.html)
Marx, K. and Engels, F. (1967), *The Communist Manifesto*, London: Penguin.
Marx, K. and Engels, F. (1970), *The German Ideology*, London: Lawrence and Wishart.
Massey, D. (1994), *State, Place and Agenda*, Cambridge: Polity Press.
Massey, D. (1995), 'Thinking Radical Democracy Spatially', *Society and Space*, Vol. 13, pp. 283-289.
Mayall, J. (1998), 'Globalisation and International Relations', *Review of International Studies*, Vol. 24, pp. 239-251.
Mclellan, D. (1986), *Marx*, London: Fontana.
McMichael, P. (2000), 'Globalisation: Trend or Project?', in Palan, R. (ed.) (2000), *Global Political Economy: Contemporary Theories*, London: Routledge, pp. 100-115.
Meiksins-Woods, E. (1996), 'A Reply to Sivanandan', *Monthly Review*, Vol. 48, pp. 21-31.
Meiksins-Woods, E. (1996a), 'Modernity, Postmodernity and Capitalism', *Monthly Review*, Vol. 48, pp. 21-40.

Melucci, A. (1984), *Nomads of the Present. Social Movements and Individual Needs in Contemporary Society*, London: Hutchison.

Middlebrook, K. (1988), 'Dilemmas of Change in Mexican Politics', *World Politics*.

Mittelman, J. (1995), 'Globalisation: Surviving at the Margins', *Third World Quarterly*, Vol. 15, pp. 427-445.

Mittelman, J. (1996) (ed.), *Globalization: Critical Reflections*, Boulder: Lynne Rienner.

Moguel, J. (1999), 'Key Elements of the Zapatista Consultation', *NCDM*, 20 March.

Moore, M. and Low, P. (2000), 'Select Committee on International Development: Examination of Witnesses Questions 83-99', 7 March.

Morris, S. (1999), 'Corruption and the Mexican Political System. Continuity and Change', *Third World Quarterly*, Vol. 20, pp. 623-645.

Mouffe, C. (ed.) (1992), *Dimensions of Radical Democracy: Pluralism, Citizenship and Community*, London, New York: Verso.

Mouffe, C. (1995), PostMarxism, Identity and Democracy', *Society and Space*, Vol. 13, pp. 259-267.

Murphy, C. and Tooze, R. (1991), *The New International Political Economy*, Boulder: Lynne Rienner.

Nash, J. (1994), 'Global Integration and Subsistence Insecurity', *American Anthropologist*, Vol. 96, pp. 7-31.

Nash, J. (1997), 'Fiesta of the World. The Zapatistas and Radical Democracy in Mexico', *American Anthropologist*, Vol. 99, pp. 261-274.

Nash, J. and Kovic, C. (1996), 'Reconstituting Hegemony. The Free Trade Act and the Transformation of Rural Mexico', in Mittelman, J. (ed.) (1996), *Globalization. Critical Reflections*, Boulder: Lynne Rienner.

NCDM, 5 February 1998, 'The Acteal Article'.

NCDM, 3 March, 1998, 'The San Andres Accords. A History of Two Years of Non-Compliance'.

NCDM, 17 and 18 July 1998, 'Zapatista Communique. Above and Below. Masks and Silences'.

NCDM, 10 September 1998, 'The State of Mexico'.

NCDM, 14 September 1998, 'Consulta. Part of the New Solution'.

NCDM, 17 September 1998, 'Fobaproa'.

NCDM, 31 October 1998, 'G7 Agrees to Boost IMF Power'.

NCDM, 2 December 1998, 'The Commandantes War'.

NCDM, 9 December 1998, 'Civil Space Destroyed in San Cristobel'.

NCDM, 15 December 1998, 'EZLN Communique from CCRC-GC'.

NCDM, 9 February 1999, 'EZLN Communique'.

NCDM, 13 March 1999, 'Consultation for the Recognition of Rights of Indian Peoples and an End to the War of Extermination'.

Norris, C. (1994), 'What is Enlightenment? Kant and Foucault', in Guttings, G. (ed.) (1994), *Cambridge Companion to Foucault*, Cambridge: Cambridge University Press.

Nugent, D. (1995), 'Northern Intellectuals and the EZLN', *Monthly Review*, Vol. 47, pp. 124-138.

Nugent, D. (1995a), 'Northern Intellectuals and the EZLN (or why the EZLN is not post-modern)' (http://flag.blackened.net/revolt/mexico/comment/north_intellect_ezln.html).

Nye, J. (1992), 'What New World Order?', *Foreign Affairs*, Vol. 72.

Ohmae, K. (1985), *The Triads. The Coming of Age of Global Competition*, New York: Free Press.

Ohmae, K. (1990), *The Borderless World*, London: Routledge.

O Neill, J. (1986), 'From Weber to Foucault. The Disciplinary Society', *British Journal of Sociology*, Vol. 37, pp. 42-61.

Oppenheimer, A. (1997), 'Interview with Andres Oppenheimer: Money, Murder and Mexico', *Documents on Mexican Politics* (http://www.cs.unb.ca/~alopez/politics/interoppenheimer.html).

Ouweneel, A. (1996), 'Away from Prying Eyes: The Zapatista Revolt of 1994', in Gosner, K. and Ouweneel, A. (eds) (1996), *Indigenous Revolts in Chiapas and the Andean Highlands*, Latin American Studies.

Overbeek, H. (2000), 'Transnational Historical Materialism: Theories of Transnational Class Formation and World Order', in Palan, R. (ed.) (2000), *Global Political Economy: Contemporary Theories*, London: Routledge, pp. 168-184.

Ovetz, R. (1994), 'First Interview with Marcos', *Native-L* (http://nativenet.uthesca.edu/archive/nl/9401/0188.html).

Owen, G. (2001), 'Who's afraid of multinationals', *The Spectator*, 12 May, p. 22.

Panitch, L. (1994), 'Globalisation and the State: Between globalism and nationalism', *Socialist Register*, pp. 60-93.

Panitch, L. (1998), 'The State in a Globalising World. A Socially Democratic Global Capitalism', *Monthly Review*, Vol. 50, pp. 11-23.

Parfitt, M. (1996), 'Chiapas: The Rough Road to Reality', *National Geographic*, Vol. 190, pp. 114-132.

Parsons, T. (1952), *The Social System*, London: Tavistock.

Pauly, I. (1997), *Who Elected the Bankers? Surveillance and Control in the World Economy*, Ithaca: Cornell University Press.

Petras, J. and Morley, M. (1983), 'Imperialism and Intervention in the Third World. US Foreign Policy in Latin America', *Socialist Register*, pp. 219-239.

Pettifer, A. (2001), cited in *Analysis*, BBC Radio 4, 15 November.

Pilger, J. (1999), *Hidden Agendas*, London: Vintage.

Pilger, J. (2001), 'John Pilger Column', *New Statesman*, 9 July, p. 15.

Poulantzas, N. (1981), 'On Social Classes', in Giddens, A. and Held, D. (eds) (1981), *Classes, Power and Conflict: Classical and Contemporary Debates*, Oxford: Blackwell.

Puig, A. (1995), 'Weaving a Fortress. Textiles from Chiapas. The Epitome of a Resistance Culture', *Voices of Mexico*, Vol. 34, p. 84.

Rachjman, J. (1985), *Michel Foucault: The Freedom of Philosophy*, New York: Colombia University Press.

Radgett, T. (1998), 'Laws of the Jungle', *Time Magazine Online* (http://www.time.com/time/magazine/1998/dom/text/world/laws_of_the_jungle 8.htm).

Ransom, D. (1997), 'Globalisation; An Alternative View, *New Internationalist Online* (http://www.oneworld.org/ni/issue296/keynote.html).

Rengger, N. (1993), *Modernity, Postmodernity and Political Theory: Beyond Enlightenment and Critique*, Oxford: Blackwell.

Robertson, R. (1992), *Globalisation and Social Theory*, London: Routledge.

Roddick, A. (2000), 'Sleepless in Seattle', *New Internationalist*, No. 322, p. 20.

Roddick, A. (2001), cited in *Analysis*, BBC Radio 4, 15 November.

Rodriguez, C. (1994), 'The Struggle of the Zapatistas Runs Clearly and Directly Against the Policies of Neo-liberalism' (http://www.actlab.utexas.edu/~Zapatistas/neo.html).

Rodriguez, C. (1999), 'All You Ever Wanted to Know About the Consulta But Were Afraid to Ask', *NCDM*, 22 February.

Rosenau, J. (1995), 'Governance in the Twenty-first Century', *Global Governance*, Vol. 1, Jan-April, pp. 13-43.

Rosenau, P. (1990), *Postmodernism and the Social Sciences*, Princeton: Princeton University Press.

Ross, J. (1994), 'Chiapas Part One: Missing the Story' (http://flag.blackened.net/revolt/mexico/comment/media94.html).

Ross, J. (1996), 'Is Zapatista Rebellion Rooted in Oil?', *Earth Island Journal* (http://www.earthisland.org/journal/s96-20.html).

Ross, J. (1998), 'Big Pulp Versus Zapatistas. Cellulose Dreams in Latin America', *NCDM*, 22 October (http://serpiente.dgsca.unam.mx/jornada/mas-ross.html).

Rosset, P. and Cunningham, S. (1994), 'Understanding Chiapas: Land and Rebellion', (http://nativenet.uthesca.edu/archive/nl/9404/0010.html).

Rouse, D. (1996), 'American Library Association: Review of Andres Oppenheimer's 'Bordering on Chaos, Guerrillas, Stockbrokers, Politicians and Mexico's Road to Prosperity' (http://www.amazon.com/exec/obidos/ISBN%30031665095l/mexicoconnectA/ 102-9432824-1918467).

Routledge, P (1998), 'Going Globile: Spatiality, Embodiment and Mediation in the Zapatista Insurgency', in Tuathail, Gerard,. O. and Dalby, D. (eds) (1998), *Rethinking Geopolitics*, London, New York: Routledge.

Routledge, P. and Simons, J. (1995), 'Embodying Spirits of Resistance', *Society and Space*, Vol. 13, pp. 471-498.

Roxborough, I. (1992), 'Neoliberalism in Latin America. Limits and Alternatives', *Third World Quarterly*, Vol. 13, pp. 421-441.

Rude, G. (1952), *The Crowd in the French Revolution*, Oxford: University Press.

Ruggiero, G. (1998), *Zapatista Encuentro: Documents from the 1996 Encounter for Humanity and Against Neoliberalism*, New York: Seven Stories Press.

Rupert, M. (1998), 'Reengaging Gramsci: a response to Germain and Kenny', *Review of International Studies*, Vol. 24.

Rupert, M. (2000), *Ideologies of Globalization: Contending Perspectives for a New World Order*, London: Routledge.

Sachs, J., Tornell, A. and Velasen, A. (1995), 'Mexican Economic Crisis' (http://www.worldbank.org/ubi/edimp/mex/stu.html).

Sane, P. (1999), 'UN Secretariat Launch of Global Sullivan Principles' (http://www.unglobalcompact.org/).

Saramago, J. (1998), 'Moral Force Versus the State. Chiapas Land of Hope and Sorrow', *NCDM*, 17 March.

Sawicki, J. (1994), 'Foucault, Feminism and Questions of Identity', in Gutting, G. (ed.) (1994), *The Cambridge Companion to Foucault*, Cambridge: University Press.

Scholte, J. (2000), *Globalization: A Critical Introduction*, London: Macmillan.

Schraeder, P. (1992), *Intervention in the 1990s: US Foreign Policy in the Third World*, London: Verso.

Schusterman, G. (1994), 'Pragmatism and Liberalism: Between Dewey and Rorty', *Political Theory*, Vol. 22, pp. 391-414.

Schwab, K. and Smadja, C. (1999), 'Globalization needs a Human Face', *International Herald Tribune*, 28 January.

Scott, A. (1990), *Ideology and New Social Movements*, London: Unwin Hyman.

Seabrook, J. (1999), 'After the Eclipse', *New Internationalist*, No. 309, Jan- Feb.

Seers, D. (ed.) (1985), *Dependency Theory: A Critical Reassessment*.

Semler, P. (2001), 'A Sword over Europe', *New Statesman*, 14 May, p. 32.

Serrill, M. (1994), 'Zapatas Revenge: Bloody Uprising in one of the Country's Poorest States seen as an Embarassing Reminder that Mexico not quite joined the 1st World Industrial Club', *Time Magazine Online* (http://www.time.com/time/magazine/archive/1994/940117/940117.mexico.html).

Shaw, M. (1994), 'Civil Society and Global Politics', *Millennium: Journal of International Studies*, Vol. 23, pp. 647-676.

Shaw, M. (2000), *Theory of the Global State: Globality as Unfinished Revolution*, Cambridge: University Press.

Short, C. (1997), 'Speech by Minister of International Development to Introduce White Paper' (http://www.gov.uk/intdev).

Short, C. (1999), 'Interview with New Internationalist' (http://www.oneworld.org/ni/issue296/short.html).

Short, C. (1999a), 'Speech to the WTO Assembly at Seattle' (http://www.developments.org.uk/data/0100/speech.html).

Short, C. (2001), 'Making Globalisation Work for the Poor, speech to the Network of International Development Organisations in Scotland', 21 January (http://www.developments.org.uk/data/0100/speech.html).

Sklair, L. (1991), *Sociology of the Global System*, London: Harvester Wheatsheaf.

Sklair, L. (1998), 'Social Movements and Global Capitalism', in Jameson, F. and Miyoshi, M. (eds) (1998), *The Cultures of Globalization*, Duke University, Durham and London.

Smadja, C. (1999), 'Global Turmoil' (http://live99.weforum.org/global).

Smart, B. (1990), *Postmodernity*, London: Routledge.

Smelser, N. (1962), *Theory of Collective Behaviour*, New York: Routledge.

Smith, D. (2001), 'The World Poor need a fair deal, not handouts', *The Sunday Times*, 28 January, p. 19.

Smith, L. (1995), 'Mexico's Glittering Bargain', *Fortune Magazine*, Vol. 131, p. 74.

Smith, S. (1992), 'The Forty Years Detour; The Resurgence of Normative Theory in International Relations', *Millennium: Journal of International Studies*, Vol. 21, pp. 489-509.

Smith, S. (1997), 'Power and Truth. A Reply to William Wallace', *Review of International Studies*, Vol. 23, pp. 507-516.

Solal-Cohen, S. (1991), *Sartre: A Life*, London: Minerva Press.

Spegele, R. (1997), 'Is Robust Globalism a Mistake?', *Review of International Studies*, Vol. 23, pp. 211-241.

Spike-Peterson, V. (ed.) (1992), *Gendered States: Feminist Revisions in International Relations*, Boulder: Lynne Rienner.

Starn, O. (1995), 'Maoism in the Andes. The Communist Party of Peru's Shining Path and the Refusal of History', *Journal of Latin American Studies*, Vol. 27, pp. 399-423.

Stephen, L. (1996), 'Democracy for Whom? Women's Grassroots Political Activism in 1990s Mexico City and Chiapas', in Otero, G. (ed.) *Neoliberalism Revisited: The Economic Restructuring of Mexican Politics*, Boulder: Westview Press, pp. 187-209.

Stern, N. (2000), 'Press Conference on World Development Report, 2000/2001: Attacking Poverty', *World Bank Group Transcripts* (http://www.worldbank.org).

Strange, S. (1985), *Casino Capitalism*, Oxford: Blackwell.

Strange, S. (1988), *States and Markets: An Introduction to IPE*, Oxford: Blackwell.

Strange, S. (1994) 'Wake up Krasner! The World has Changed', *Review of International Political Economy*, Vol. 1.

Strange, S. and Stopford, J. (1991), *Rival States, Rival Firms*, Cambridge: Cambridge University Press.

Swift, R. (1998), 'Just Do It!', *New Internationalist Online* (http://www.oneworld.org/ni/issue296/just.html).

Tabb, W. (1997), 'Globalisation is an Issue, Power of Capital is the Issue', *Monthly Review*, Vol. 49, pp. 20-31.

Tarleton, J. (1996), 'May Day in Mexico City: A Second Look at Neoliberalism' (http://myhouse.com/pub/bigjohn/STORY94.html).

Taylor, P. (1991), 'The Crisis of the Movements and the State as Quisling', *Antipode*, Vol. 23, pp. 214-229.

Tilly, C. (1978), *From Mobilisation to Revolution*, Reading, Mass.: Addison Wesley.

de Toqueville, A. (1966) (originally published 1856), *The Ancien Regime and the French Revolution*, London: Collins/Fontana.

Touraine, A. (1981), *The Voice and the Eye: An Analysis of Social Movements*, Cambridge: University Press.

Trujillo, G. (1994), 'Chiapas Digest: Statement of 6th January 1994', *Native-L* (http://nativenet.uthesca.edu/archive/nl/9401/0188.html).

Tuathail, G.O. and Dalby, S. (eds) (1998), *Rethinking Geopolitics*, London, New York: Routledge.

Van Der Pijl, K. (1984), *The Making of the Atlantic Ruling Class*, London: Verso.

Vilas, C. (1989), 'Revolution and Democracy in Latin America', *Socialist Register*.

Wachtel, H. (1990), *The Making of a Supranational Economic Order*, London: Pluto.

Wagar, W. (1996), 'Towards a Praxis of Integration', *Journal of World Systems Research*, Vol. 7, pp. 1-16.

Walker, R.B.J. (1988), *One World, Many Worlds: Struggles for a Just World Peace*, Boulder: Lynne Rienner.

Walker, R.B.J. (1991), 'State Sovereignty and the Articulation of Political Space/Time', *Millennium: Journal of International Studies*, Vol. 23, pp. 445- 461.

Walker, R.B.J. (1993), *Inside/Outside: International Relations as Political Theory*, Cambridge: University Press.

Walker, R.B.J. (1994), 'Social Movements/World Politics', *Millennium: Journal of International Studies*, Vol. 23.

Walker, R.B.J. (2000), 'International Relations Theory and the Fate of the Political', in Ebata, M. and Neufeld B. (eds) (2000), *Confronting the Political in International Relations*, London: Macmillan, pp. 212-239.

Wallace, W. (1996), 'Truth and Power. Monks and Technocrats. Theory and Practice in International Relations', *Review of International Studies*, Vol. 22, pp. 301-321.

Wallerstein, I. (with Arrighi, G. and Hopkins, T.) (1991), *Antisystemic Movements*, London: Verso.

Wallerstein, I. (1992), 'The Collapse of Liberalism', *Socialist Register*, pp. 96-111.

Wallis, D. (1997), 'Democracy, the Only Game in Town', *World Today*, No. 53, pp. 285-288.

Waltz, K. (1979), *Theory of International Politics*, Reading: Addison Wesley.

Ward, P. (1993), 'Social Welfare Policy. Political Opening in Mexico', *Journal of Latin American Studies*, Vol. 25, pp. 613-629.

Warnock, J. (1998), 'Letter to *The Economist* On Chiapas'
(http://www.criscenzo.com/jaguar/ccrp2.html).

Warren, B. (1985), 'Nietzsche and Political Philosophy', *Political Theory*, Vol. 13, pp. 183-213.

Warren, M. (1997), 'Mexico: Elections Usher in New Era'
(http://www.polyconomics.com/searchbase/g7-7-97.html).

Waterman, P. (1993), 'Social Movement Unionism: A New Union Model for a New World Order? The New Internationalisms', *Review*, Vol. XVI, pp. 245-279.

Waterman, P. (1998), *Social Movements, Globalisation and the New Internationalisms*, London: Mansell/Cassell.

Waters, M. (1994), *Globalization*, London: Routledge.

Watson, I. (2001), 'Politics, Resistance to Neoliberalism and the Ambiguities of Globalisation', *Global Society: Journal of Interdisciplinary International Relations*, Vol. 15, pp. 201-218.

Watson, I. (2001a), 'Rethinking Strategy and Geopolitics: Critical Responses to Globalization', *Geopolitics*, Vol. 6, pp. 97-106.

Watson, I. (2002), 'Contesting Neoliberalism: Perspectives on a Politics of Inclusion from Chiapas', *Manchester Papers in Politics Series* (forthcoming).

Watson, I. (2002a) 'An Examination of the Zapatista Army of National Liberation (EZLN) and New Political Participation', *Democracy and Nature: The International Journal of Inclusive Democracy*, Vol. 8, pp. 63-86.

Watson, I. (2002b), 'Rethinking Resistance: Contesting Neoliberal Globalisation and the Zapatistas as a Critical Social Movement', in Abbott, J. and Worth, O. (2002), *Critical Perspectives on International Political Economy*, London: Macmillan, pp. 108-139.

Wehlings, G. (1995), 'Zapatismo. What is the EZLN Fighting For?'
(http://flag.blackened.net/revolt/mexico/comment/why.html).

Wehlings, G. (1995a), 'Chiapas Report'
(http://flag.blackened.net/revolt/mexico/reports/jan95.html).

Weinberg, B. (1996), 'Latin America Drug War Update: Narco Traffic Colombia and Mexico' (http://www.mediafilter.org/Shadow/S40/S40.DrugWar.html).

Welch, J. (1993), 'New Forces of Latin America.Financial Flows, Markets, and Investment in the 1990s', *Journal of Latin American Studies*, Vol. 25, pp. 1-23.

Welker, G. (1994), 'Chiapas is Mexico', *Native-L*
(http://nativenet.uthesca.edu/archive/nl/9405/0067.html).

Welker, G. (1995), 'Carlos Fuentes Speaks on Chiapas', *Native-L*
(http://nativenet.uthesca.edu/archive/ni/9503/0114.html).

Wendt, A. (1987), 'The Agent Structure Problem in International Relations', *International Organisation*, Vol. 41, pp. 335-370.

Whalen, C. (1995), 'Mexico: Whats Next?', *Documents on Mexican Politics*
(http://www.cs.unb.ca/~alopez/politics/whatsnext.html).

Wheen, F. (1999), *Karl Marx*, London: Harpercollins.

Wickham, G. (1990), 'The Political Possibilities of Postmodernism', *Economy and Society*, Vol. 19.

Wight, C. (1996), 'Beyond Incommensurability. What's the Frequency Kenneth?', *Millennium: Journal of International Studies*, Vol. 25, pp. 291-321.

Wight, C. (1999), 'Meta Campbell: the epistemological problematics of perspectivism', *Review of International Studies*, Vol. 28, pp. 311-317.

Wilson-Brian, S. (1995), 'US Military Moves in to Mexico', *Earth Island Journal Online* (http://www.oneworld.org/ni/index4.html).

Wintour, P. (2001), 'Blair Gets Tough on Europe', *The Guardian*, 6 August, p. 19.

Wired News Report (1998), 'Zapatista Rebels Support Wages Virtual War', *Wired Magazine Online* (http://www.wired.com/news/news/politics/story/10085.html).

Wodall, P. (1999), 'The World Economy. A Survey', *The Economist*, 25 September.

Wodall, P. (2000), 'The New Economy Goes Global', *The World in 2001 (The Economist)*, p. 21.

World Bank Development Report (1995), 'Mexico: National Development Plan for 1995-2000' (http://www.demon.co.uk/mexuk/july95/plan9520.html).

World Bank Development Report (1995a), 'Mexico: Economic Indicators' (http://www.demon.co.uk/mexuk/econ_ind.html).

World Bank Development Report (1996), 'Mexico's Economic Outlook for 1996' (http://www.demon.co.uk/mexuk/feb96/outlook.html).

World Bank Annual Report (1996a), 'Section Four: 1996 Regional Perspectives: Latin America and the Caribbean' (http://www.worldbank.org/html/extpb/annrep96/annrep96.htm).

The World Bank, *World Development Report 2000/2001* (http://www.worldbank.org/html/extpb/annrep00/annrep00.htm).

Wright, R. (2000), 'Planet Earth Goes for the Big One', *The Sunday Times News Review*, 27 February, p. 7.

Younts, G. (1998), 'Mexicos Rebels Problems Mounting', *NCDM*, 30 June.

Zald, M. and McCarthy, J. (1977), 'Resource Mobilization Theory', *American Journal of Sociology*.

Zapatista Army of National Liberation (EZLN) (1994), 'First Declaration of the Lacandon Jungle' (http://www.ezln.org/fzln/1st-decl.html).

Zapatista Army of National Liberation (EZLN) (1994a), 'Second Declaration of the Lacandon Jungle' (http://www.ezln.org/fzln/2nd-decl.html).

Zapatista Army of National Liberation (1996), 'The San Andres Accords' (http://flag.blackened.net/revolt/mexico/ezln/san_andres.html).

Zapatista Army of National Liberation (1998), 'Fifth Declaration of the Lacandon Jungle' (http://flag.blackened.net/revolt/mexico/ezln/ccri_5_dec_lj_july98.html).

Zapatista Army of National Liberation (2000), 'Letter to Senor Vicente Fox' (http://flag.blackened.net/revolt/mexico/ezln/2000/letter_to_fox_dec00.html).

Zapatista Net on Autonomy and Liberation (1995)
(http://www.actlab.utexas.edu/~zapatistas/).

Zedillo Prince do Leon, President of the Federal Republic of Mexico (1995),
'Federal Budget Project and the Economic Policy Criteria for 1996'
(http://www.demon/mexuk/press/gbr0475.html).

Zedillo Prince de Leon, President of the Federal Republic of Mexico (1996),
'Second State of the Nation Address'
(http://www.demon/mexuk/press/gbr0296.html).

Zedillo Prince de Leon, President of the Federal Republic of Mexico (1996a),
'Address to the Annual Dinner of the National Foreign Trade Council of the
United States, New York, 9 December 1996'
(http://www.demon/mexuk/press/gbr02996.html).

Zedillo Prince de Leon, President of the Federal Republic of Mexico (1998),
'Initiatives for Constitutional Reform Regarding Indigenous Rights and Culture
Presented to Congress'
(http://precsidentia.gob.mx/chiapas/document/initiati.html).

Zedillo Prince de Leon, President of the Federal Republic of Mexico (1998a),
'Speech to Mexican Congress'
(http://precsidentia.gob.mx/chiapas/speeches/23jan98.html).

Zedillo Prince de Leon, President of the Federal Republic of Mexico (1999),
'Speech to Mexican Nation'
(http://world.precsidentia.gob.mx/statereport/1999/text.end.html).

Zermano, S. (1994), 'State/society and Dependent Neoliberalism in Mexico: The
Case of the Chiapas Uprising', in Smith, W. and Korzeniewick, P. (eds) (1996),
Politics, Social Change and Economic Restructuring in Latin America,
Boulder: Westview Press.

Zerzan, J. (1997), 'The Catastrophe of Postmodernism'
(http://www.teleport.com/jaberiot/pomo/html).

Zinser, A. (1987), 'Mexico. The Presidential Problematic', *Foreign Policy*,
Vol. 69, pp. 40-61.

Zysman, J. (1996), 'The Myth of the Global Economy Enduring National
Foundations and Emerging Regional Realities', *New Political Economy*, Vol. 1,
pp. 157-184.

Index